MUSIC

TEACHER'S EDITION Grade 1

Eunice Boardman Meske
Professor of Music and Education
University of Wisconsin—Madison
Madison, Wisconsin

Barbara Andress
Professor of Music Education
Arizona State University
Tempe, Arizona

Mary P. Pautz
Assistant Professor of Music
  Education
University of Wisconsin—Milwaukee
Milwaukee, Wisconsin

Fred Willman
Professor of Music and Education
University of Missouri—St. Louis
St. Louis, Missouri

Holt, Rinehart and Winston, Publishers
New York, Toronto, Mexico City, London, Sydney, Tokyo

Acknowledgments for previously copyrighted material
and credits for photographs and art begin on page 232.
ISBN 0-03-005262-9
7890 032 98765432

HOLT MUSIC

It's the leader of the band!

CONSIDER THE ADVANTAGES . . .

☐ *Dozens of the world's finest songs in each level—the songs your students want to sing!*

☐ *Exciting activities that enable students to interact with the music and acquire musical knowledge.*

☐ *Exceptionally motivating listening lessons that really get students involved in learning.*

☐ *Flexibly organized Teacher's Editions, rich with background information and no-nonsense teaching strategies.*

☐ *A wealth of supplementary materials that enhance, extend, and enrich.*

Music That Motivates

Every song in HOLT MUSIC builds on the natural enthusiasm young children have for singing, dancing—expressing themselves in creative ways! You'll find hundreds and hundreds of authentic songs that students really *want* to sing—songs with built-in appeal.

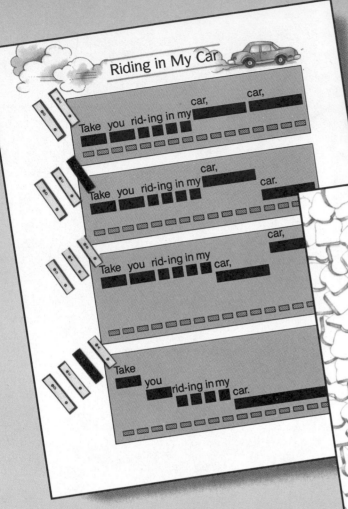

Lively, colorful photographs and illustrations provide the perfect visual accompaniment.

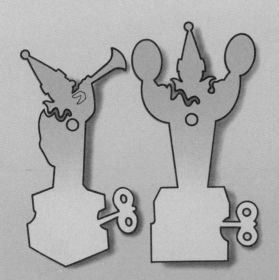

Just look at some of these favorites:

Little Sir Echo
Jack-in-the-Box
The Merry-go-round
Reuben and Rachel
Five Angels
Heigh-Ho
Redbird
Stay Awake
Hey, Lolly, Lolly
Rudolph, the Red-Nosed Reindeer

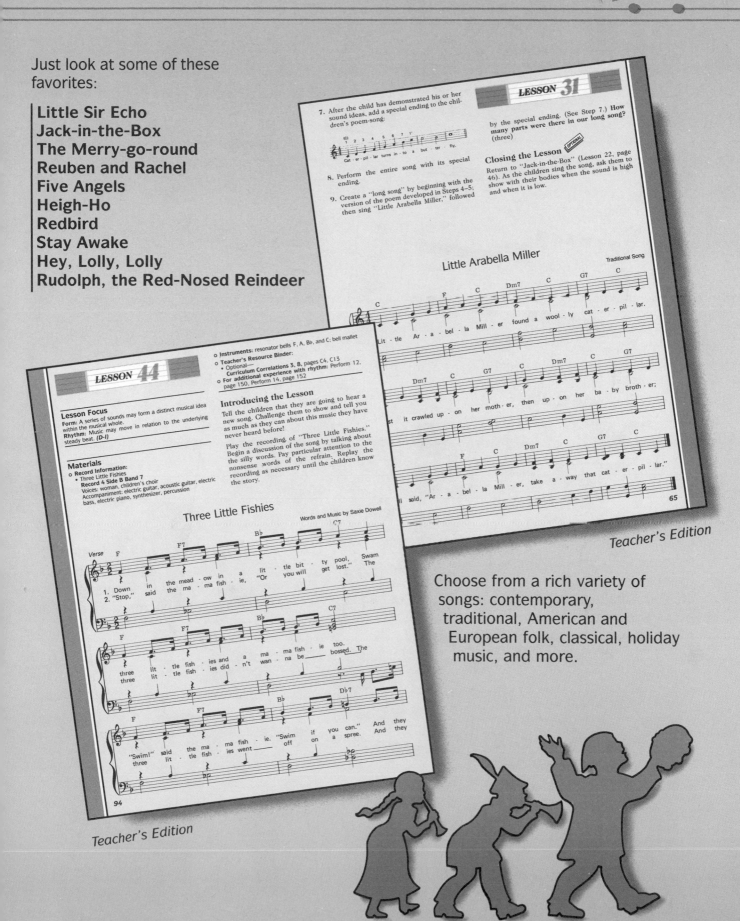

Choose from a rich variety of songs: contemporary, traditional, American and European folk, classical, holiday music, and more.

Teacher's Edition

Teacher's Edition

Music to Learn From

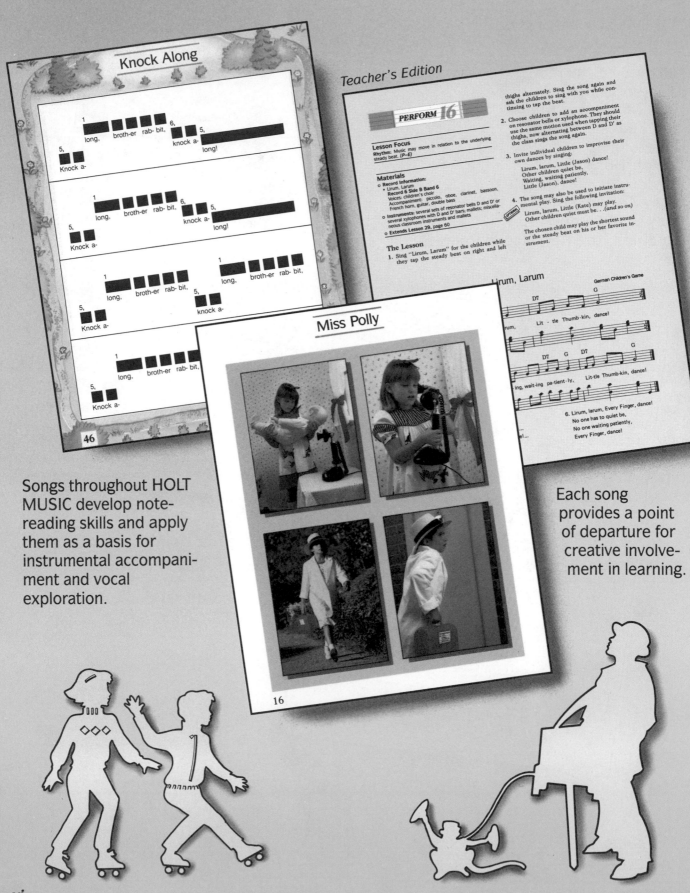

Songs throughout HOLT MUSIC develop note-reading skills and apply them as a basis for instrumental accompaniment and vocal exploration.

Each song provides a point of departure for creative involvement in learning.

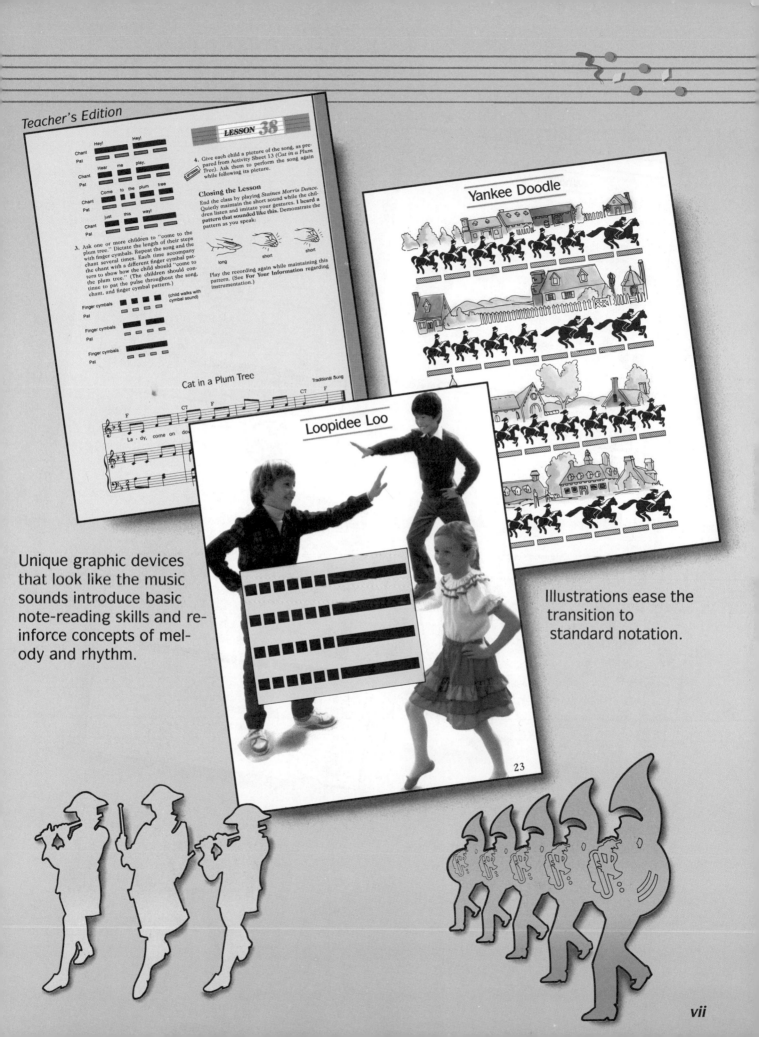

Unique graphic devices that look like the music sounds introduce basic note-reading skills and reinforce concepts of melody and rhythm.

Illustrations ease the transition to standard notation.

Music to Interact With

Whole and Parts

How Long?

1

A Walk in the Zoo

Amy and Greg went for a walk in the zoo.
What did they see?
What did they hear?

36

Going for a Walk

Picture 1

52

Irresistible activities inspire singing, clapping, making up melodies and rhymes, and more— the true exhilaration of musical expression. Many activities involve poetry or related arts.

Short instrumental experiences begin at Kindergarten, employing readily available instruments.

Music Worth Listening To

Many activities call upon students to move to rhythms and melodic patterns or to listen critically and make judgments about mood, instrumentation, melody, and form.

The Cuckoo in the Woods

38

Song of the Narobi Trio

Play your ukulele as you listen to the music. Can you play a different way for each part?

rum   Tap with your fingers   Play like a violin

e a cello   Shake   Tap with your hand

r ways to play!   33

The Three Little Pigs

1

8

Listening lessons in HOLT MUSIC keep students tuned in with appealing graphics, follow-along activities, and professional performances. Recordings use a wide variety of vocal and instrumental sounds to heighten awareness of form, mood, melody, and musical styles.

The focus is on active participation to make music exciting, involving, and fun!

The listening selections include a wide variety of musical styles and eras.

Thinking About Music

Both activities and listening lessons supply ample opportunities to develop and reinforce thinking skills. Exercises are designed to improve students' ability to think, through analysis and evaluation, comparison and contrast, choosing alternatives, and more.

Music That's Realistic to Teach!

Whatever your musical background, you'll find all the backup help you need in HOLT MUSIC Teacher's Editions: concrete information, strategies you can rely on, and solid, flexible lesson plans with many optional suggestions. Every page is designed to bring musical understanding and appreciation within reach of all your students.

Each lesson begins with a clear objective and a complete list of program materials, including a detailed summary of recordings and the voices and instruments used.

Each of the extension lessons in Unit 2 is cross-referenced to a core lesson.

"Introducing the Lesson" includes a simple-to-perform motivator that leads naturally into the lesson content.

"Developing the Lesson" gives step-by-step teaching suggestions to ensure that the lesson objective is met. Commentary and questions to the student are highlighted in boldface type.

 A special logo signals when activity sheets are available for the lesson.

LESSON 14

Anybody There?

Lesson Focus
Expression: The expressiveness of music is affected by the way timbre contributes to the musical whole. *(D–E)*

Materials
- o **Piano Accompaniment:** page 203
- o **Record Information:**
  - The Happy Train
    (Record 1 Side B Band 7)
  - Knock! Knock! Anybody There?
    Record 2 Side A Band 4
    Voices: children's choir
    Accompaniment: synthesizer, percussion
- o **Instruments:** sand blocks; drum and mallet; rhythm sticks; woodblock and mallet; guiro with scratcher; finger cymbals
- o **Other:** paper; feathers or ribbons
- o **Teacher's Resource Binder:**
  - Optional—
    Enrichment Activity 3, page E5
- o **For additional experience with timbre:** Perform 16, page 153; Special Times 5, page 190

Introducing the Lesson

Tell the children to open their books to page 3, or show page 3 of the Jumbo Book. Review "The Happy Train" (Lesson 10, page 20); recall the many ways that we can make music. Ask some children to step to the beat and others to clap the shortest sound. One child could play the shortest sound on sand blocks.

Have the children look at pupil pages 4–5. Name the different creatures (bird, cricket, rabbit, frog, snake). Discuss the places these creatures make their homes: trees, cracks, holes, and ponds.

Developing the Lesson

1. **Let's visit the homes of these creatures. Listen; can you sing this tune?**

Knock! Knock! An-y-bod-y there?

28

Repeat the tune as necessary until the children can sing it with confidence.

2. Point to each picture on the pupil pages and ask the children to sing their new tune. (See Step 1.) Follow each performance of the tune by reading to the class the appropriate poem from **For Your Information.**

3. Add the sounds of instruments as you again "visit" each home. Follow this sequence: The children sing their tune; the teacher says the poem; one or more children then softly play instruments to suggest the sound of the creature:

   Bird: waving paper for rustling feathers
   Cricket: rhythm sticks or woodblock for cricket chirp
   Rabbit: drum for thumping feet
   Frog: guiro for "ribbit"
   Snake: sand blocks for slithering sound

x

Freedom of choice is truly yours—lesson plans are designed for maximum flexibility. Each level is divided into two units. Unit 1, the core, contains 60 lessons for a minimum program. Unit 2 contains four chapters for reinforcement, enrichment, and special performances.

LESSON 14

For Your Information
Poems for use in Step 2:

BIRD: I want to see a bird
With a bright red vest,
Who rustles his feathers
When he sits in his nest.

CRICKET: A cricket lives
In a deep, dark crack,
Under a rock,
Way to the back.

RABBIT: Who lives down deep
In a hole in the ground,
And thumps her foot
When she looks around?

FROG: I've come to the pond
For a very short visit,
With a frog who just sits
And occasionally says,
"ribbit"!

SNAKE: A green snake's house
Is a long, skinny place,
'Cause his tail won't fit
In any other place.

5

When a score is given in graphic notation in the pupil book, the music notation appears on the teacher's page.

"For Your Information" provides a quick, convenient reference for background information about lesson contents.

A colored band designates the core pages. Optional steps are labeled with a logo.

"Closing the Lesson" offers activities to apply what has been learned.

A special logo indicates when performance cas-　settes are available.

Listen to the recording and learn the complete song, "Knock! Knock! Anybody There?". During the song sections the children could dramatize the action. Have one child live in the "home" and dispense the feathers and ribbons. A different child comes to the door for each statement of the song and pantomimes receiving the gifts. The visiting child then sings a short, improvised "thank you" melody during the recorded interlude.

losing the Lesson [OPTIONAL]

eturn to the song, "The Old Gray Horse" (Les-
n 8, page 16). Repeat the first verse several
mes and change the name of the animal with
ch repetition. Have the children select an in-
rument to represent each animal's sound. Then
k the children to use each instrument to ac-
mpany the appropriate repetition. (Possible
oices might include: fed my horse—wood-

block for hoofs; fed my chick—finger cymbals for peeps; fed my bee—sand blocks for buzzing.)

Knock! Knock! Anybody There?
Words by Clyde Watson
Traditional Melody

29

xi

Music That's Manageable

The **Teacher's Resource Binder** makes classroom management uncommonly convenient. Blackline masters help teachers structure the course to match individual preferences.

Teachers who use the **Kodaly** approach will find creative teaching ideas and fun-filled student charts — all correlated to HOLT MUSIC.

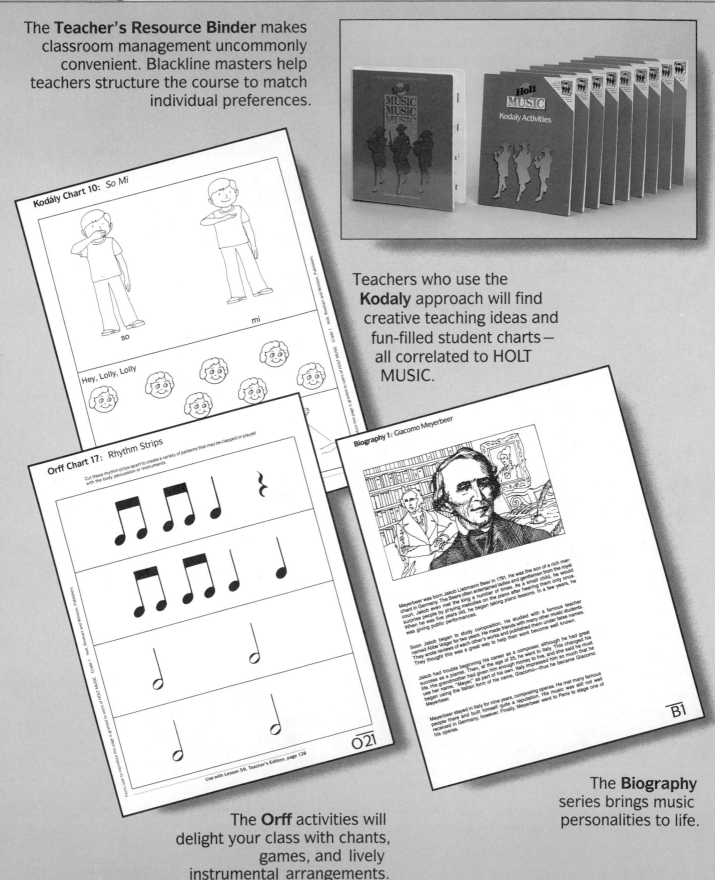

The **Orff** activities will delight your class with chants, games, and lively instrumental arrangements.

The **Biography** series brings music personalities to life.

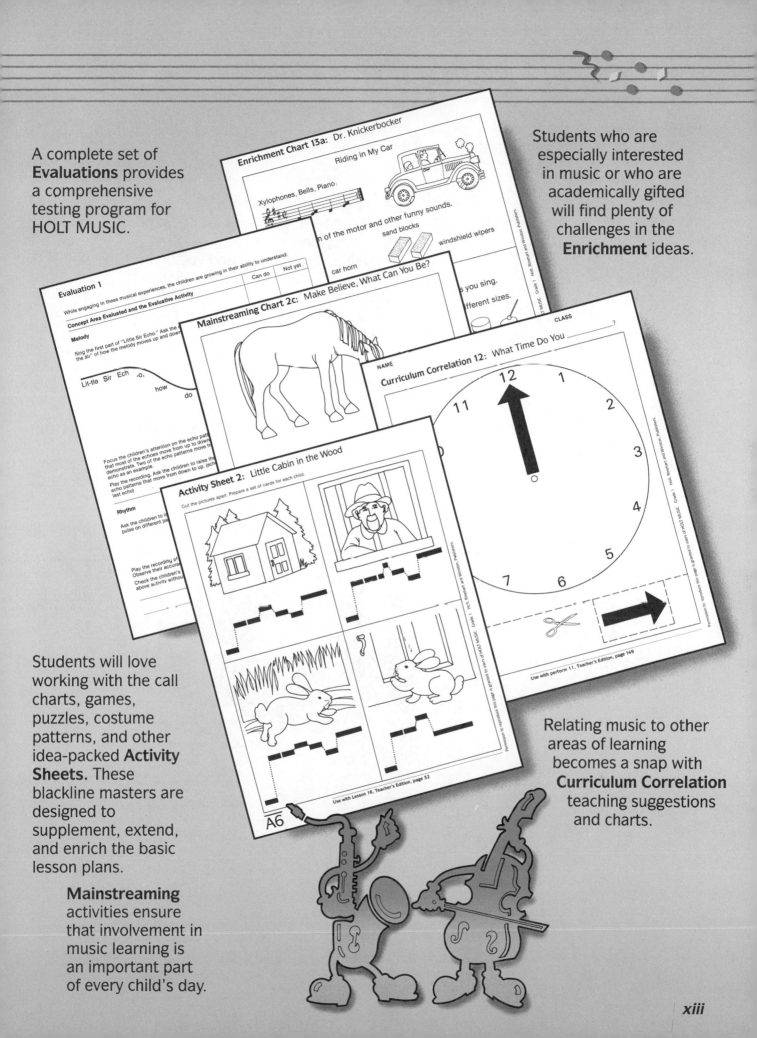

A complete set of **Evaluations** provides a comprehensive testing program for HOLT MUSIC.

Students who are especially interested in music or who are academically gifted will find plenty of challenges in the **Enrichment** ideas.

Students will love working with the call charts, games, puzzles, costume patterns, and other idea-packed **Activity Sheets.** These blackline masters are designed to supplement, extend, and enrich the basic lesson plans.

Mainstreaming activities ensure that involvement in music learning is an important part of every child's day.

Relating music to other areas of learning becomes a snap with **Curriculum Correlation** teaching suggestions and charts.

Music to Play

Recordings

A set of first-quality recordings serves a dual purpose: to give students a model for performance and to provide a valuable instrumental and vocal resource. Dual-track stereo allows separation of recorded voice and accompaniment. Recordings are digitally mastered.

A sturdy carrying case includes an index cross-referenced to lessons in the Teacher's Edition.

Song and listening selections appear in lesson order.

Extra Features!

Performance cassettes contain instrumental tracks specially edited for optimum sound in public performance.

Rehearsal cassettes in Grades 4–8 help students learn part songs by hearing each vocal part alone.

Supplementary Items

Wait Until You Hear This! Music software uses songs from HOLT MUSIC to encourage active experimentation with musical elements. Students can rearrange phrases, alter rhythms, tempo, and timbre, and change key or mode to create new musical works. Three separate programs are available: Grades K–2, 3–5, and 6–8.

The *Holiday Song Book* includes lyrics and piano accompaniments for an additional 50 songs celebrating a year's worth of holidays— Mother's Day, Columbus Day, the Fourth of July, and more.

COMPONENTS CHART

	K	1	2	3	4	5	6	7	8
Pupil Book		✓	✓	✓	✓	✓	✓	✓	✓
Jumbo Book	✓	✓							
Teacher's Edition	✓	✓	✓	✓	✓	✓	✓	✓	✓
Recordings	✓	✓	✓	✓	✓	✓	✓	✓	✓
Teacher's Resource Binder	✓	✓	✓	✓	✓	✓	✓	✓	✓
Holiday Song Book	✓	✓	✓	✓	✓	✓	✓	✓	✓
Computer Software	✓	✓	✓	✓	✓	✓	✓	✓	✓
Performance Cassettes	✓	✓	✓	✓	✓	✓	✓	✓	✓
Rehearsal Cassettes				✓	✓	✓	✓	✓	✓

HOLT MUSIC offers you a total package for your classroom needs. A list of components is given in the chart at the left.

TABLE OF CONTENTS

CORE UNIT 1 Music to Explore xxxii

UNIT 2 *More Music to Explore*..... 132

Meet the Authors

Eunice Boardman Meske is Director of the School of Music and Professor of Music and Education at the University of Wisconsin, Madison. She works with university students in a "lab school" where she and her students teach grades K-8. Meske holds a Ph.D. from the University of Illinois.

EUNICE BOARDMAN MESKE

BARBARA ANDRESS

Barbara Andress is Professor in the School of Music at Arizona State University, Tempe. She received a B.A. and M.A. in education from Arizona State University. Andress has taught general music and instrumental music and for over twenty years was a district music supervisor.

Mary Pautz is Assistant Professor of Music Education at the University of Wisconsin, Milwaukee. In addition to teaching music education methods, she also teaches elementary music classes as part of a practicum for music majors. Pautz is a doctoral candidate at the University of Wisconsin, Madison.

MARY PAUTZ

FRED WILLMAN

Fred Willman is Professor of Music Education at the University of Missouri, St. Louis. Willman holds a Ph.D. from the University of North Dakota, Grand Forks. He has worked extensively in the development of computer software for use in music education.

Consultants

Nancy Archer
Forest Park Elementary School
Fort Wayne, Indiana

Joan Z. Fyfe
Jericho Public Schools
Jericho, New York

Jeanne Hook
Albuquerque Public Schools
Albuquerque, New Mexico

Danette Littleton
University of Tennessee at Chattanooga
Chattanooga, Tennessee

Barbara Reeder Lundquist
University of Washington
Seattle, Washington

Ollie McFarland
Detroit Public Schools
Detroit, Michigan

Faith Norwood
Harnett County School District
North Carolina

Linda K. Price
Richardson Independent School District
Richardson, Texas

Buryl Red
Composer and Arranger
New York, New York

Dawn L. Reynolds
District of Columbia Public Schools
Washington, D.C.

Morris Stevens
A.N. McCallum High School
Austin, Texas

Jack Noble White
Texas Boys Choir
Fort Worth, Texas

Contributing Writers

Hilary Apfelstadt
University of North Carolina at Greensboro
Greensboro, North Carolina

Pat and Tom Cuthbertson
Professional Writers
Santa Cruz, California

Louise Huberty
(*Special Kodaly Consultant*)
Milwaukee Public Schools
Milwaukee, Wisconsin

Susan Kenney
Brigham Young University
Salt Lake City, Utah

Janet Montgomery
Ithaca College
Ithaca, New York

Richard O'Hearn
Western Michigan University
Kalamazoo, Michigan

Diane Persellin
Trinity University
San Antonio, Texas

Arvida Steen
(*Special Orff Consultant*)
The Blake School
Minneapolis, Minnesota

Field Test Sites

While HOLT MUSIC was being developed, parts of the program were field tested by 25 teachers in 18 states. These teachers played a crucial role in the program's development. Their comments, suggestions, and classroom experiences helped HOLT MUSIC become the workable, exciting program it is. Our grateful appreciation goes to the following teachers who used our materials in their classrooms.

ARKANSAS
Judy Harkrader
Vilonia Elementary School
Vilonia

COLORADO
Nancylee Summerville
Hutchinson Elementary School
Lakewood

Robert Horsky
Goldrick Elementary School
Denver

Joan Tally
Eiber Elementary School
Lakewood

Germaine Johnson
University of Northern Colorado
  Laboratory School
Greeley

GEORGIA
Angela Tonsmeire
Cartersville Elementary School
Cartersville

Nancy Clayton
Norman Park Elementary School
Norman Park

INDIANA
Nancy Archer
Forest Park Elementary School
Fort Wayne

Elizabeth Staples
School #92
Indianapolis

Pat Gillooly
School #90
Indianapolis

KANSAS
Shelli Kadel
El Paso Elementary School
Derby

KENTUCKY
Patricia Weihe
Wright Elementary School
Shelbyville

MASSACHUSETTS
Marya Rusinak
Kennedy School
Brockton

MISSISSIPPI
Dottie Dudley
Crestwood Elementary School
Meridian

Mira Frances Hays
Forest Seperate School District
Forest

MISSOURI
Elizabeth Hutcherson
Parker Road Elementary School
Florissant

NEW JERSEY
Lorna Milbauer
North Cliff School
Englewood Cliffs

NEW YORK
Ruthetta S. Smikle
Hillary Park Academy
Buffalo

NORTH CAROLINA
Julie Young
Burgaw Elementary School
Burgaw

OKLAHOMA
Cindy Newell
Washington Irving Elementary School
Durant

OREGON
Larry Verdoorn
Hall Elementary School
Gresham

PENNSYLVANIA
Marianne Zimmerman
Steele School
Harrisburg

TENNESSEE
Sarah Davis
Powell Elementary School
Powell

WEST VIRGINIA
Eva Ledbetter
Cross Lanes Elementary School
Cross Lanes

WISCONSIN
Jill Kuespert Anderson
Lannon Elementary School
Lannon

A Guide To Holt Music

The HOLT MUSIC program can help you provide rich and enjoyable experiences for all of your students. The information given below will help you get acquainted with the Pupil Book, the Teacher's Edition, the Teacher's Resource Binder, and the Recordings.

Organization Of The Program

Each level of HOLT MUSIC is divided into two units. Unit 1, "Music to Explore," is the "core" unit. The core lessons are divided into four quarters, or chapters, of fifteen lessons each. Each quarter ends with an evaluation. If time for music class is limited, we suggest that you concentrate on the core, which provides a comprehensive program in itself.

Unit 2, "More Music to Explore," contains an additional four chapters for review, reinforcement, extension of core concepts, and seasonal music. Lessons in Unit 2 are cross-referenced in the Teacher's Edition to lessons in Unit 1. However, these cross-references are only suggestions; you will also be guided by the interests of your students and available class time.

Types Of Lessons In The Book

☐ **Song lessons**—Most lessons in HOLT MUSIC are song-based. Songs in the Pupil Book are identified by a gray band above and below the song title. When the song does not appear in standard notation in the Pupil Book, the notation can be found in the teaching copy for that lesson. For song-based lessons that do not use pupil pages a piano accompaniment is printed on the Teacher's Edition lesson page. Many songs in the Pupil Book are notated with ikons (pictures of musical sound). Because the ikons are used to help the children gradually acquire note-reading skills, it is strongly recommended that the core unit be followed in page order.

☐ **Listening lessons**—These lessons are built around a recording of a classical, folk, or contemporary work. Listening lessons featured in the Pupil Book are identified by a logo. Complete titles, composers, and performer credits are listed in the "Materials" section of the Teacher's Edition.

Many of the listening lessons have a chart or an illustration designed to help guide the children through the listening experience. In some lessons the recording includes "call numbers"—spoken numbers recorded over the music. The call numbers correspond to the numbers on the chart and help to focus attention on important features as the music continues.

☐ **Activities**—Many activity-based lessons are included in HOLT MUSIC. The type of activity in the Pupil Book is identified by a special logo: a quill pen and an ink bottle for creative activities, a

French horn for performance activities, and a human figure for activities involving movement.

The activity is always structured in some way; for example, a poem, a story, or a picture in the Pupil Book might serve as a focal point for creative exploration, or the students could be invited to explore certain sounds on instruments.

Using The Recordings

The recordings are essential teaching aids for HOLT MUSIC. The song recordings may be used in various ways: to help students learn words and melody if songs are beyond their current reading level; and to provide examples of appropriate tempo, diction, expression, and vocal tone quality. For teaching flexibility, song recordings have voices on one channel and instruments on the other. By turning the balance control completely to the right, you will hear instruments only. The grooves between all selections are locked.

Special Helps For The Teacher

☐ The **Scope and Sequence Chart,** page xxviii–xxxi, summarizes concepts, terms, and skills covered in each grade level.

☐ The teacher's **Glossary,** page 230, gives definitions of musical terms used in the text.

☐ Complete **Classified and Alphabetical Indexes,** starting on page 234, provide a convenient way to locate songs, poems, listening lessons, and particular skills and concepts.

☐ Step-by-step **lesson plans** are provided for each page of the Pupil Book. The **Lesson Focus** indicates the concept to be studied and gives, in abbreviated form, an indication of the primary behavior and mode stressed. **P–I,** for example, means "perform" in the "ikonic mode." (See "The Generative Approach to Music Learning," page xxvi.)

☐ The **Teacher's Resource Binder** includes Activity Sheets, Biographies, Evaluations, and suggestions for Curriculum Correlation, Enrichment, Kodaly, Mainstreaming, and Orff. All binder materials are cross-referenced to lessons in the Teacher's Edition. This enables you to adapt or expand individual lessons to fit your special needs.

☐ **Instrumental accompaniments**—Most songs contain chord names for autoharp or guitar accompaniment, and many lesson plans include accompaniments for students to perform on classroom instruments. Piano accompaniments, provided in the back of the Teacher's Edition, are cross-referenced to each lesson plan. The piano score includes markers showing where a new line begins in the Pupil Book. The symbol ♪ above the score, for example, indicates that the second line of music in the Pupil Book begins at this point.

To the Classroom Teacher

The classroom teacher's role in music education varies from school to school. Whatever the situation in your district, the classroom teacher is vital to the success of the total music program.

Many teachers approach music with mixed feelings: enthusiasm, apprehension, curiosity, or insecurity. These attitudes are influenced by the musical knowledge the teacher possesses, the memory of music in his or her own school experience, and by heavy demands on the teacher's time.

HOLT MUSIC welcomes the classroom teacher's participation. The suggestions that follow are provided with the hope that they will alleviate fears and encourage the teacher to enjoy and learn music with the students.

1 "I Don't Know How To Teach Music!"

Every classroom teacher can teach music with HOLT MUSIC—if he or she is willing to learn with the students and read through the lessons in the Teacher's Edition. The "generative" approach used in HOLT MUSIC can help the teacher learn along with the students.

Music presents a special challenge because of the need to occasionally demonstrate by singing, moving, or playing. HOLT MUSIC helps the teacher as much as possible with

- comprehensive, easily understood lesson plans
- quality demonstration recordings
- a teaching sequence that works
- appealing songs, listening lessons, and poetry
- activities that are fun for students to do

2 "There Isn't Time To Teach Music!"

The pressure for students to achieve in all curricular areas is intense. However, music can be interspersed throughout the school day. Sing a song to begin or end the day; create an instrumental accompaniment to enrich a story; share the music from the culture being highlighted in social studies.

The Curriculum Correlation section in the Teacher's Resource Binder provides many suggestions for integrating music into your day. To expand class time for music, set up music centers where small groups may work on their own.

However, a scheduled time devoted to music is just as important as time scheduled for other subjects. Just as reading throughout the day does not take the place of reading class, neither should the use of music throughout the day be considered sufficient. To achieve an understanding of music there must be a sequential course of study.

3 "I Don't Have Time To Hunt For Materials!"

The authors of HOLT MUSIC have gathered and organized all materials for you. You will find

- Complete lesson plans that include a lesson focus, an introduction, a development and a conclusion. Usually a lesson can be completed in 20 to 30 minutes.
- Integration of all types of activities—listening lessons, dances, creative experiences, and songs—within a lesson.
- Boldfaced dialogue in the lesson plans that may help you in presenting the lesson, especially if you are not familiar with musical concepts and terms.

4 "The Kids Will Laugh If I Sing!"

Students may need encouragement at first. However, young people will eventually sing if a positive atmosphere is created. Common teaching errors that hinder singing include

- expecting students to sing before they are ready (A new song must be heard several times before the students sing it.)
- expecting students to sing too loud

The students may laugh the first time they hear you sing. You are not alone: They are even more likely to laugh at a music specialist who has a trained voice! If you can laugh with the class and proceed with the song, the laughter is soon forgotten and the music enjoyed. Or if you prefer, you can rely on the recordings. By adjusting the balance on the stereo, the voice only may be heard; this is especially helpful in teaching a new song.

5 "What Will I Do With the Boys?"

There is nothing inherent in the genes of boys that causes them to have an aversion to music! Often they will be the most enthusiastic supporters. Expect all students to enjoy music; expect everyone to learn. You will find that an activity-based, hands-on experience in music will spark enthusiasm in both boys and girls. They will never tire of opportunities to play bells and autoharps, to use props such as streamers, wands, and balloons, or to work with the activity sheets provided in the Teacher's Resource Binder.

6 "I Can't Play the Piano!"

While playing the piano is helpful, it is not essential for teaching music. Instead, you can play the recordings or use autoharp accompaniments.

7 "I Remember How I Hated Music When I Was In School!"

Teachers who have had pleasant experiences with music are likely to approach music teaching with enthusiasm. Others, unfortunately, may have less pleasant memories. What was it in the experience that caused the bad feelings? You can prevent another generation from having unpleasant experiences by avoiding those stressful practices you recall.

The Generative Approach To Music Learning

HOLT MUSIC's generative approach is based on the recognition that

Learning begins with a "need to know." Real learning occurs only to the extent that the student willingly makes a commitment to the act of learning. Learning based on intrinsic "need to know" goals, which the learner personally identifies, is more permanent than learning based on extrinsic goals such as rewards or adult approval.

Learning leads to more learning. Once the student is personally committed to learning, each achievement is "generative"; it provides the foundation and the impetus for further learning.

Learning is future-oriented. The student who becomes enthralled with the learning process continues to seek opportunities to learn as long as each experience leads toward personal independence and self-actualization. Music learning thus approached allows the learner to become

☐ more deeply involved in the aesthetic experience

☐ aware of music as an avenue of one's own personal expression

☐ musically independent

The Generative Instructional Theory

The Generative Instructional Theory recognizes that music learning, whether formal or informal, involves four components. These components include

1. The musical concept to be learned. Musical understanding emerges gradually as the learner develops musical concepts, that is, principles or ways of categorizing musical sounds.

Concepts stressed in the generative approach include

☐ those related to musical elements
  ■ pitch (melody and harmony)
  ■ duration (rhythm and tempo) ■ dynamics
  ■ articulation ■ timbre (qualities of sound)

☐ those that reflect the way musical elements are organized into a complete musical statement that has ■ form ■ texture ■ an expressive nature ■ a cultural context (time and place)

The Scope and Sequence chart beginning on page xxviii gives the concepts covered in HOLT MUSIC.

2. A musical example that embodies the concept to be learned. Examples are selected for their musical value reflecting

  ■ diverse musical heritages
  ■ diverse times and places
  ■ many forms of human emotion
  ■ many different combinations of voices and instruments

3. A musical behavior through which the learner interacts with music, gradually developing essential musical concepts by
  ■ performing music through singing and playing

  ■ describing music through moving, visualizing, and verbalizing
  ■ creating music through improvisation or composition

4. A conceptual mode that enables the learner to communicate understanding and move through three stages of conceptualization:

☐ **The enactive mode:** The learner begins to associate concept with example through observation, manipulation, and experimentation. Understanding is "acted-out" as the student interacts directly and nonverbally with the musical sound.

☐ **The ikonic mode:** The learner internalizes musical sound images that can be recalled even when the musical sound is absent. The learner demonstrates understanding through pictorial representations that "look like" the music sounds or with simple verbal imagery such as up-down, longer-shorter, or smooth-jerky.

☐ **The symbolic mode:** The learner builds on previous enactive and ikonic experiences until verbal and musical symbols gradually become associated with the sound.

The Lesson Focus

Lesson plans in HOLT MUSIC are built on the recognition that these four components must be present in order for learning to take place. The **Lesson Focus** for each plan identifies the concept, the behavior, and the conceptual mode. An example follows.

Lesson Focus
Melody: A series of pitches may move up, down, or remain the same. *(P–I)*

  ■ The **behavior** is identified at the end of the concept statement by the first letter.
  P Perform (singing/playing)
  D Describe (move/verbalize/visualize)
  C Create (improvise/compose)
  ■ The **conceptual mode** at which it is expected that most students will be functioning in this lesson is identified by the second capital letter.
  E Enactive *I* Ikonic *S* Symbolic

Thus in the example given above, the designation *(P–I)* at the end of the concept statement indicates that the behavior stressed in the lesson is **Perform** and that the students will be primarily using the **Ikonic** mode in that lesson.

The Generative Approach To Music Reading

Lessons that help develop music-reading skills are an integral part of any learning sequence that leads toward musical independence. The generative approach to music reading used in HOLT MUSIC

☐ is based on a cyclic process that takes the learner through three stages corresponding to the three modes of conceptualization (See chart.)

- provides a lesson sequence that recognizes that a learner may be functioning at different stages of the cycle simultaneously—for example, a student might be reading simple rhythms from notation (symbolic stage) while associating melodies with ikons (ikonic stage) and learning harmonies aurally (enactive stage).
- presents each new skill in relation to the musical whole, rather than through pattern drill alone.
- distinguishes between sight-reading (playing an instrument from notation) and sight-singing.

Reading Rhythm

The generative approach to reading rhythm

- recognizes that reading of rhythm depends on the perception of durational relationships
- is based on a two-dimensional approach
  - sensing durations within the melodic rhythm in relation to the underlying beat, and
  - sensing durations in the melodic rhythm in relation to the shortest sound within that rhythm

The **additive approach** described above is used because

- it is the rhythmic relationship to which the young person seems to respond most readily
- it allows the student to solve rhythmic problems by using addition rather than division
- it is the basis for rhythmic organization used in the music of many non-Western cultures, as well as in much of the popular music of today.

Reading Melody

The generative approach to reading melody

- begins with melodies based on major or minor modes because these are most familiar to the contemporary American child
- uses the body scale (see below) to help the beginning student internalize pitch relationships
- stresses the hearing and performing of melodies in relation to the underlying harmony
- makes use of scale numbers to describe tonal relationships because numbers

  - provide the learner with a way of internalizing and recalling melodic pitches in relation to a tonal center
  - build on a numerical concept that most children have when this stage is introduced
  - allow for meaningful transfer to the reading of staff notation
  - are commonly used to describe chord structure, thus helping the student to understand the relation of melody to harmony

---

Lessons that develop reading skills take the student through the three conceptual modes.

ENACTIVE MODE The student performs the rhythm of a melody and metric grouping by imitating what is heard.

IKONIC MODE The student associates rhythms with ikons that represent duration in relation to

- the shortest sound
- the beat and accent

As the student associates these ikons with sound patterns, vocabulary is introduced to describe

- sounds that make up the melodic rhythm (short, long, lo-ong)

short short long   short short long   lo-ong

- sounds in relation to the beat (shorter than, longer than)

shorter same   longer   lo-ong

- the accent (moves in twos, moves in threes)

moves in twos   moves in threes

SYMBOLIC MODE The process is completed as the child transfers the ability to read ikons to reading traditional music notation.

ENACTIVE MODE The student performs in response to melodies heard. During this stage the body scale is introduced, providing the child with another means of sensing and responding to pitch relationships.

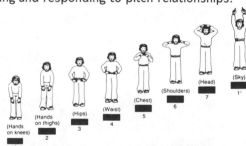

(Hands on knees) 1 (Hands on thighs) 2 (Hips) 3 (Waist) 4 (Chest) 5 (Shoulders) 6 (Head) 7 (Sky) 1'

IKONIC MODE The child first associates melodies with ikons that represent the up-down, step-skip relationship of pitches. Later, pitches are labeled with scale numbers to show their relationship to the tonal center.

SYMBOLIC MODE The student transfers the ability to read a new melody from scale numbers to staff notation.

Scope and Sequence

As students grow in their understanding of musical concepts, they acquire skills for manipulating their own musical environments. Page numbers following each concept statement guide the teacher to lessons in HOLT MUSIC, Level 1, that focus on that concept. Boldfaced numbers represent lessons where that concept is dealt with as a primary focus of the lesson. Other numbers indicate

	Concept	Ikon	Musical Symbol
RHYTHM	■ Music may be comparatively fast or slow, depending on the speed of the underlying pulse. *Pages:* **38–39**, 40–41, 100–101 ■ Music may become faster or slower by changing the speed of the underlying pulse. *Pages:* 4–5, 6–7, **38–39**, 100–101 ■ Music may move in relation to the underlying steady beat or shortest pulse. *Pages:* 6–7, **8–9**, 10–11, **12–13**, **14–15**, 16–17, **20–21**, **22–23**, 26–27, 48–49, **72–77**, 86–87, **94–95**, 102–103, 106–107, 112–113, **148–149**, **150**, **151**, **154**, **165**, 172–173, 187, **191**, **194–195** ■ A series of beats may be organized into regular or irregular groupings by stressing certain beats. *Pages:* **48–49**, **50–51**, **110–111**, 160–161 ■ Individual sounds and silences within a rhythmic line may be longer than, shorter than, or the same as other sounds within the line. *Pages:* 26–27, 40–41, **56–57**, **68–69**, **122–123**, **124–125**, **128–129**, **152**, **155**, **167**, **168–169**, **170**, **172–173**, 185 ■ Individual sounds and silences within a rhythmic line may be longer than, shorter than, or the same as the underlying steady beat or shortest pulse. *Pages:* 14–15, 20–21, **60–61**, **70–71**, **82–83**, **84–85**, 86–87, 90–91, 112–113, 118–121, **156**, **166**, **175**, **176**, **178**, **181**, 188, 191, **196–197**, **198–199**, 200 ■ Accented sounds within a rhythmic line may sound with, before, or after the accented underlying beat.		
MELODY	■ A series of pitches may move up, down, or remain the same. *Pages:* 6–7, 8–9, **10–11**, 12–13, 14–15, 16–17, 20–21, 22–23, **24–25**, 40–41, **46–47**, **52–53**, **54–55**, 56–57, **58–59**, **60–61**, **62–63**, 66–67, 98–99, 112–113, **126–127**, 130–131, 136, **138–139**, **140–141**, 143, **174**, 188 ■ A series of pitches may move up or down by steps or skips. *Pages:* 64–65, **72–77**, **78–79**, 94–95, **106–107**, **108–109**, 110–111, 112–113, **128–129**, 130–131, **170**, 174, **178**, **200** ■ Each pitch within a melody moves in relation to a home tone. *Pages:* **182–183** ■ A series of pitches bounded by the octave "belong together," forming a tonal set. *Pages:* 64–65, **78–79**, **80–81**, **108–109**, **110–111** ■ A melody may be relatively high or low. *Pages:* **64–65**, **138–139**, 179, 185 ■ Individual pitches, when compared to each other, may be higher, lower, or the same. *Page:* 200		
TIMBRE	■ The quality of a sound is determined by the sound source. *Pages:* 14–15, 16–17, **18–19**, 28–29, 100–101, **104–105**, 118–121, 137, 147, 150, 151, **157**, 158–159, 171, 177, 179 ■ The quality of a sound is affected by the material, shape, and size of the source. *Pages:* 14–15, 16–17, 28–29, 100–101, 179 ■ The quality of a sound is affected by the way the sound is produced. *Pages:* 140–141, **142**, 147, 151, 171, 177		

lessons where the concept is dealt with, but not as the primary focus.

The skills list gives a sampling of representative behaviors for Level 1. Page numbers listed give only one example of a lesson where that skill is developed. For a comprehensive listing of skills, refer to the Classified Index of Activities and Skills, page 236.

Terms for Grade 1   Skills/Behaviors for Grade 1

Terms for Grade 1	Skills/Behaviors for Grade 1	
fast–slow faster–slower short–long same shorter–longer beat short sound steady beat heavy–light twos threes sounds–silence notes rests rhythm patterns	**Perform**	Maintain a steady beat when chanting, walking, tapping, clapping, and playing classroom instruments. THROUGHOUT Sing songs and chant rhymes with rhythmic accuracy. THROUGHOUT Play simple ostinato patterns on classroom instruments. 151
	Describe	Respond to fast-slow by clapping, chanting, moving, and playing instruments. 4–5 Identify tempo using terms such as fast, slow, getting faster, or getting slower. 100–101 Use ikons to identify fast-slow and faster-slower. 38–39 Identify sounds within rhythm patterns as same, short, long, shorter than, and longer than. 72–77 Associate ikons with short and long sounds within a rhythm pattern. 122–123 Respond to music grouped in twos or threes by playing and moving. 50–51
	Create	Improvise rhythm patterns in relation to a steady beat. 181 Compose original music using simple rhythm patterns. 150–151
up–down step–skip high–low higher–lower shape of melody scale scale steps	**Perform**	Develop ability to vocally match pitches. 1–3 Sing a repertoire of songs with tonal accuracy. THROUGHOUT Sing or play short melodic patterns showing awareness of up-down-same, step-skip, and higher-lower. 80–81 Sing songs using the body scale. 108–109 Use a range of vocal inflections when performing poetry, chants, and nursery rhymes. 66–67
	Describe	Show melodic contour with body and hand movements. 62–63 Match a variety of visual images with melody patterns heard. 58–59 Devise own visual images to indicate awareness of melodic shape. 170 Use own vocabulary to describe high-low and melodic direction and contour. 46–47
	Create	Improvise melodic "conversations." 134–135 Improvise original melodies using the pentatonic and whole-tone scales. 185
classroom instrument names (triangle, resonator bells, drum, woodblock, autoharp, finger cymbals, tambourine, jingle bells) orchestral instrument names (trumpet, violin, flute, double bass, oboe, clarinet, bassoon, French horn) speaking voice–singing voice	**Perform**	Sing with a pleasing vocal quality. 138–139 Use the voice, classroom instruments, body sounds, and environmental objects to produce a variety of timbres. 147
	Describe	Recognize the difference between talking and singing. 134–135 Respond to differences in sound quality with appropriate movement. 171

	Concept	Ikon	Musical Symbol	
TIMBRE (continued)	▪ The total sound is affected by the number and qualities of sounds occurring at the same time. *Page:* **190**			
DYNAM-ICS	▪ Music may be comparatively loud or soft. *Pages:* 16–17, 30–31, 40–41, 100–101, 136, 138–139 ▪ Music may become louder or softer. *Pages:* 66–67, 165		*f* *p*	
ARTICULA-TION	▪ A series of sounds may move from one to the next in either a smoothly connected or a detached manner. *Pages:* 100–101 ▪ The quality of a sound is affected by the way the sound begins, continues, and ends. *Pages:* 177, 179			
HARMONY	▪ Chords and melody may move simultaneously in relation to each other. *Pages:* 6–7, **153**, 182–183 ▪ A series of simultaneous sounds may alternate between activity and rest. *Pages:* **160–161** ▪ Two or more pitches may be sounded simultaneously. *Pages:* 102–103, 160–161 ▪ Two or more musical lines may occur simultaneously. *Pages:* **104–105**, 130–131, 179, **185, 200**			
TEX-TURE	▪ Musical quality is affected by the distance between the musical lines. ▪ Musical quality is affected by the number of or degree of contrast between musical lines occurring simultaneously. *Page:* **190**			
FORM	▪ A musical whole begins, continues, and ends. *Pages:* **88–89, 112–113** ▪ A musical whole is a combination of smaller segments. *Pages:* 12–13, **32–33, 44–45, 54–55, 64–65, 86–87,** 88–89, **90–91, 92–93, 114–117, 143,** 160–161, **164,** 189, **192–193** ▪ A musical whole may be made up of same, varied, or contrasting segments. *Pages:* 22–23, **42–43,** 68–69, 102–103, **112–113, 137,** 165, **168–169, 172–173** ▪ A series of sounds may form a distinct musical idea within the musical whole. *Pages:* 2–3, **94–95** ▪ A musical whole may include an introduction, interludes, and an ending segment. *Pages:* 4–5, 42–43, 86–87, **92–93,** 104–105, **114–117,** 148–149, 150, 156, 168–169, 181, **187,** 188, 189, 190			
EXPRES-SION	▪ Musical elements are combined into a whole to express a musical or extramusical idea. *Pages:* 2–3, 4–5, 6–7, 26–27, 34–37, 66–67, 98–99, 100–101, 102–103, 118–121, 136, 144–145, 150, 171, **186, 189** ▪ The expressiveness of music is affected by the way timbre, dynamics, articulation, rhythm, melody, harmony, form, tempo, and texture contribute to the musical whole. *Pages:* **16–17, 28–29, 134, 135,** 138–139, **140–141, 147,** 150, **151, 158–159, 177, 179, 184, 185, 188, 189**			
TIME & PLACE	▪ The way musical elements are combined into a whole reflects the origin of the music. *Pages:* 40–41 ▪ A particular use of timbre, dynamics, articulation, rhythm, melody, harmony, and form reflects the origin of the musical whole.			

Terms for Grade 1	Skills/Behaviors for Grade 1	
		Recognize by ear and by sight common orchestral instruments. 179
	Create	Improvise original music using a variety of sound sources. 100–101
loud–soft louder–softer	**Perform**	Sing or play with dynamics appropriate to the musical mood or style. 138–139
		Use dynamic levels to enhance poetry, chants, drama, and musical stories. 16–17
	Describe	Show dynamic changes with movement. 4–5
		Use the terms loud and soft to identify volume changes. 30–31
		Use ikons to reflect dynamic changes. 40–41
smooth connected detached	**Perform**	Chant and sing in a manner that reflects sensitivity to articulation. 138–139
	Describe	Respond to varying articulation with appropriate movement. 177
		Discuss the way sounds begin, continue, and end. 88–89
accompaniment chord ostinato	**Perform**	Sing a melody while hearing an accompaniment. 14–15
		Play drones or simple melodic patterns to accompany songs. 196–197
	Describe	Demonstrate recognition of chord changes with movement. 153
		Use visual images to show awareness of multiple harmonic strands. 104–105
	Create	Improvise pentatonic or whole-tone accompaniments. 200
heavy–light thick–thin	**Describe**	Respond to varying textures with appropriate movements. 104–105
		Use visual images to show awareness of texture. 190
whole–part same–different phrase verse–refrain beginning: introduction interlude special ending: coda	**Describe**	Show recognition of phrase changes with movement. 32–33
		Demonstrate awareness of whole-part structure and repetition and contrast. 114–117
		Organize geometric shapes to indicate understanding of same-different. 92–93
	Create	Plan a long song by combining short songs. 42–43
		Develop introductions, interludes, and endings for songs. 148–149
mood feeling	**Perform**	Express mood by choosing instruments, planning simple accompaniments, and singing appropriately. 186
		Use musical expression to enhance art, poetry, and drama and to assist in the study of language and social studies. 66–67
	Describe	Use visual images, movement, and words to express own responses to music. 4–5
	Create	Improvise music to represent different moods. 184
long ago far away	**Perform**	Sing or play chants and songs of many times and places. 40–41
		Sing selected songs with correct foreign language pronunciation. 166
	Describe	Discuss music about people, neighborhoods, jobs, places, and so on. 137

UNIT 1 *Music to Explore*

Unit Overview

In this unit the children will be introduced to major concept areas—expression, rhythm, melody, timbre, form, harmony, and time and place —while engaging in a variety of activities— moving, chanting, singing, playing instruments, listening, describing music, and creating their own musical events. By listening to *The Three Little Pigs* and by dramatizing with puppets, the children will be initiated into the world of the music drama. Other lessons further illustrate how musical materials may be used to tell a story or express non-musical ideas.

Throughout *Music to Explore*, the children are guided toward reading musical notation. Most of the notational material is in the form of ikons— graphic devices (pictures) that represent musical sounds. The children are first introduced to rhythm bars and melody contours, through both kinesthetic activities (such as use of the body scale) and reading activities. The ikons are then displayed together with traditional musical notation to help the children make a transition from the pictorial realm to symbolic notation. Finally, the children apply their newly developed skills to read musical notation for simple songs.

Come All You Playmates

Traditional

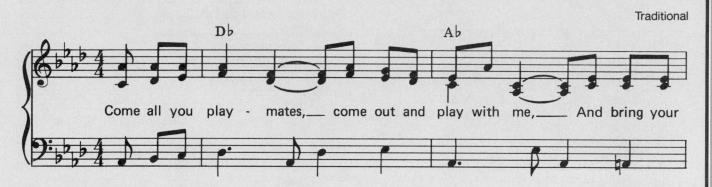

Come all you play - mates,__ come out and play with me,__ And bring your

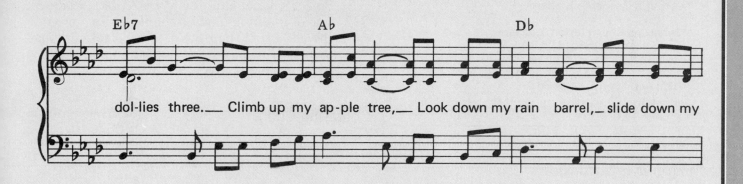

dol-lies three.__ Climb up my ap-ple tree,__ Look down my rain barrel,__ slide down my

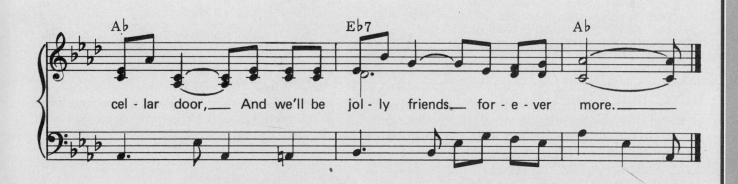

cel - lar door,__ And we'll be jol - ly friends__ for - e - ver more._____

LESSON 1

Lesson Focus

Expression: Musical elements are combined into a whole to express a musical or extramusical idea. *(P–E)*

Materials

o **Record Information:**
  • Come All You Playmates
  📠 **Record 1 Side A Band 1**
    Voices: children's choir
    Accompaniment: flute, clarinet, saxophone, cornet, trombone, violin, double bass, banjo, percussion
  • *Children's Symphony,* First Movement, by Harl McDonald, 1899–1955
    Record 1 Side A Band 2
    Philadelphia Orchestra
    Harl McDonald, conductor

o **Other:** masking tape

o **Teacher's Resource Binder:**
  • Optional —
    Curriculum Correlation 2, page C2
    Enrichment Activity 1, page E2
    Kodaly Activity 5, page K8
    Mainstreaming Suggestion 1, page M7
    Orff Activity 13, page O16

o **For additional experience with expression:** Describe 12, page 177

For Your Information

Structure of *Children's Symphony*:
  Introduction
  Section A: "London Bridge Is Falling Down"; drum cadence signals transition to new section.
  Section B: "Baa, Baa, Black Sheep"; drum cadence again announces transition to next section.
  Section A: Original song returns.

Introducing the Lesson

Welcome the children to music class by playing the recording of "Come All You Playmates" or singing the song for them. Suggest that there are many games that can be played to music. **Let's be playmates and sing some song games together.**

Developing the Lesson

1. Share the joy of music with your class by playing some familiar song games with them. Many children will have learned versions of the rhymes included here; encourage them to share their versions with you as you introduce each rhyme. Use the simplified game ideas suggested here or create your own games.

2. Select games from among the following that you feel will be the most enjoyable for you and your class. Sing each rhyme for the class and then have the children join in. These simple melodic ideas can also provide opportunities for you to check the children's pitch-matching skills.

Jack, Jump Over the Candlestick

Jack be nim - ble, Jack be quick,

Jack jump o - ver the can - dle - stick!

Select several children to be "Jack." Place a line of masking tape on the floor. As you and the class sing the rhyme, each "Jack" jumps over the line at the appropriate time (as indicated by the words of the rhyme).

Teasing Chant

Nyeh! Nyeh! You can't catch me,

Can't catch a tur - tle sit - tin' in a tree!

The children should be seated with one arm pointing straight "to the sky." The teacher is "it." While the class sings the chant, the teacher covers her or his eyes with one hand while trying to catch the hand of a child with the other hand.

Allee, Allee Outs in Free

One, two, three. Al - lee, Al - lee outs in free. ___

The children close their eyes and sing the chant, while the teacher chooses one child to hide behind the piano or the teacher's desk. When the children have finished singing the chant, they may open their eyes; they must

2

then determine the name of the child who is hiding. When they have identified the hidden child, the class can sing the chant again, inserting the name of the hidden child in place of the numbers.

Ring Around a Rosy

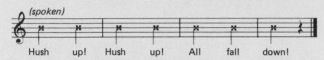

Ring a-round a ro-sy, Pock-et full of po-sies.

(spoken)

Hush up! Hush up! All fall down!

To play this game the teacher and the class sing while seated. All cover their mouths on the words "Hush up," and let their heads fall toward their laps on the words, "All fall down."

3. After the children have enjoyed some of the preceding activities, end this part of the lesson by singing and playing the following traditional song game.

London Bridge Is Falling Down

Lon - don Bridge is fall - ing down,

Fall - ing down, fall - ing down, Lon - don Bridge is

fall - ing down, My fair la - dy.

To play the game, choose two children to form an arch with their clasped hands. Assign one child the color "red" and the other child the color "blue." The class marches under the arch (in a circle) until the words, "My fair

lady." On these words the children forming the arch drop their hands around the child marching under the arch at that moment. The child who is "caught" is then asked which color he or she prefers (i.e., red or blue). The caught child whispers the answer so that the others cannot hear. He or she then stands behind the child forming the arch who was assigned that color. Continue the game until all have been caught.

4. **Our game songs are sometimes played on instruments. Listen to this music. Which of our game songs is the orchestra playing?** Play through Section A of *Children's Symphony* and have the children identify the song ("London Bridge Is Falling Down").

5. **This orchestra can play another song that you know! Listen while they play "London Bridge" again. Then see if you can name the next song you hear.** Play from the beginning of *Children's Symphony* through Section B. The children may identify the melody in Section B as "Baa, Baa, Black Sheep," "Twinkle, Twinkle, Little Star," or "ABC."

6. **Let's listen once more. Make a bridge with your hands when you hear "London Bridge." Put your hands in your lap when you hear "Baa, Baa, Black Sheep."** Play the complete recording. Observe which children recognize the return of "London Bridge."

Closing the Lesson

End the class by returning to the first song of the day, "Come All You Playmates." Replay the recording or sing the song for the class. **I hope you'll be my musical playmates again!**

LESSON 2

Lesson Focus

Expression: Musical elements are combined into a whole to express a musical or extramusical idea. *(D–E)*

Materials

o **Record Information:**
  • Come All You Playmates **(Record 1 Side A Band 1)**
  • A-Hunting We Will Go
    Record 1 Side A Band 3
    Voices: children's choir
    Accompaniment: two oboes, two clarinets, two bassoons, French horn
  • *Children's Symphony* **(Record 1 Side A Band 2)**

o **Instruments:** hand drum and mallet; large cymbal and mallet; finger cymbals; sand blocks

o **Teacher's Resource Binder:**
  • Optional —
    Mainstreaming Suggestion 2, page M7

o **For additional experience with expression:** Special Times 4, page 189

For Your Information

Form of recording of "A-Hunting We Will Go":
Introduction: Horn announces hunt
Song
Interlude: Walking tempo
Song
Interlude: Walking tempo, pause, walking tempo
Song
Interlude: Slow tempo (as though looking cautiously)
Song
Interlude: Fast tempo (chasing fox)
Song and **Coda:** Song returns at original tempo and gets softer as hunters disappear down trail

Introducing the Lesson

Play the recording of "Come All You Playmates." Review the words of the song. Invite the class to choose and play one of the song games played during the previous class session.

Here's a new game. Listen! What does the song tell us to do? Sing or play the recording of "A-Hunting We Will Go." Listen to the song several times to familiarize the children with the words of the song.

Developing the Lesson

1. **How will you move as you hunt for the fox?** Play the recording again. **Listen carefully! The music will tell you how to move.** Play the recording several times to help the chil-

dren determine that they must move in a different way during each repetition of the song. (See **For Your Information.**)

2. Invite the class (or a small group of children) to dramatize the hunt. They should listen during each repetition of the song and dramatize a part of the hunt during each interlude.

   Can you sing and move this time? Some children may sing the song while others dramatize during both the song sections and the interludes.

3. **You showed the way that music expresses ideas very well with your movements. What ideas do these sounds express?** Sing the following phrase:

Make be - lieve, what can you be?

Play an instrument in the manner indicated below. Have the children respond with movement to each sound pattern. Invite the children to sing the phrase, "Make believe, what can you be?", with you after each action. The words shown in each example suggest ideas the children might have in response to each sound pattern. Ask them to verbalize the idea that each sound suggests to them.

I'm a straight stick.

I'm a big, round balloon.

I'm a tree in the gentle wind.

4

I'm a thundercloud.

I'm a slithering snake.

(Roll fingertips over drum head)

Let's pretend we are in "sleeping land."

I'm a horse standing up to sleep.

(Rub drum head)

I'm falling asleep in a rocking chair.

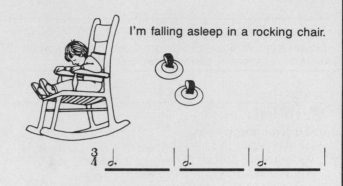

I'm a little kitten . . . sound asleep.

Closing the Lesson

You expressed ideas that you heard in the sounds so well! Rest while you listen to the orchestra's sounds. Think about the ideas the instruments are expressing! Play the recording of *Children's Symphony* to end the class.

A-Hunting We Will Go

Traditional

Oh a - hunt-ing we will go, A - hunt-ing we will go, We'll catch a lit-tle fox and put him in a box, And then we'll let him go.

5

LESSON 3

Lesson Focus

Expression: Musical elements are combined into a whole to express a musical or extramusical idea. *(P–E)*

Materials

o **Record Information:**
  - Come All You Playmates **(Record 1 Side A Band 1)**
  - A-Hunting We Will Go **(Record 1 Side A Band 3)**
  - Circus Music from *The Red Pony* by Aaron Copland, 1900– **Record 1 Side A Band 4** Little Orchestra Society Thomas K. Scherman, conductor

o **Instruments:** autoharp; hand drum and mallet; woodblock and mallet; sand blocks; finger cymbals

o **Teacher's Resource Binder:**
  - Optional — **Biography 1,** pages B1–B2 **Enrichment Activity 1,** page E2 **Mainstreaming Suggestion 3,** page M7

o **For additional experience with expression:** Perform 20, page 158

For Your Information

Game instructions for "Come All You Playmates":
Form a circle. At the start of the game, the children face the center of the circle and join hands.

Phrases 1–2:	Walk to center of circle while raising joined hands; walk backwards to original position while lowering hands
Phrase 3:	Drop hands, "rock" dolly; hold up three fingers
Phrase 4:	Pretend to climb tree
Phrase 5:	Cup hands around mouth as though shouting into barrel
Phrase 6:	Make "scooping" motion with hands
Phrases 7–8:	Join hands; walk to center of circle and back as in Phrases 1–2

Introducing the Lesson

Begin the class by playing the recording of "Come All You Playmates." **We can play a game with this song!** (See **For Your Information** for instructions.)

Play the game. Make sure that the children change their movements at the beginning of each new word pattern.

Developing the Lesson

1. **Let's review another game! Do you remember how to move to this music?** Play "A-Hunting We Will Go" while the children move in response to tempo changes during the interludes. (See **For Your Information** in Lesson 2 for form of recording.)

2. **Can you sing the song for me?** Establish the tonality on the autoharp by strumming the chords F-C7-F. Softly play a chordal accompaniment as the children sing. If the children have any problems singing the song, have them listen again to the recording. Then guide their singing by mirroring the melodic contour with hand gestures.

Mirroring

3. **You can sing without the recording. Can you add the sounds of the hunt without the recording?** Draw attention to the instruments you have on display (hand drum, woodblock, sand blocks). **Which instrument would be good for the walk at the beginning of our hunt?** Children may choose the same or different instruments for each interlude.

4. **Who can play steady walking sounds on the hand drum? Who can play a slow walking sound on the sand blocks? Who can play a fast rhythm on the woodblock?** Choose a child to play each instrument. The instrument players play during the interludes; the rest of the class sings the song sections.

5. Sing the following to the class:

Let's pretend we're in a circus! What can you be?

I'm a tightrope walker.

6

I'm a balancing clown holding an umbrella.

1) Move one foot slowly forward and back.

2) Move one foot slowly backward, then stop.

3) Move one foot slowly back and forth without stopping.

Always look at the umbrella (to help maintain balance).

I'm a piece of popcorn starting to pop!

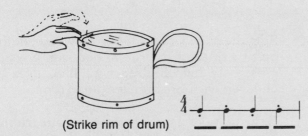

(Strike rim of drum)

$\frac{4}{4}$

I'm a galloping horse!

$\frac{6}{8}$

I'm on a trapeze swinging back and forth!

$\frac{3}{4}$

6. While the children are still pretending, begin to play the recording of "Circus Music." **What circus ideas does this music suggest? What can you be now?** Give the children the freedom to show ideas in movement without insisting that they verbalize what they are showing. Replay the recording as the children take their seats to rest.

Closing the Lesson OPTIONAL

End the class by returning to "sleeping land." (See Lesson 2, page 4, Step 3.)

7

LESSON 4

Lesson Focus

Rhythm: Music may move in relation to the underlying steady beat. *(D–E)*

Materials

○ **Record Information:**
  • Hello
    Record 1 Side A Band 5
    Voices: man, child
    Accompaniment: whistler, synthesizer, electric piano, electric bass, percussion
  • A-Hunting We Will Go **(Record 1 Side A Band 3)**
  • *Gavotte*
    by George Frederick Handel, 1685–1759
    Record 1 Side A Band 6
    Paul Sheftel, piano

○ **Instruments:** autoharp

○ **Teacher's Resource Binder:**
  • Optional —
    Biography 2, pages B3–B4
    Curriculum Correlation 4, page C8
    Enrichment Activity 13, page E21
    Mainstreaming Suggestion 4, page M11
    Orff Activity 5, page O5

Introducing the Lesson *OPTIONAL*

Welcome the class by singing "Hello" or playing the recording. **Listen while I sing again. The song asks a question. What is it?** ("How are you?") **Is there an answer? Listen again.** Discover that the answer is "I'm fine."

Some children may be familiar with a similar song, "Hello, Ev'rybody." You may wish to review or teach this welcome song also.

Hello Ev'rybody
Words by Eunice Holsaert
Music by Charity Bailey

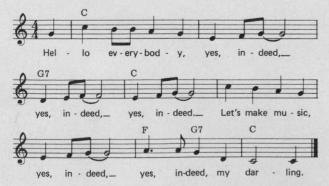

Developing the Lesson

1. Sing "Hello" to the children several times as you walk around the room shaking hands. When the class has heard the song many times, ask them to sing the question phrase ("Hello, Hello, Hello and how are you?") while you sing the answer phrase. Using hand gestures mirror the melodic contour as you sing; encourage the children to imitate your movements. Then reverse singing roles — you sing the question phrase and the class answers.

Mirroring

Ask the class to sing the entire song; accompany them on the autoharp, emphasizing the underlying steady beat.

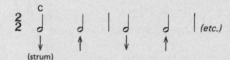

Sing the song as a dialogue between children on two sides of the room; between boys and girls; between children with blue eyes and children with brown eyes; and so on.

2. **Can you take a walk to call on your friends?** Choose some children to walk around the room "calling" on friends while singing the question phrase from the song. Those "at home" sing the answer. **Can you step with the sound of my autoharp's steady beat as you go calling?**

Help the children sense the steady beat. Stress it with your autoharp accompaniment or lightly clap as the children listen to the recording.

3. **You stepped nicely to the beat of that song. Can you step with the beat as we pretend to go hunting?** Review "A-Hunting We Will Go." As they dramatize the hunt during the interludes, step the beat for the children as necessary to help them sense its changing speed.

4. Play the recording of *Gavotte* (or play *Gavotte* on the piano). **Show me the steady beat of this music with your hands. Here's a spe-**

cial way to clap. Show the children how to clap the beat: Hold one hand (left for most children) palm up, like a tabletop. This hand remains still. The other hand moves up and down to make the clapping sound.

Play the recording while the children lightly clap the beat. **Now show me how you might step to the steady beat of this piano music.** Children may respond by stepping lightly, or tiptoeing to show the beat.

Closing the Lesson

End the class by singing the following words to the melody of "Hello."

> Goodbye, Goodbye,
> Goodbye to all my friends.
> I'm sad, I'm sad,
> Music class is at an end.

As before, mirror the melodic contour while singing; exaggerate the downward movement of the melody on the words "Goodbye" and "I'm sad."

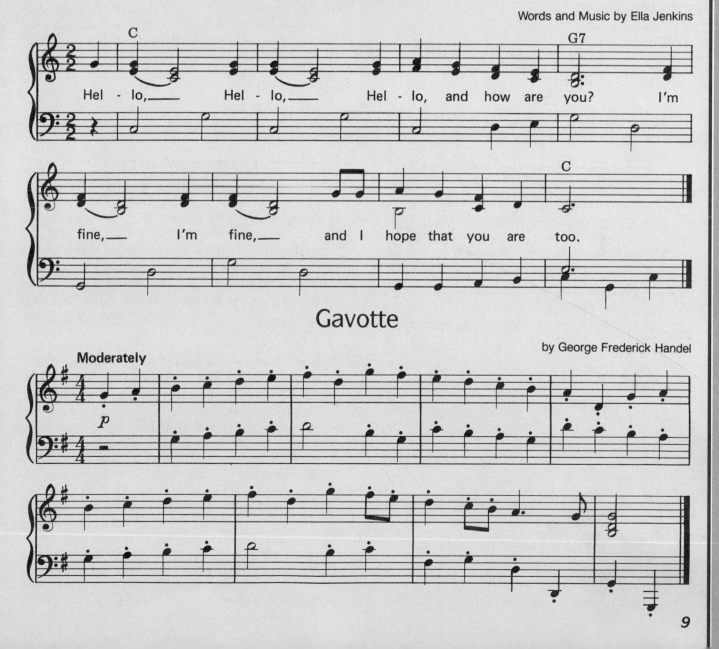

Hello

Words and Music by Ella Jenkins

Hel - lo,___ Hel - lo,___ Hel - lo, and how are you? I'm fine,___ I'm fine,___ and I hope that you are too.

Gavotte

by George Frederick Handel

Moderately

LESSON 5

Lesson Focus

Melody: A series of pitches may move up, down, or remain the same. *(D–E)*

Materials

o **Record Information:**
  • Hello **(Record 1 Side A Band 5)**
  • Dog and Cat
    Record 1 Side A Band 7
    Voices: children's choir
    Accompaniment: dulcimer, autoharp, guitar, double bass, percussion
  • *Gavotte* **(Record 1 Side A Band 6)**

o **Instruments:** resonator bells E, F, G, and A; bell mallet

o **Other:** bell stairsteps for major scales (See Binder, page A2, for instructions.)

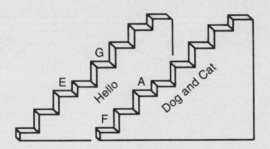

o **Teacher's Resource Binder:**
  • Optional —
    Biography 2, pages B3–B4
    Enrichment Activities 12, 13, pages E13, E21
    Mainstreaming Suggestion 5, page M11

o **For additional experience with melody:** Describe 9, page 174

For Your Information

Structure of *Gavotte*:
  Four phrases, each 8 beats long
  Form—**A B A B'**
  Melodic contour of each phrase:

Introducing the Lesson

Begin by reviewing "Hello" (Lesson 4, page 8). As the class sings the song, move about the room shaking hands.

Listen! I'm going to change the song. Sing the song and insert a child's name at the end of Phrase 1. (See the examples below.) **What did I do?**

Invite the child whose name you have inserted to sing the answer phrase. **Let's show the up-down movement of the melody with our hands as we sing.** Repeat the activity; give several children the opportunity to sing alone while the class shows the contour of the melody.

Developing the Lesson

1. **We can add something more to our song.** Place resonator bells E and G on the stairsteps. (See **Materials** for placement.) Invite a child to locate the sound of the first "Hello" on the bells. **(Joshua) started at the top, on this bell, and then he moved down to make his tune sound like the melody we sang.** Allow several children to play the melodic pattern of the first two "Hellos" while the class sings the song.

2. **Let's learn a new song!** Sing "Dog and Cat," and listen to the recording as necessary. **When we sang "Hello," the melody moved down at the beginning of the song. Show me how the beginning of *this* song moves.** Sing "Dog and Cat" again, and with hand gestures show the upward skip in the first two measures.

3. **Can we find this melody on the bells?** Place the F and A bells on the stairsteps. (See **Materials** for placement.) Choose a child to experiment with the bells. Sing the melodic pattern of the first two measures as necessary until the class agrees that the bell player has found the correct pattern.

4. Challenge the class to sing the entire song while different children play the opening pattern. **The beginning of this song goes up; the beginning of "Hello" went down.**

Closing the Lesson

Review *Gavotte.* Play the recording and have the children step lightly to the steady beat.

Can you show the up-down of this music? Model the melodic contour of *Gavotte* with your upper body and arms; have the children imitate your actions. Exaggerate your up-down move-

ment to emphasize the melodic direction. (See **For Your Information** for pictures showing the melodic direction of the four phrases.)

Can you do two things at once? Can you step the beat with your feet and show the melody with your body? Play the recording of *Gavotte* as necessary until the children are able to combine the two movements.

Dog and Cat

American Folk Song

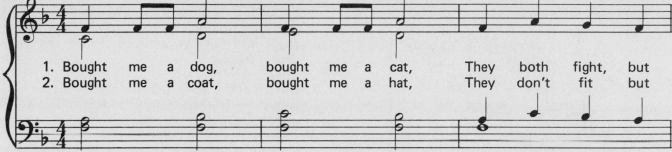

1. Bought me a dog, bought me a cat, They both fight, but
2. Bought me a coat, bought me a hat, They don't fit but

don't mind that___ Hi - o, my dar - lin'.
don't mind that___ Hi - o, my dar - lin'.

LESSON 6

Lesson Focus

Rhythm: Music may move in relation to the underlying steady beat. *(D–E)*

Materials

○ **Record Information:**
- *Gavotte* **(Record 1 Side A Band 6)**
- Dog and Cat **(Record 1 Side A Band 7)**
- Hello **(Record 1 Side A Band 5)**
- If You're Happy
  Record 1 Side A Band 8
  Voices: children's choir
  Accompaniment: string quartet

○ **Instruments:** resonator bells E, F, G, and A; bell mallet; a variety of percussion instruments (rhythm sticks, drums, jingle bells, and so on)

○ **Other:** bell stairsteps for major scales (See Binder, page A2, for instructions.)

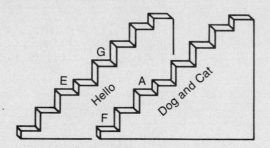

○ **Teacher's Resource Binder:**
- Optional —
  Biography 2, pages B3–B4
  Mainstreaming Suggestion 6, page M11

○ **For additional experience with rhythm:** Perform 13, page 151

Introducing the Lesson

Begin the class with *Gavotte.* Play the recording. **Can you show me the up-down melody as you step to the beat?**

Guess what song my hand is "singing." Can you hear it in your head by watching the up-down movement of my hand? Show the beginning of "Dog and Cat." If a child guesses the wrong song, sing the words of the suggested song to the melody of "Dog and Cat." **Does that sound right?** When the correct song is named, invite the class to sing while one child plays the opening pattern on resonator bells F and A. (See **Materials** for placement of bells on stairsteps.)

Continue the guessing game with "Hello." When the correct song is guessed, one child can play

"Hello" on bells E and G while the class sings. **How can you show that you feel fine?** (smile, turn thumbs up, walk with bouncy step)

Developing the Lesson

1. **What does this song tell you to do to show that you are feeling fine?** Play the recording of "If You're Happy." Repeat until the class has identified all three motions.

2. Play the recording again. Invite the children to follow the instructions in the song. Guide them to sense the underlying beat by modeling each movement as they perform.

3. Perform the song as a dialogue. The children sing the first two phrases; the teacher sings the last two phrases.

4. **What other motions could we use to show that we are happy?** (swing around, bend and stretch, wink an eye) Add verses to the song for each new movement. The teacher should continue to sing the last two phrases — the range will not be comfortable for the children's voices.

5. Have half the class march while the other half sings, "If you're happy and you know it, march around."

6. **I know another way to show I'm happy.** Hand out percussion instruments and make up special verses: "If you're happy and you know it, play the sticks (drum; jingle bells)."

Closing the Lesson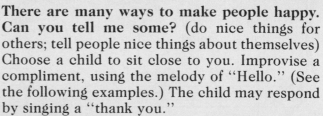

There are many ways to make people happy. Can you tell me some? (do nice things for others; tell people nice things about themselves) Choose a child to sit close to you. Improvise a compliment, using the melody of "Hello." (See the following examples.) The child may respond by singing a "thank you."

Encourage class members to sing a compliment to another child in the room. The chosen child responds with the "thank you" phrase. If any children are uneasy about singing the melody, reassure them by saying that they may instead choose to speak their phrase.

End the class by singing "If You're Happy" once again.

If You're Happy

Traditional

Lesson Focus

Rhythm: Music may move in relation to the underlying steady beat. *(D–E)*

Materials

o **Record Information:**
   • Step in Time
   • **Record 1 Side B Band 1**
     Voices: children's choir
     Accompaniment: small show orchestra
   • *Zingarese*, (Gypsy Dance) No. 1
     by Franz Joseph Haydn (**hide**-n), 1732–1809
     Record 1 Side B Band 2
   • *Mango Time*
     Trinidad Folk Tune
     Record 1 Side B Band 3

o **Instruments:** hand drum; tambourine; autoharp

o **Teacher's Resource Binder:**
   • Optional —
     Biography 3, pages B5–B6
     Kodaly Activity 3, page K5
     Mainstreaming Suggestion 7, page M12
     Orff Activity 2, page O2

o **For additional experience with rhythm:** Special Times 8, page 194

For Your Information

Structure of *Zingarese,* No. 1:
This dance, in the style of Hungarian Gypsy music, moves in twos. The violin melody usually moves with tones that are shorter than the beat.

Structure of *Mango Time*:
This is a country-style dance from Trinidad. Instruments that can be identified include a harmonica (playing the melody), a wooden trumpet, a coconut grater scraped with a spoon, and a knife tapped on a pick-blade. Other instruments include bottles and pipe-joints.

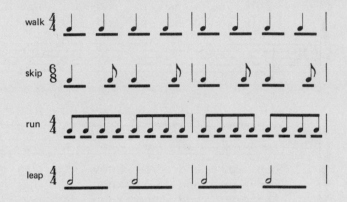

Introducing the Lesson

Begin the class with a familiar chant:

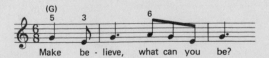

Review some of the make-believe actions from Lessons 2 and 3 (pages 4–7). End by playing a steady beat on the hand drum. Sing:

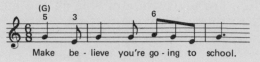

Invite a child to show how he or she might come to school. Ask the child to move across the room in whatever way he or she chooses. On a drum or tambourine, pick up the rhythm of the child's movement. **That's a good way to go to school! Who can show another way?** Continue to imitate with instrument sounds the rhythm of each child's movements.

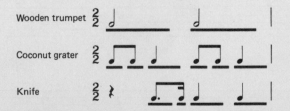

Sing the following chant to the children:

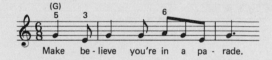

Beat a steady beat on the hand drum. As the children step around the room in time to the beat of the drum, begin to sing, "Step In Time."

Developing the Lesson

1. **Listen to the recording of this marching song. What does it tell you to do?** Ask the children to listen carefully until they can identify the action for each verse.

2. Invite the children to listen again and make up motions to fit the words (while standing in place).

3. **You've heard this melody many times. Do you think you can sing it? Let's listen one more time. Pay careful attention to the way the melody moves up and down.** Play the recording again and mirror the melodic contour. Then invite the children to sing while you play the autoharp (or the accompaniment channel on the recording).

4. **Let's march around the room as we sing our song one last time.** Reinforce the beat on the autoharp as the children march and sing.

5. **You've moved well to a march's steady beat. Can you move to the beat in this dance music?** Play the recording of *Zingarese*, No. 1. Help the children hear the steady beat by tapping the beat in the palm of your hand.

steady pulse of the wooden trumpet by clapping. Invite the children to find a way to show the beat as they sit in their seats. They could pretend to play an instrument, conduct, swing their arms, nod their heads, and so on.

Closing the Lesson

Good! Let's find the beat in this music. Play the recording of *Mango Time* and respond to the

Step in Time

Words and Music by Richard M. Sherman and Robert B. Sherman

1. Kick your knees up, step in time! Kick your knees up, step in time!
2. Link your el-bows, step in time! Link your el-bows, step in time!
3. Spin a-bout and step in time! Spin a-bout and step in time!
4. 'Round the chim-ney step in time! 'Round the chim-ney step in time!

Nev-er need a rea-son, nev-er need a rhyme, Kick your knees up, step in time!
Nev-er need a rea-son, nev-er need a rhyme, Link your el-bows, step in time!
Nev-er need a rea-son, nev-er need a rhyme, Spin a-bout and step in time!
Nev-er need a rea-son, nev-er need a rhyme, 'Round the chim-ney step in time!

LESSON 8

Lesson Focus

Expression: The expressiveness of music is affected by the way timbre contributes to the musical whole. *(D–E)*

Materials

o **Record Information:**
  - A-Hunting We Will Go **(Record 1 Side A Band 3)**
  - The Old Gray Horse
    Record 1 Side B Band 4
    Voices: solo children's voices, children's choir
    Accompaniment: clarinet, trumpet, trombone, tenor banjo, double bass, piano, percussion
  - *Gavotte* **(Record 1 Side A Band 6)**
  - *Mango Time* **(Record 1 Side B Band 3)**
  - *Zingarese*, No. 1 **(Record 1 Side B Band 2)**

o **Instruments:** jingle bells; jingle clogs; cymbals; rhythm sticks; woodblocks and mallets; claves; maracas; drums and mallets; autoharp

o **Other:** Prepare three boxes of small percussion instruments grouped by sound quality: RINGING SOUNDS (jingle bells, jingle clogs, cymbals); CLICKING SOUNDS (rhythm sticks, woodblocks, claves, maracas); and THUDDING SOUNDS (various small drums).

o **Teacher's Resource Binder:**
  - Optional —
    Biographies 2–3, pages B3–B6
    Mainstreaming Suggestion 8, page M12
    Orff Activity 4, page O4

o **For additional experience with expression and timbre:** Perform 19, page 157; Create 5, page 186

Introducing the Lesson

Review "A-Hunting We Will Go." Sing the song with autoharp accompaniment. Invite three children to play interludes on percussion instruments of their choice. You may wish to have the children imitate the form of the recording. (See **For Your Information** in Lesson 2, page 4.) Remind the child who performs the final coda to play more softly as the hunters disappear into the forest.

Developing the Lesson

1. **Here is a song about another animal. Listen! What happens?** Listen to the recording of "The Old Gray Horse" several times to acquaint the children with the story.

2. **Part of our song changes words each time to tell a different part of the story. Part of our song has the same words every time. Listen carefully to the part that stays the same. As you listen, show me with your** hands how that melody moves. After the children have listened carefully to the recording, invite them to sing the repeated part (the refrain).

3. **Let's add some funny sounds to the funny refrain. Can you remember when to listen?** (during the verse) **when to play?** (during the refrain) Distribute instruments from the first box to children seated near each other. Give the children time to experiment with the instruments' sounds. **All these instruments make ringing sounds. Play these instruments when I pretend to ring a bell.** (See **Materials.**)

Distribute "clicking sound" instruments to a second group of children; they will play when you tap two fingers together. Finally, distribute the instruments that make thudding sounds. Have these children play when you make a "hammering" motion.

Practice signaling each group to play.

4. Perform "The Old Gray Horse." (Use the recording or sing the verse and have the children sing the refrain.) Signal a different group to play on each refrain.

5. Invite a child to be the conductor. The conductor signals which group is to play during the refrains by using the motions you have been using. Perform the song once again.

6. Read or sing the following poems to the children. Ask them to decide which of the instrument groups should play to best express the ideas in each poem. They should also decide whether to play during the entire poem or only during certain sections.

TWINKLE, TWINKLE, LITTLE STAR
(ringing sounds)

Twinkle, twinkle, little star,
How I wonder what you are.
Up above the world so high,
Like a diamond in the sky.
Twinkle, twinkle, little star,
How I wonder what you are.

HICKORY, DICKORY, DOCK
(clicking sounds, ringing sound for clock chime)

Hickory, dickory, dock,
The mouse ran up the clock;
The clock struck one,
The mouse ran down,
Hickory, dickory, dock.

16

A RIDE
(thudding sounds)

Lumpity, lumpity, lump!
I ride on a camel's hump;
I down go up when he up goes down,
Lumpity, lumpity, lump!

Lumpity, lumpity, lump!
I ride on a camel's hump;
I under go out from side to side,
Lumpity, lumpity, lide!

7. After the children have selected instruments for each poem, discuss other decisions that need to be made. **When should you play very loudly? softly?** Plan other conducting signals to indicate loud and soft (mouth open in an "O" for loud; lips closed tightly for soft). Repeat each poem. Have the children

follow your conducting signals. Indicate when each group of instruments is to be played and whether the instruments should be played loudly or softly.

Closing the Lesson

Listen again to *Gavotte*, *Mango Time*, and *Zingarese*, No. 1. Have several children choose a ringing, clicking, or thudding sound to accompany each piece. These children should play a steady beat while the rest of the class moves to show the beat (by stepping, nodding their heads, and so on).

The Old Gray Horse

Nursery Song

1. Fed my horse in an old wood trough, Fed my horse in an old wood trough,
2. Fed my horse with a sil - ver spoon, Fed my horse with a sil - ver spoon,
3. Fed my horse 'til_ he got sick, Fed my horse 'til_ he got sick,
4. Doc - tor said, "He's_ al - most dead," Doc - tor said, "He's_ al - most dead,"

Fed my horse in an old wood trough, And there he caught the whoop - ing cough.
Fed my horse with a sil - ver spoon, And then he kicked it o - ver the moon.
Fed my horse 'til_ he got sick, _ Called for the Doc - tor quick, quick, quick.
Doc - tor said, "He's_ al - most dead, _ Put this horse to bed, bed, bed!"

Refrain

Koy ma - lin - go, kil - ko, kil - ko, Koy ma - lin - go, Kil - ko kee.

17

LESSON 9

Lesson Focus

Timbre: The quality of a sound is determined by the sound source. *(D–E)*

Materials

o **Record Information:**
  • This Little Light of Mine
  📼 **Record 1 Side B Band 5**
  Voices: children's choir
  Accompaniment: electric organ, electric guitar, electric bass, piano, percussion
  • Ghost Dance from *Ancient Voices of Children* by George Crumb, 1929–
  Record 1 Side B Band 6
  Jan DeGaetani, mezzo soprano
  Stephen Bell, mandolin
  Contemporary Chamber Ensemble
  Arthur Weisberg, conductor

o **Instruments:** hand drum and mallet; triangle and striker; woodblock and mallet

o **Teacher's Resource Binder:**
  • Optional —
  Mainstreaming Suggestion 9, page M12

o **For additional experience with timbre:** Perform 10, page 147

For Your Information

Structure of "Ghost Dance":
  The dance is performed using only two instruments — the mandolin and the maracas. The unusual mandolin sounds are created by plucking a string and then moving the left hand up and down on the string while it is still vibrating. The instruments are heard in the order shown below.

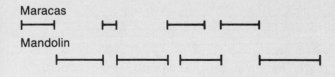

Introducing the Lesson

Review one of the game songs from Lesson 1 (page 1). Invite a child to choose a game; that child should be the leader and sing the song while others perform the game actions. Guide the child's singing by mirroring the melodic contour of the chosen game song.

Developing the Lesson

1. **Listen to a new song! How many different things "of mine" does it tell about?** Play the recording of "This Little Light of Mine" and ask the children to identify all five things (light, drum, triangle, block, song).

2. Hold up a triangle, a hand drum, and a wood-block. **Listen again. Which instrument plays first? second? last?** After determining the order of the instruments, ask the children to listen again to find out how many times each instrument plays. (six times, always on the word that describes the sound)

3. Choose three children to play the instruments in Verses 2–4 at the appropriate times. Other children can "show with their bodies" their favorite sound each time it is played.

   Play the recording while the children play the instruments or perform appropriate motions. **Be sure you play or move only when it is your time. Listen carefully!**

4. **What could we do to show the words in the first verse?** (pretend to hold a candle) **the last verse?** (sing) Play the recording while the children either play the instruments or perform the appropriate motions. When the last verse begins, turn down the voice-channel volume and have the class sing the verse. If the children have any problems singing the melody, listen to the recording with the voice channel again. Then learn the entire song.

5. **Listen! Here are some more sounds!** Play approximately the first minute of "Ghost Dance" while the children listen quietly.

   Did you hear different sounds? Can you "show" me each sound? Can you show when the sounds change?

6. Play "Ghost Dance" again while the children move to show when the sounds change. Observe those children who change movements when the sound qualities change. **How many different kinds of sounds did we hear?** (two)

7. Play the music again, through the first entrance of the mandolin. Divide the class into two groups. Group 1 moves with the maraca sounds. Group 2 moves with the sound of the mandolin. **Move when you hear your sound. Freeze when you hear other sounds!**

Closing the Lesson

Play the recording through the first segment in which the two instruments play simultaneously. Observe which children recognize that both groups must now move.

18

Play the complete recording of "Ghost Dance."
This is called a "Ghost Dance." Can you make
your movements very ghostly?

This Little Light of Mine

Spiritual
Words and Melody adapted by F.W.

1. This lit - tle light of mine, I'm gon-na let it shine.

This lit - tle light of mine, I'm gon-na let it shine.

This lit - tle light of mine, I'm gon-na let it shine, let it

shine, let it shine, let it shine. ____

2. This little drum of mine, I'm gonna let it beat...
3. This little triangle, I'm gonna let it ring...
4. This little block of mine, I'm gonna let it tap...
5. This little song of mine, I'm gonna let it sing...

LESSON 10

Lesson Focus

Rhythm: Music may move in relation to the underlying steady beat or shortest pulse. *(D–E)*

Materials

o **Record Information:**
  • If You're Happy **(Record 1 Side A Band 8)**
  • The Happy Train
    Record 1 Side B Band 7
    Voices: man, children's choir
    Accompaniment: guitar, piano, double bass, percussion
  • *Mango Time* **(Record 1 Side B Band 3)**
o **Instruments:** hand drum and mallet; woodblock and mallet; C' resonator bell and bell mallet
o **For additional experience with rhythm:** Describe 2, page 165; Special Times 10, page 198

Introducing the Lesson

Review "If You're Happy" (Lesson 6, page 12). Invite the children to perform the verses and motions they especially like.

Developing the Lesson

1. **People can be happy. This song tells about something else that is happy!** Play the recording of "The Happy Train."

2. **Show me a happy train!** Allow each child to find a space in the room where he or she can move without disturbing others. Play the recording. Comment on those children who move with the underlying shortest sound.

(Samantha's) "train" was moving with really short steps. Can we all move that way? Play the recording again; ask all the children to move with short steps.

3. **I saw others moving with this happy movement.** Play the recording and demonstrate stepping to the longer sound of the beat. **This time let's step to the beat.**

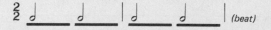

4. **Can you find short and long sounds in this music?** Play *Mango Time*. Help the children hear the long sound of the wooden trumpet and the shorter sounds of the coconut grater.

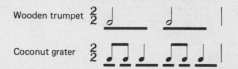

Two children may play these patterns on a drum and a woodblock while other children choose one pattern to lightly clap.

The Happy Train

Words and Music by Ruth Roberts and Ralph Stein

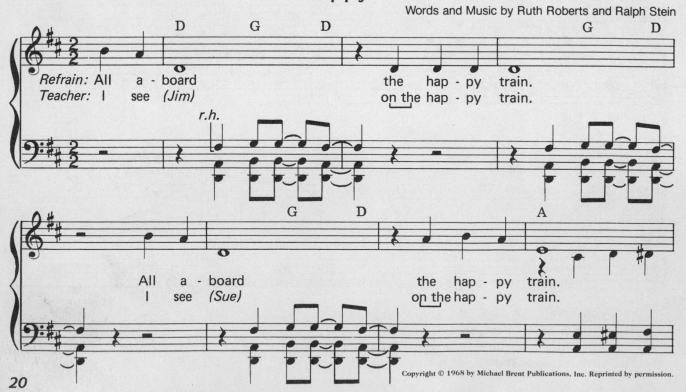

5. Return to "If You're Happy." Begin to sing, showing the shortest sound by tapping lightly against your thigh.

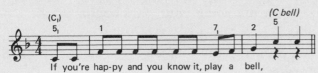

Find a place on your body to tap the shortest sound while we sing our happy song. The children should try different ways to show the shortest sound. (They could tap hands, arm, head, thigh, knees, and so on.)

6. I have a new verse. Sing, "If you're happy and you know it, play a bell." Give one child a C′ resonator bell. **Can you play two long sounds after you hear the words, "play a bell"?** Have the rest of the class tap the short sounds and sing, while the bell player plays after each statement of "play a bell."

Closing the Lesson

Return to "The Happy Train." Listen to the recording again, this time focusing attention on the melody by mirroring the melodic contour with hand gestures. **There are three places where the melody stays down low. Let's see if we can hear those places.** Listen to the recording once again and move your hands to show the melodic contour; exaggerate by leaning over on the patterns sung on D ("the happy train," Measures 2–3; "clack, clack, clack," Measures 9–10; and the last two measures of the song). **Can you sing just those parts and listen to the rest of the song?**

LESSON 11

Lesson Focus

Rhythm: Music may move in relation to the underlying shortest pulse. *(P–E)*

Materials

o **Record Information:**
  • The Happy Train **(Record 1 Side B Band 7)**
  • Chatter With the Angels
    Record 2 Side A Band 1
    Voices: man, children's choir
    Accompaniment: electric organ, piano, guitar, double bass, percussion
  • *Children's Symphony* **(Record 1 Side A Band 2)**

o **Instruments:** tambourines

o **For additional experience with rhythm:** Create 1, page 181; Special Times 9, page 196

Introducing the Lesson

Have the recording of "The Happy Train" playing as the children enter the classroom. Pantomime to show the children that they are to move to their seats in step with the shortest sound.

Sing Verse 2 for the class, inserting the names of various children. Have each child stand up and move about the room when his or her name is sung. Suggest that they move their arms back and forth to suggest the movement of the train's wheels.

Invite the class to sing the first verse with you. If the children have any problems singing the melody, listen to the recording again.

Developing the Lesson

1. **Can you find the shortest sound in this music?** Play the recording of "Chatter With the Angels." Encourage the children to find a way to tap the shortest sound.

2. **How many times do you hear the words, "chatter with the angels"?** Replay the recording until the children determine that these words are repeated six times.

3. **Listen carefully! How many times do the words, "chatter with the angels" have the same up-down melody?** As the children listen, use exaggerated hand motions to show the melodic contour; agree that the first four statements have the same melody. Ask the

class to sing those patterns while you sing the remaining parts of the song.

4. Invite the children to accompany the music by tapping an imaginary tambourine against their thighs. Tap the shortest unit of sound:

Some children may find it easier to alternate thighs:

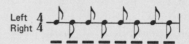

Play your imaginary tambourine when the music begins. When the music seems to change, stop playing. Listen carefully! Show me when your part begins again.

Play the recording again. The children should tap during the first eight measures of each verse.

5. **Can we sing the song by ourselves this time? You sing the part you've been playing on your tambourines. I'll sing the other part.** Perform all the verses in this manner. Then challenge the children to sing the complete song.

6. When the children can sing the whole song, distribute tambourines so that the children may accompany the first eight measures.

7. Add movements to the song:

Section A (first eight measures)
Standing in place, clap the shortest unit of sound. Find a different place to clap for each verse:

Section B (last four measures, repeated)
Move to the long sounds of the accompaniment:

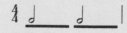

Step with hands at sides as though in a procession.

22

During the last two measures ("chatter with the angels all day long"), turn in a circle.

Closing the Lesson OPTIONAL

While the children rest after their busy class, play the recording of *Children's Symphony* and quietly enjoy the lovely music.

Chatter With the Angels

Spiritual

- Optional —
  Curriculum Correlation 8, page C13
  Mainstreaming Suggestion 10, page M13
o **For additional experience with melody:** Perform 2, page 135

Lesson Focus

Melody: A series of pitches may move up, down, or remain the same. *(P–E)*

Materials

o **Record Information:**
  - Chatter With the Angels **(Record 2 Side A Band 1)**
  - Dog and Cat **(Record 1 Side A Band 7)**
  - Three Little Kittens
    Record 2 Side A Band 2
    Voices: woman, children's choir
    Accompaniment: harpsichord, crumhorn, viola da gamba

o **Instruments:** resonator bells F, A, C, D, and F′; bell mallet

o **Other:** 4 lunch-size paper sacks; 3 brads; bell stairsteps for major scales (See Lessons 5 and 29, pages 10 and 60, regarding placement of bells on stairsteps for "Dog and Cat" and "Chatter With the Angels.")

o **Teacher's Resource Binder:**
  | Activity Sheets | • **Activity Sheet 1,** page A5 (Prepare one set of puppets — see instructions on activity sheet.) |

Introducing the Lesson

Begin singing "Chatter With the Angels." Ask the children to join in if they remember the song.

Place the C, D, and F′ resonator bells on the stairsteps. Ask a child to experiment with the bells and find the melody for "chatter with the angels." **Should the bell player start at the top and move down or start at the bottom and move up?** (start at top and move down)

Ask the rest of the class to sing the song while the bell player plays the pattern for the first four statements of "chatter with the angels."

Developing the Lesson

1. Review "Dog and Cat" (Lesson 5, page 10). Give several children the opportunity to play

Three Little Kittens

Words from Mother Goose

Traditional English Melody

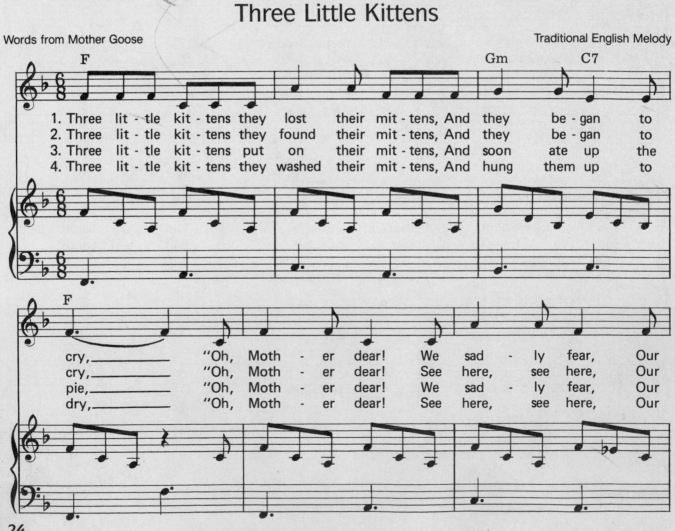

1. Three lit-tle kit-tens they lost their mit-tens, And they be-gan to cry,_____ "Oh, Moth-er dear! We sad-ly fear, Our
2. Three lit-tle kit-tens they found their mit-tens, And they be-gan to cry,_____ "Oh, Moth-er dear! See here, see here, Our
3. Three lit-tle kit-tens put on their mit-tens, And soon ate up the pie,_____ "Oh, Moth-er dear! We sad-ly fear, Our
4. Three lit-tle kit-tens they washed their mit-tens, And hung them up to dry,_____ "Oh, Moth-er dear! See here, see here, Our

the F–A pattern that begins each verse.

2. "Dog and Cat" begins with a melody that goes up. Let's turn that pattern upside down! Play the pattern A–F. Can you find this upside-down pattern in a new song? Play the recording of the first verse of "Three Little Kittens." Agree that "meow" (Measures 13–14) is the "upside-down" pattern.

3. Play the complete recording of "Three Little Kittens." Ask the children to mirror the melodic contour for each "meow" refrain.

4. Play the recording again, or sing without the recording. Ask the children to sing the refrain

while you sing the story part of the song.

5. Challenge the children to perform the entire song. Listen to the recording again if needed.

Closing the Lesson

Dramatize the story. Choose four children to be the kittens and the mother cat. The class may sing the song while the characters pantomime the words, using Activity Sheet 1 (*Kitten Paper-Sack Puppets*).

mit - tens we have lost." "What! Lost your mit - tens, you
mit - tens we have found." "What! Found your mit - tens, you
mit - tens we have soiled." "What! Soiled your mit - tens, you
mit - tens we have washed." "What! Washed your mit - tens, you

naugh - ty kit - tens, Then you shall have no pie."
love - ly kit - tens, Then you shall have some pie."
naugh - ty kit - tens, And she be - gan to cry."
love - ly kit - tens, And she be - gan to sigh."

Me - ow, me - ow, me - ow, meow.

25

Lesson Focus

Expression: Musical elements are combined into a whole to express a musical or extramusical idea. *(P–E)*

Materials

o **Piano Accompaniment:** page 202

o **Record Information:**
  • That's Nice
  Record 2 Side A Band 3
  Voice: woman
  Accompaniment: synthesizer, electric guitar, electric bass, percussion
  • Chatter With the Angels **(Record 2 Side A Band 1)**

o **Instruments:** drum and mallet; woodblock and mallet; finger cymbals; jingle bells; one maraca; tambourines

o **Other:** Prepare two "secret" boxes: Place the jingle bells in one box and the maraca in the other box.

o **Teacher's Resource Binder:**
  • Optional —
  Enrichment Activity 2, page E4

o **For additional experience with expression:** Special Times 2, page 188

Introducing the Lesson

Greet the children by singing the first verse of "That's Nice" or by playing the recording. Comment that when music time comes we always find many ways to make music.

Developing the Lesson

1. Tell the children to open their books to page 3 or show page 3 of the Jumbo Book. Ask the children to identify the different ways the children in the pictures are making music. As each way is identified, sing the appropriate verse of "That's Nice."

2. Invite the children to "make music" in different ways as you point to a picture on the pupil page and sing the corresponding verse of the song. Begin by singing Verses 3 and 4 as the children clap and walk at the appropriate times. **Can you help me make music by singing?** Suggest that you will sing the first part of Verse 2 and that they may sing the last part of the song ("singing Hi-de-lee, Hi-de-lee, Hi-de-lee? That's nice!").

3. Continue to "make music" with the other verses of the song. For Verse 5 you could

"talk" the first part of the song and then ask the children to chant the last part. For Verse 6 choose a few children to improvise an accompaniment on drum, woodblock, or finger cymbals. As before, you can sing the first part of the song, and the children may join in at the end.

4. Look again at the pictures on the pupil page. Explore different ways to make music.
(a) Clap hands: Play an echo game.

(b) Talk: Chant "Had a Little Car." (The rhythm bars show the underlying pulse.) The children could initially learn to chant the last two lines and then learn the complete rhyme.

Had a little car, license 4-8,

Went to the station to fix my brake.

Station man said, "You can't drive this machine

'Til you fill it up with gas–o–line."

I said, "Hey man, nooooo way!

I'll just get a horse that runs on hay."

(c) Walk: **Walk with the beat of the drum. Stop when the drum is silent.**

(d) Play: Place the two "secret" boxes on a table. (See **Materials.**) One child chooses a box and shakes it while you speak the following poem. The rest of the class tries to guess what is inside. If the class cannot correctly identify the contents of the box, the child holding the box looks inside and describes the instrument.

I had a little box,
That held a secret sound;
I shook it and turned it (*pause*)—
Just look at what I found!

Music Is Fun!

Share it with others.

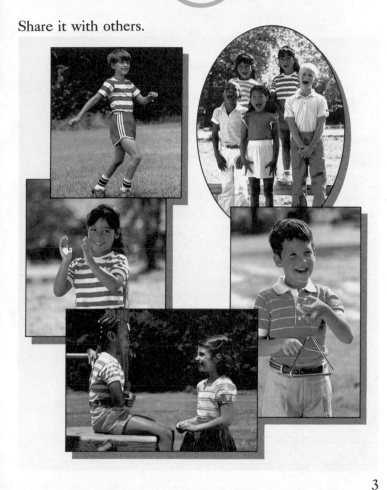

3

The children may go to the instrument cupboard and find a new instrument to hide in the secret box. The guessing game can then be repeated.

(e) Sing: Invite children to choose their favorite songs from among those they have learned this year. Share this music by singing the songs together.

Closing the Lesson

End the class by combining several of the music activities pictured on the pupil page. Review "Chatter With the Angels" (Lesson 11, page 22). Choose several children to walk with the beat, several to play the shortest sound on tambourines, and several to clap the beat during the second section. **How can we add talking to our song?** Decide that one child can introduce the song by saying, "Listen to our first-grade class sing 'Chatter With the Angels'."

That's Nice
Words and Music by B.A.

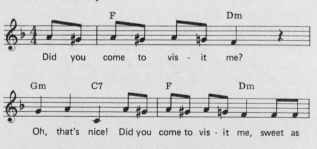

Did you come to vis - it me?

Oh, that's nice! Did you come to vis - it me, sweet as

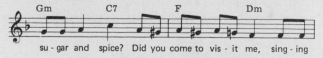

su - gar and spice? Did you come to vis - it me, sing - ing

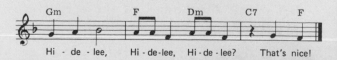

Hi - de - lee, Hi - de - lee, Hi - de - lee? That's nice!

2. ... sing with me?   3. ... clap with me?   4. ... walk with me?
5. ... talk with me?   6. ... play with me?

27

Anybody There?

Lesson Focus

Expression: The expressiveness of music is affected by the way timbre contributes to the musical whole. *(D–E)*

Materials

o **Piano Accompaniment:** page 203

o **Record Information:**
  • The Happy Train
    (Record 1 Side B Band 7)
  • Knock! Knock! Anybody There?
    Record 2 Side A Band 4
    Voices: children's choir
    Accompaniment: synthesizer, percussion

o **Instruments:** sand blocks; drum and mallet; rhythm sticks; woodblock and mallet; guiro with scratcher; finger cymbals

o **Other:** paper; feathers or ribbons

o **Teacher's Resource Binder:**
  • Optional—
    Enrichment Activity 3, page E5

o **For additional experience with timbre:**
  Special Times 5, page 190

Introducing the Lesson

Tell the children to open their books to page 3, or show page 3 of the Jumbo Book. Review "The Happy Train" (Lesson 10, page 20); recall the many ways that we can make music. Ask some children to step to the beat and others to clap the shortest sound. One child could play the shortest sound on sand blocks.

Have the children look at pupil pages 4–5. Name the different creatures (bird, cricket, rabbit, frog, snake). Discuss the places these creatures make their homes: trees, cracks, holes, and ponds.

Developing the Lesson

1. **Let's visit the homes of these creatures. Listen; can you sing this tune?**

Knock!   Knock!   An-y-bod-y there?

Repeat the tune as necessary until the children can sing it with confidence.

2. Point to each picture on the pupil pages and ask the children to sing their new tune. (See Step 1.) Follow each performance of the tune by reading to the class the appropriate poem from **For Your Information**.

3. Add the sounds of instruments as you again "visit" each home. Follow this sequence: The children sing their tune; the teacher says the poem; one or more children then softly play instruments to suggest the sound of the creature:

   Bird: waving paper for rustling feathers
   Cricket: rhythm sticks or woodblock for cricket chirp
   Rabbit: drum for thumping feet
   Frog: guiro for "ribbit"
   Snake: sand blocks for slithering sound

For Your Information

Poems for use in Step 2:

BIRD: I want to see a bird
          With a bright red vest,
          Who rustles his feathers
          When he sits in his nest.

CRICKET: A cricket lives
          In a deep, dark crack,
          Under a rock,
          Way to the back.

RABBIT: Who lives down deep
          In a hole in the ground,
          And thumps her foot
          When she looks around?

FROG: I've come to the pond
          For a very short visit,
          With a frog who just sits
          And occasionally says,
          "ribbit"!

SNAKE: A green snake's house
          Is a long, skinny place,
          'Cause his tail won't fit
          In any other place.

4. Listen to the recording and learn the complete song, "Knock! Knock! Anybody There?". During the song sections the children could dramatize the action. Have one child live in the "home" and dispense the feathers and ribbons. A different child comes to the door for each statement of the song and pantomimes receiving the gifts. The visiting child then sings a short, improvised "thank you" melody during the recorded interlude.

Closing the Lesson

Return to the song, "The Old Gray Horse" (Lesson 8, page 16). Repeat the first verse several times and change the name of the animal with each repetition. Have the children select an instrument to represent each animal's sound. Then ask the children to use each instrument to accompany the appropriate repetition. (Possible choices might include: fed my horse—wood-block for hoofs; fed my chick—finger cymbals for peeps; fed my bee—sand blocks for buzzing.)

Knock! Knock! Anybody There?
Words by Clyde Watson
Traditional Melody

Knock! Knock! An-y-bod-y there? I've fea-thers for your caps and rib-bons for your hair. If you can't pay you can sing me a song. But if you can't sing I'll just run a-long!

29

LESSON 15

Lesson Focus

Evaluation: Review concepts and skills studied in the First Quarter.

Materials

o **Piano Accompaniment:** page 204
o **Record Information:**
  • Little Sir Echo
  ▭ **Record 2 Side A Band 5**
  Voice: child
  Accompaniment: four French horns
  • *Fanfare for Three Trumpets, Three Trombones, and Timpani*
  by Daniel Speer, 1636–1707
  Record 2 Side A Band 6
  The London Brass Players
  Joshua Rifkin, director
o **Teacher's Resource Binder:**
  Evaluation • **Evaluation 1,** pages Ev1–Ev2
  • **Musical Progress Report 1,** page Ev3
  • Optional—
  Curriculum Correlation 14, page C24

The King Is Coming

Introducing the Lesson

Listen to the recording of "Little Sir Echo." Inquire if anyone has ever heard a car horn honked when passing through a tunnel. **What happened?** (heard the sound repeated) **Was the sound louder or softer when it was repeated?** (softer) **You heard an echo!** Explain that an echo is the sound that was bounced back from the tunnel walls.

Invite the children to be the echo as you play the recording. **Will you sing loudly or softly when you echo?** (softly) Play the recording.

Developing the Lesson

1. Begin a musical story. **The king is coming. We must tell all the people. But how?** Tell the children to open their books to pages 6–7 or show pages 6–7 of the Jumbo Book.

   How are people at one castle telling the people at the next castle that the king is coming? (by playing trumpets) **If the people in each far castle hear the trumpets, they will have their musicians play back the same sound—the far group of musicians will "echo" the near musicians.**

2. **Listen to this music. Do the musicians echo each other?** Play the recording of *Fanfare for Three Trumpets, Three Trombones, and Timpani.* As the music is played, point to the near (loud) or far (soft) castles depicted on the pupil pages. The final melodies are represented by the pictures showing the entrance of the king and his court.

Closing the Lesson

Administer *Evaluation 1* to check the children's understanding of ideas studied in the First Quarter. The evaluation may be conducted with the children individually or in small groups. If

For Your Information

Structure of *Fanfare for Three Trumpets, Three Trombones, and Timpani*:

A	*(loud)*	Fanfare-type melody played by all instruments.
A	*(soft)*	Melody repeated by same instruments, now played with less energy, less forcefully.
B	*(loud)*	New melody played forcefully by all instruments.
B	*(soft)*	Same melody is echoed, as though faraway.
A *(loud)* **B**		Composition is ended by repeating both fanfares in a loud, stately style.

the evaluation is conducted as a small group activity, make sure to observe the progress of individual children as they participate in each part.

Complete the *Musical Progress Report 1* for each child. This report may be sent home as a report to parents or simply retained by the teacher as a record of each child's progress.

Little Sir Echo

Original Version by Laura R. Smith and J. S. Fearis
Verse and Revised Arrangement by Adele Girard and Joe Marsala

Lesson Focus

Form: A musical whole is a combination of smaller segments. *(D–I)*

Materials

- o **Record Information:**
  - Three Little Kittens **(Record 2 Side A Band 2)**
  - Little Cabin in the Wood
    Record 2 Side A Band 7
    Voice: man
    Accompaniment: English horn, violin, harp
- o **Instruments:** autoharp
- o **Other:** puppets prepared for Lesson 12 (page 24); overhead projector
- o **Teacher's Resource Binder:**

  - **Activity Sheet 2**, pages A6–A7 (Prepare one set of picture cards for each child; cut pictures apart and scramble order of each set before distributing.)
  - Optional—
    Enrichment Activity 4, page E5
    Mainstreaming Suggestion 11, page M13

Introducing the Lesson

Begin class by reviewing "Three Little Kittens." Play the recording and invite the children to dramatize the story by using puppets. (See **Materials.**)

Developing the Lesson

1. **Here is some more music that tells a story. Listen! Can you tell me what the story is about?** Play the recording of "Little Cabin in the Wood." Listen to the recording again as necessary. After each listening, question the children about some aspect of the story until they are familiar with both the story and the music.

2. **We can help tell this story with motions!** Play the recording and demonstrate the motion for each phrase:

   Phrase 1   Form a peaked roof with hands, fingertips touching.
   Phrase 2   Shade eyes with hands; peer out the "window."

   Phrase 3   Middle finger and forefinger up for rabbit's ears, other fingers tucked under thumb; make rabbit "hop."
   Phrase 4   Pantomime knocking on door.
   Phrase 5   Wave hands in air on each "help!".
   Phrase 6   Pantomime shooting a gun.
   Phrase 7   Beckon rabbit to come near.
   Phrase 8   Pantomime warming hands by the fire.

3. **That story had several parts. How many different parts were there? You can decide by counting the number of different motions you make to tell the story.** Listen to the recording again and help the children learn the motion for each phrase. Listen and move again until the children determine that the story has eight parts.

4. **I believe you could sing the song now!** Set the tonality by playing the chord sequence **F-C7-F** on the autoharp. Then help the children sing the song and perform the motions. Listen to the recording as necessary to correct "problem spots."

Closing the Lesson

Give each child a set of cards prepared from Activity Sheet 2 *(Little Cabin in the Wood)*. **Can you arrange the pictures to tell the story?** Listen to the recording one more time and put the cards in order. **How many cards did you use?** (eight) **Yes, eight, one for each part of the whole song!**

Little Cabin in the Wood

Words by Betty Welsbacher

German Folk Song

Playfully

Lit - tle cab - in in the wood, Lit - tle man by the win - dow stood.

Lit - tle bun - ny hop - ping by, Knock - ing at the door.

"Help me! Help me! Help!" said he, "'Ere the hunt - er shoots at me!"

"Come on in," the lit - tle man cried, "Warm up by the fire."

LESSON 17

The Three Little Pigs

Lesson Focus

Expression: Musical elements are combined into a whole to express a musical or extra-musical idea. *(D–I)*

Materials

o **Record Information:**
- *The Three Little Pigs*
  by Fred Willman
  Record 2 Side B Band 1
  Voices: children's choir, solo child, man
  Accompaniment: synthesizer, electric piano, electric bass, percussion

o **Other:** tongue depressors or popsicle sticks; glue or tape; overhead projector

o **Teacher's Resource Binder:**

Activity Sheets
- **Activity Sheets 3a–e,** pages A8–A12 (Prepare a set of puppets from the figures on Activity Sheets 3a–d; cut out each figure and glue or tape it to a tongue depressor or popsicle stick. Prepare a transparency from Activity Sheet 3e.)
- Optional—
  Curriculum Correlation 10, page C16
  Mainstreaming Suggestion 12, page M14

o **For additional experience with expression:** Describe 14, page 179

Introducing the Lesson

If you were going to build a new house, what materials would you use? What kind of materials do you think would make the strongest house? After the children have offered their ideas, tell them to open their books to page 8, or show page 8 of the Jumbo Book.

Developing the Lesson

1. **These pictures tell a story about building a house. Do you know whose house the story is about?** Some children may recognize from the pictures that the story is about the "Three Little Pigs." The children may wish to tell their versions of the traditional story. **Music can make a story much more exciting; let's listen! Put your finger on Picture Number 1 as the music starts. Then use your finger to follow the path to the other pictures as you listen to this musical story.**

2. Play the recording of *The Three Little Pigs.* Signal to the children (as necessary) to move their fingers along the path at the appropriate times. (The numbers shown on the path are also found in **For Your Information** to help you identify major events in the story.)

3. After the children have listened to the entire story, invite their comments. **What part of the story did you like best? Can you remember times when the music made the story more interesting than hearing the story without music? What sounds told you when the wolf was trying to blow the houses in? Could you tell whether the pigs were frightened or happy by the sound of the music? When did you hear "frightened" music? "happy" music?** (See For Your Information regarding the sounds used to depict these parts of the story.)

4. **Let's listen again!** As the recording is played

34

2

3

4

9

For Your Information

Narration for *The Three Little Pigs*:

1 Once upon a time there were three little pigs. Their mother decided they were old enough to go out into the world on their own.

So the three lit-tle pigs went walk-ing,

on a sun-ny day. The

three lit-tle pigs went walk-ing. They

rest-ed a-long the way.

2 When the first little pig had rested enough, he walked on down the road. Soon he met a man with a bundle of straw. "What a fine house I could make with that straw," the pig thought. So he said,

Please, man, give me some straw. I'll

build a house with-out a saw.

Please, man, give me some straw, so

I can build my house.

again, help the children (as necessary) to "stay with" the music as they move their fingers from one picture to the next. **Did you hear anything special in the music this time that you missed before?** Repeat this step as often as needed and as time allows.

Closing the Lesson

End the class by distributing the puppets prepared from Activity Sheets 3a–d *(The Three Little Pigs)*. Play the recording and have the puppeteers dramatize the story by moving their puppets in appropriate ways and at appropriate times in front of the projected transparency prepared from Activity Sheet 3e. Remaining members of the class may sing each of the short songs along with the recording. Ask the class to watch the puppeteers carefully and to be ready to make suggestions for improvement of the dramatization. If time allows, repeat the activity with new puppeteers.

3 When the man gave the little pig the straw, the pig was so pleased that he began to build his house right away. After it was finished, he went inside and sat down to rest and enjoy his new house. But then he heard a wolf outside:

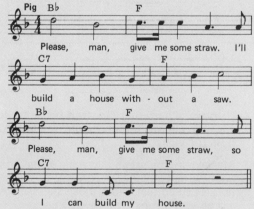

Lit-tle pig, lit-tle pig,

let me come in. Lit-tle pig,

lit-tle pig, let me come in.

(continued on next page)

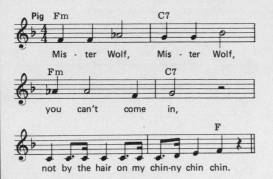

LESSON 17

For Your Information (continued)

He was afraid! He didn't trust the wolf at all.

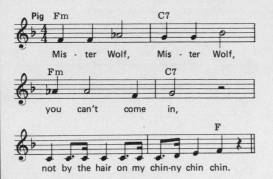

Pig Fm / C7
Mis-ter Wolf, Mis-ter Wolf,

Fm / C7
you can't come in,

F
not by the hair on my chin-ny chin chin.

The wolf was very angry now!

Wolf Fm
I'll huff and I'll puff and I'll

C7
blow your house in. _____ I'll

Fm
huff and I'll puff and I'll

C7 Fm
blow your house in. _____

7

6

5

10

4 He blew so hard that the straw house fell to the ground. The little pig was frightened and ran to the forest to hide from the wolf.

5 Meanwhile, the second little pig walked down the road. Soon he met a man with a bundle of sticks. "What a fine house I could make with those sticks—a wooden house will be very strong." So he said,

Pig B♭ / F
Please, man, give me some sticks.

C7 F
if you do, I'll do some tricks.

B♭ F
Please, man, give me some sticks, so

C7 F
I can build my house.

6 When the man gave him the sticks, the little pig could hardly wait to finish his house. He carefully fastened them together so his house would be strong. After he went inside, he heard the wolf calling:

(wolf's "little pig" song—see Part 3)

He knew his house was strong, but he didn't trust the wolf.

(pig's "Mister Wolf" song—see Part 3)

The wolf was angry!

(wolf's "huff and puff" song—see Part 3)

7 This house was much stronger. But the wolf blew, and he blew, and he blew, and finally he blew the house to the ground. The little pig quickly ran to the forest to hide.

8 The third little pig had been resting a long time, and he knew that it was time to walk down the road and find something he could use to make a strong new house. Soon he met a man with a cart full of bricks. "This is just what I need," he thought. So he said,

Answers to questions in Step 3:

WOLF TRYING TO BLOW HOUSES IN—accompanied by synthesized wind and huffing-puffing sounds and by vocal huffing-puffing sounds

"FRIGHTENED" MUSIC—end of Events 4 and 7, when the pigs run to hide in the forest

"HAPPY" MUSIC—throughout Event 1; beginning of Events 2, 5, and 8, when each pig starts off on his walk; end of Event 10, when the three pigs are safely inside the brick house

Please, man, give me some bricks.

Bricks are much strong-er than __ sticks.

Please, man, give me some bricks, so

I can build my house.

9 The man gave the pig enough bricks to build a fine, strong house. Soon the little pig had the house finished, and he went inside and closed the door. No sooner had he closed the door than he heard a wolf outside:

(wolf's "little pig" song—see Part 3)

He wasn't worried—brick houses are very strong!

(pig's "Mister Wolf" song–see Part 3)

The wolf thought he was pretty tough, so he said,

(wolf's "huff and puff" song–see Part 3)

10 He huffed and he puffed and he puffed and he huffed, but no matter how hard he blew, the house didn't move. Finally the wolf gave up and went home. The first little pig and the second little pig scrambled out of the forest and ran to the third little pig's brick house. All three pigs were safely inside where the wolf couldn't reach them.

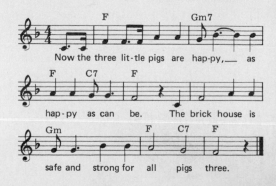

Now the three lit-tle pigs are hap-py, __ as

hap-py as can be. The brick house is

safe and strong for all pigs three.

37

LESSON 18

Lesson Focus

Rhythm: Music may be comparatively fast or slow, depending on the speed of the underlying pulse.
Rhythm: Music may become faster or slower by changing the speed of the underlying pulse. *(D–I)*

Materials

- ○ **Piano Accompaniment:** page 206
- ○ **Record Information:**
  - • The Hurry Song
    Record 2 Side B Band 2
    Voices: children's choir
    Accompaniment: harp, synthesizer, percussion
  - • Run, Run! from *Scenas Infantis* (Memories of Childhood) by Octavio Pinto, 1890–1950
    Record 2 Side B Band 3
    Nelly and Jaime Ingram, pianists
- ○ **Instruments:** sand blocks; woodblocks and mallets; hand drum and mallet
- ○ **Teacher's Resource Binder:**
  - • Optional —
    Enrichment Activities 1, 5, pages E2, E8
    Mainstreaming Suggestion 13, page M14

The Hurry Song

12

Introducing the Lesson

Play the following game with the children:

One little man said, "Oh dear me,
I want to hear your hands
clap fast as can be!"
(clap hands very fast)
The little old lady said, "Oh, no! no! no!
I want to hear your hands clap slow, so slow."
(clap hands very slowly)
So when the man was near,
This is what you'd hear—
(fast claps)
But when the lady came walkin',
We would quickly stop 'em!
(pull hands behind back)

Developing the Lesson

1. Tell the children to open their books to pages 12–13, or show pages 12–13 of the Jumbo Book. Play the recording of "The Hurry Song". As the children listen, have them follow the pictures on the pupil pages. Point to the legs in the boxes on pupil page 12 as each number of legs is mentioned in the song. Trace the contour of each ikon (picture of music) on pupil page 13. Follow the "fast" ikon and then the "slower" ikon when indicated in Phrase 3 of the song (at the *ritard*).

2. Invite the children to sing the song. Play the recording again as necessary. Discuss the fast and slow ideas in the song. **When was the song fast? slower? Look at page 13. Can you find the fast picture? the slower picture?**

3. Play the recording again. Focus the children's attention on the fast and slower sounds heard during the interlude. Have the children identify these sounds by pointing to the appropriate ikon on pupil page 13.

Fast

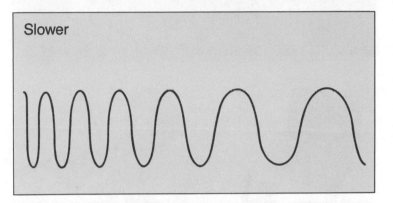

Slower

13

For Your Information

Structure of "Run, Run!":

A Melody moves rapidly with short, "detached" tones, four to a beat. The meter is in twos.

B Melody moves more smoothly and softly. The triple meter, uneven rhythmic pattern, and undulating melody suggest a different mood.

A Return to mood of first section.

The Hurry Song
by B.A.

Briskly

Two, four, six, eight, Man-y legs I see, They real-ly are pe - cu -liar when they aren't on me! Hur-ry, hur - ry, run-ning fast then slow-ly 'til we're through, Eight, six, four legs do just like my two!

---

4. Invite the children to sing the song and move in response to the recording. Select one child to be the "two-legged" leader and to indicate to the rest of the class when to move fast and when to move slower. Group the other children to form four-, six-, and eight-legged creatures that copy the actions of the leader.

5. Ask the children to name things that can move both fast and slow. (trains, horses, children) Help the children make up "fast and slow" stories about the things they name. One child might tell a story while another plays instrumental sounds to reflect the tempo, using an appropriate timbre: train— **OPTIONAL**

sand blocks; horses—woodblocks; or children—hand drum.

Closing the Lesson

Close your eyes and listen to this music! Does it remind you of some of the fast or slow things we described in our stories? Play the recording of "Run, Run!"

What did you see as you listened? Did you see things that sometimes moved quickly and sometimes slowly? Show me! Play the recording again. Observe the children's responses to changes in tempo, dynamics, and overall mood.

Lesson Focus

Time and Place: The way musical elements are combined into a whole reflects the origin of the music. *(D–I)*

Materials

○ **Piano Accompaniment:** page 207
○ **Record Information:**
  • Happy Birthday
    Record 2 Side B Band 4a
    Voices: children's choir
    Accompaniment: brass ensemble
    Band 4b: celesta
    Band 4c: violin
    Band 4d: piano, double bass, percussion
○ **Teacher's Resource Binder:**
  • Optional —
    Curriculum Correlation 16, page C26

Happy Birthday

① ② ③

14

Introducing the Lesson

Tell the children to open their books to page 14, or show page 14 of the Jumbo Book. Point out the boy pictured at the upper right of the page. **Why is today special for this boy?** (It is his birthday.) **How can you tell?** (birthday hat, birthday decorations) Discuss the special feelings that a person might have on his or her birthday.

Listen to the sung version of "Happy Birthday." **How old is the boy?** (six) As they listen, ask the children to point to the pictures of the girls and boys singing to the birthday child.

Developing the Lesson

1. **You could tell by looking at the pictures that the boy was having a birthday and that he was six years old. What do you think the other pictures tell you?** Invite suggestions

from the children. **Listen to this music. Which picture matches it?** Play, in any order, "Happy Birthday" as performed on an instrument that sounds like a music box (Picture 1), by a solo violinist (Picture 2), and by a jazz trio (Picture 3). Play each version several times so that the children can match the sounds with the pictures on page 14. Ask the children to comment on the different versions—do they have different feelings as they hear each version?

2. **The pictures helped us know what sounds we were hearing. What do you think these pictures might tell us?** Examine the pictures on page 15 and invite the children's suggestions.

3. Play the sung version of "Happy Birthday." As each repetition of the melody is heard, draw attention to the different aspects of the

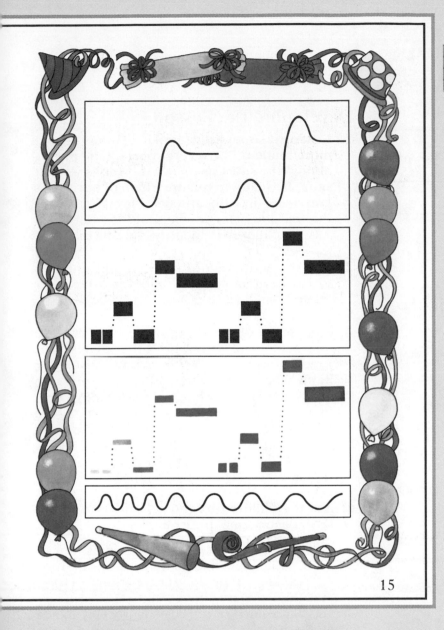

15

music represented by the pictures on page 15. (Each picture shows the first two phrases of the song.) Comment as each repetition is heard:

Picture 1—**We can make a picture of the ups and downs in our song!**

Picture 2—**We can make a picture of the long and short sounds in the music.**

Picture 3—**We can make a picture of the loud and soft sounds in our song.**

Picture 4—**We can make a picture of the fast and slow in the music.**

Closing the Lesson

Listen again to the sung version of the song. Have the children find the appropriate picture on page 15 as they hear each repetition of the song.

Happy Birthday
Words and Music by Mildred and Patty Hill

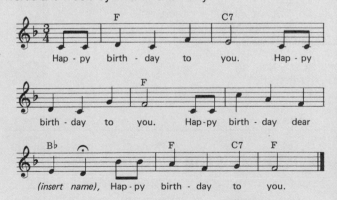

Hap - py birth - day to you. Hap - py birth - day to you. Hap-py birth - day dear (insert name), Hap - py birth - day to you.

LESSON 20

Lesson Focus
Form: A musical whole may be made up of same, varied, or contrasting segments. *(D–I)*

Materials
○ **Record Information:**
- It's Raining
  Record 2 Side B Band 5
  Voices: children's choir
  Accompaniment: percussion
- What Shall We Do on a Rainy Day?
  Record 2 Side B Band 6
  Voices: children's choir
  Accompaniment: flute, piccolo, brass ensemble, celesta, percussion
- *Kid Tunes*
  Record 2 Side B Band 7
  The Pummill Family Singers

○ **Teacher's Resource Binder:**
| Activity
| Sheets |
- **Activity Sheets 4a–c,** pages A13–A15 (Cut out 3 examples of each geometric shape, each in a different color poster board.)
- Optional—
  Kodaly Activities 16, 17, 19, pages K23, K26, K29
  Orff Activities 8, 16, pages O8, O19

○ **For additional experience with form:** Perform 4, page 137; Describe 5, page 168

For Your Information
Form of *Kid Tunes*:
  Introduction
  A "It's Raining"
  Transition
  B "Twinkle, Twinkle, Little Star"
  A "It's Raining"
  Transition
  C "Clap Your Hands"
  A It's Raining"
  Transition
  D "Prettiest Little Baby"
  A "It's Raining"
  Coda

Introducing the Lesson
Raise your hand if you know these songs! Play the recordings of "It's Raining" and "What Shall We Do on a Rainy Day?" Then sing the following chant. As the children indicate that they recognize any of the songs, invite them to sing them for you.

Talk about similarities among the songs. Agree that they all are about rain.

Developing the Lesson
1. **Listen to some more music. This is a long piece made up of several parts. One part is almost the same as one of the songs we just sang. Be ready to tell me which of our songs you hear in this music!** Play *Kid Tunes* through the first statement of "It's Raining." Ask the children to identify and sing the song.

2. Play the entire recording. Invite the children to raise their hands whenever they hear "their song." (four times)

3. **Four parts of this long piece of music use our song. Did you hear other parts that used different songs? This time, raise your hand when you hear a different song. Be ready to tell me what the other songs are.** Play the recording as necessary until the children have in some way identified the three melodies, "Twinkle, Twinkle, Little Star," "Clap Your Hands," and "Prettiest Little Baby."

4. Ask the children to choose a motion to describe each song, for example:

   "It's Raining" **(A)**—move hands downward, "wiggling" fingers to suggest raindrops
   "Twinkle, Twinkle, Little Star" **(B)**—"twinkle" fingers above head
   "Clap Your Hands" **(C)**—lightly clap hands on the beat
   "Prettiest Little Baby" **(D)**—tilt head to side and rest on hands in "sleeping" gesture

   Play the recording and observe which children readily change motions as each new melody begins.

Closing the Lesson
Could we make a long song out of short songs? Ask the children to suggest three songs they would like to combine to make a very long song. (You might suggest the songs and the chant heard at the beginning of class.) Decide the order in which the songs will be sung. Choose one song to repeat, imitating the form of *Kid Tunes.* (See **For Your Information.**)

Prepare geometric shapes using Activity Sheets 4a–c *(Geometric Shapes).* Choose one shape to represent each song. Place the shapes in a row to show the order in which the children wish to sing the songs. An example is provided below.

This very long song is made up of five parts. Let's perform our long song!

(It's Raining)

(What Shall We Do
on a Rainy Day?)

(It's Raining)

(Rain, Rain
Go Away)

(It's Raining)

It's Raining

Traditional

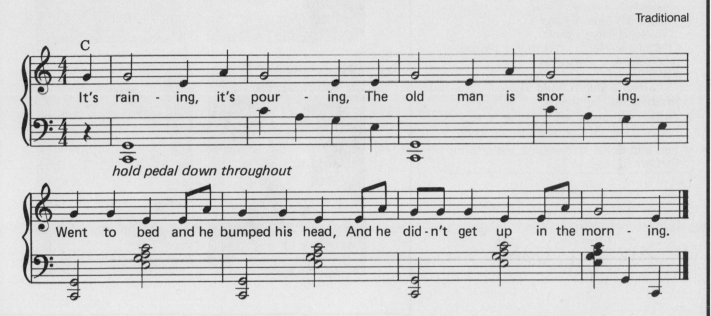

hold pedal down throughout

It's rain - ing, it's pour - ing, The old man is snor - ing.

Went to bed and he bumped his head, And he did-n't get up in the morn - ing.

What Shall We Do on a Rainy Day?

Traditional

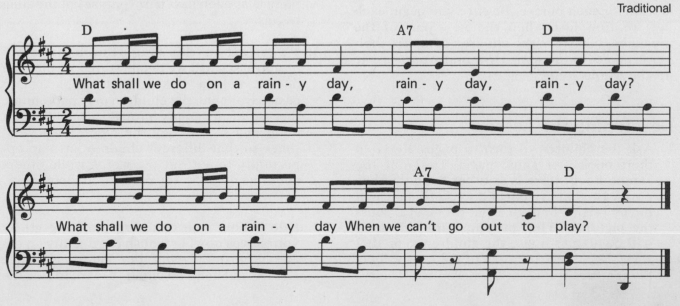

What shall we do on a rain - y day, rain - y day, rain - y day?

What shall we do on a rain - y day When we can't go out to play?

Lesson Focus

Form: A musical whole is a combination of smaller segments. *(D–I)*

Materials

o **Piano Accompaniment:** page 208
o **Record Information:**
  • Little Cabin in the Wood
    (Record 2 Side A Band 7)
  • Miss Polly
  💾 **Record 3 Side A Band 1**
    Voices: children's choir
    Accompaniment: recorder, bassoon, harpsichord, percussion
  • *Kid Tunes*
    (Record 2 Side B Band 7)
o **Instruments:** autoharp
o **Other:** telephone, hat, "doctor's bag," pad of paper, pen or pencil (all optional)
o **For additional experience with form:** Perform 8, page 143

Austrian West Yodeling!

Miss Polly

16

Introducing the Lesson OPTIONAL

Review "Little Cabin in the Wood" (Lesson 16, page 32). Invite the class to do the appropriate motion for each phrase. **Be sure you begin each new motion just when the new part of the music begins!** Have the children complete their performance of the song. **How many parts make up the whole song?** (eight)

Developing the Lesson

1. Ask the children to turn to pages 16–17 in their books, or show pages 16–17 of the Jumbo Book. **Here is another song that has parts. How many parts do you think it will have?** (eight, one for each picture) Discuss the pictures. **What do you think this song will be about?** Invite the children to predict what they think the topic of the song will be. Play the recording of "Miss Polly."

2. Decide whether the children's predictions were correct. Listen to the recording again. This time ask the children to point to each picture as each new part (phrase) of the song begins.

3. **We can act out this song. How many actors or actresses will we need?** (three—Polly, the doctor, and the sick dolly) If props are not easily available, the children may pantomime the use of imaginary props—a telephone, a door, and so on. Play the recording several times so that different children have an opportunity to act out the words while others continue to follow the pictures in their books.

4. **I do believe you can sing the song all by yourselves now!** Establish the tonality on the autoharp by playing the chord sequence **F-C7-F** and help the children learn to sing the

17

song independently. Some children may wish to dramatize the song again; this time the doctor might sing the conversational sections.

Closing the Lesson

End the lesson by quietly listening to *Kid Tunes*. **Can you show me when each new part begins? Let's use the same motions we used when we last heard this music!** Review with the children the motions used in Lesson 20 (page 42). Replay the recording while the children move to show each section of the music.

Miss Polly
Old English Nursery Song

1. Miss Pol - ly had a dol-ly who was sick, sick, sick, So she
2. She looked___ at the dol-ly and she shook her head; Then she

phoned for the doc-tor to be quick, quick, quick. The
said, "Miss___ Pol - ly, put her straight to bed." She

doc - tor came___ with her bag and her hat, And she
wrote on a pa - per for a pill, pill,___ pill. "I'll be

rapped at the door___ with a rat - ta - tat.
back in the morn-ing with my bill, bill, bill."

45

LESSON 22

Lesson Focus

Melody: A series of pitches may move up, down, or remain the same. *(C–I)*

Materials

o **Record Information:**
  • *Gavotte* **(Record 1 Side A Band 6)**
  • Jack-in-the-Box
  ▭ **Record 3 Side A Band 2**
   Voices: children's choir
   Accompaniment: two clarinets, two bass clarinets, percussion

o **Instruments:** resonator bells C, D, E, F, G, A, B, and C'; bell mallet

o **Other:** bell stairsteps for major scale (See Binder, page A2, for instructions.)

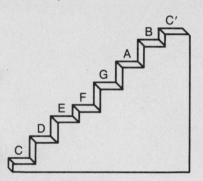

o **Teacher's Resource Binder:**

  [Activity Sheets]
  • **Activity Sheet 5,** page A16 (Prepare one copy for each child.)
  • Optional —
    Biography 2, pages B3–B4
    Enrichment Activity 6, page E7
    Orff Activity 12, page O15

o **For additional experience with melody:** Perform 6, page 140

Introducing the Lesson

Begin by playing the recording of *Gavotte*. Ask the children to show the up-down movement of the melody with their bodies. (See **For Your Information** in Lesson 5, page 10, for melody contours of *Gavotte*.)

Can you think of things that go up or down? (airplanes taking off and landing; elevators; a person climbing steps; a snowball rolling down a hill) **Let's describe with our voices things that go up and down. I'll do one for you. I'm an elevator!** Sing on "ooh." Start on as high a pitch as possible and slowly descend to as low a pitch as possible. **Where did I start? Where did I end?**

Show me! Observe children who respond with appropriate motions.

Who could be a plane taking off? landing? Give several children the opportunity to perform alone and to direct the entire class in making the up-down sounds.

Developing the Lesson

1. **Listen to a new song.** Sing or play the recording of "Jack-in-the-Box." **Who can tell me how this new tune moved? Did it go up or down most of the time?** (down, except for the ending) Sing or play the song again and have the children verify the answer by moving their arms appropriately. **Who can show what happens to our tune at the end?** (melody goes up)

2. Ask the class to move in a different manner as they listen to the recording again. Have the children start in a standing position; as the song continues they should crouch lower and lower into their imaginary boxes. When the answer, "Yes, I will!", is sung, they may spring up out of their boxes.

3. Repeat the "Jack-in-the-box" movements. This time vary the activity by telling the children to listen carefully for the answer. **Sometimes Jack says "Yes, I will!"; sometimes he says, "No, I won't!" What kind of tune would be good for the "no" answer?** (one that goes down) Sing the song several times and vary the ending at random. Observe which children quickly recognize in which direction they should move. To add to the fun, intersperse your "yes" and "no" versions with "can't decide." The children could be in a crouched position, halfway up and halfway down!

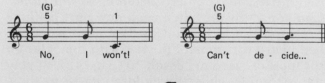

4. Challenge the class to "trade jobs." **I'll be the "Jack-in-the-box"; you must be the singers.**

Closing the Lesson

Distribute a copy of Activity Sheet 5 (*Up-Down*) to each child. Invite a child to "play the picture" of his or her choice on the resonator bells. The player chooses a picture, announces the choice to the class, and then improvises a melody on the bells. The class decides if the melody matches the picture. Give several children the opportunity to create their own "pictures."

Jack-in-the-Box

Words by Louise B. Scott

Music by Lucille F. Wood

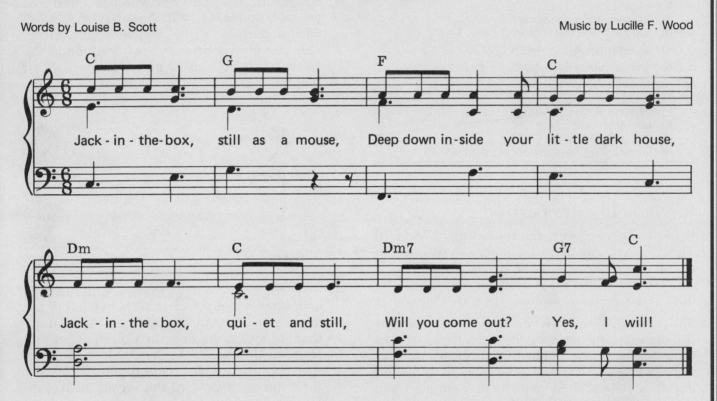

LESSON 23

Lesson Focus

Rhythm: A series of beats may be organized into regular or irregular groupings by stressing certain beats. *(D–E)*

Materials

o **Record Information:**
  • Step in Time **(Record 1 Side B Band 1)**
  • The Lion Game
    Record 3 Side A Band 3
    Voices: two men
    Accompaniment: percussion
  • *Mango Time* **(Record 1 Side B Band 3)**
o **Instruments:** small (high-pitched) drum
o **Other:** large rubber balls (or beach balls); a pebble
o **Teacher's Resource Binder:**
  • Optional —
    Enrichment Activity 7, page E9
    Kodaly Activity 8, page K11
    Orff Activity 18, page O22
    Mainstreaming Suggestion 14, page M14

Introducing the Lesson

Begin class by playing the recording of "Step in Time." Invite the children to step in time to the music. Reinforce the beat by lightly tapping a small drum. **How well you are stepping with the beat!**

Show me how well you can step with the beat of my drum! Continue a steady beat; then begin to alternate heavy and light beats. **Show me what you hear!** Observe and comment as to which children change their manner of stepping when they hear the heavy drum beats.

Developing the Lesson

1. **You stepped to the heavy-light sounds of my drum. We can make heavy-light sounds with a ball too. Watch! When is my ball making a heavy sound? When is it making a light sound?** As you talk, bounce the ball on the floor. The ball should hit the floor as you say the word "heavy"; catch the ball as you say the word "light."

2. **Can you use a pretend ball and bounce and catch with me?** Play the recording of "The Lion Game" while continuing to bounce (heavy) and catch (light). As the recording

continues hand balls to children who appear to have mastered the necessary motor-coordination skill to bounce in time with the beat of the music.

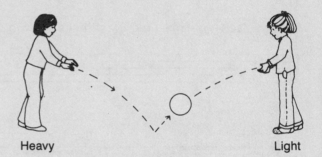

Heavy   Light

3. Suggest to those children who have mastered the ball-bouncing skill that they may work with a partner, using a single ball. (Other children may continue to work alone as described in Step 2, using either a "pretend" or real ball.) Listen to the recording or sing the song again.

Heavy   Light

4. After the children have worked with the balls and gained control of the "heavy-light" sequence in time to the music's beat, invite them to sit on the floor in a circle. **Can you sing our lion song?** As the children sing with the recording, invite them to alternately pat their knees in time to the steady beat: left-HEAVY; right-LIGHT.

5. **This lion song comes from Africa. When boys and girls there sing the song, they play a game.** Show the children how to pass a pebble around the circle in time to the steady beat.

$\frac{2}{4}$ Way,   way,   oh   way,   Oh the   li   on,
(steady beat)

Whoever is holding the pebble at the end of each verse must drop out of the circle. Repeat the song until only one child is left. She or he is the lion. **Be sure you are moving the pebble in time with the music!**

48

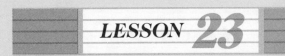

Closing the Lesson OPTIONAL

Boys and girls who live in Africa play the game
we just played. Do you remember this music?
It also comes from outside our country. People
in every country like to make music and play
singing games together, just like we do! Play
the recording of *Mango Time*. Hand out the balls
again. Have each child bounce the ball by him-
self or herself or to a partner, trying to bounce-
catch in time with the steady beat of the music.

The Lion Game

Zulu Game Song

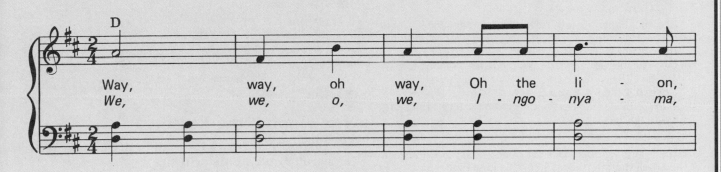

Way, way, oh way, Oh the li - on,
We, we, o, we, I - ngo - nya - ma,

One and one and one and one and Put a peb - ble here.
Mu - nye, mu - nye, mu - nye, mu - nye, Fa - ka mu - nye la.

LESSON 24

Lesson Focus

Rhythm: A series of beats may be organized into regular or irregular groupings by stressing certain beats. *(D–E)*

Materials

○ **Record Information:**
  • Whoo-ee! Whoo-ee!
  Record 3 Side A Band 4
  Voices: children's choir
  Accompaniment: wind, rain, and thunder sound effects
  • Menuetto, from *Five Divertimenti in B-Flat Major for 3 Basset Horns,* K. 439b, No. 2
  by Wolfgang Amadeus Mozart (**moet**-sahrt), 1756–1791
  Record 3 Side A Band 5
  Hans-Rudolf Stalder, Rolf Kubli, and Hansjürg Leuthold, basset horns

○ **Instruments:** resonator bells E♭ and B♭; bell mallet

○ **Other:** large rubber balls (or beach balls)—one for each child; bell stairsteps for major scale (See Binder, page A2, for instructions.)

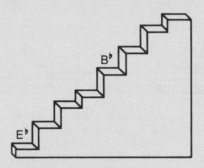

○ **Teacher's Resource Binder:**
  • Optional —
  Enrichment Activity 7, page E9
  Kodaly Activity 12, page K17
  Orff Activity 16, page O19

Introducing the Lesson

Review the ball-bouncing activity from Lesson 23 (page 48). To review the activity, have the children use either real or "pretend" balls. Sing the following chant:

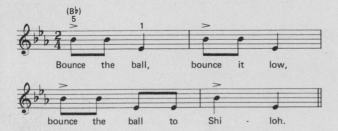

Change the words of the chant; sing "heavy-light, heavy-light." **How many different motions did we make?** (two) **How many different words did I chant?** (two) **This chant moves in twos!** Continue the activity. Alternate the words of the chant between "heavy-light" and "one-two."

Put the balls away. Ask the class to devise other motions that move in twos. (pat alternate knees; head down–head up)

Ask one child to add an ostinato (a repeated pattern) on resonator bells while the class sings the following chant and continues to devise movements in twos.

Developing the Lesson

1. **Listen. I'm going to change my chant. Will your movements still fit?**

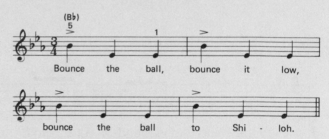

   Guide the children to realize that they now need three motions: one heavy motion, followed by two light motions. (Examples might include: tap on knees–left, right, right; hands together, apart, apart.) **This chant moves in threes!**

2. As the children repeat the "threes" chant, a child may add a "threes" ostinato:

3. Play the recording of "Whoo-ee! Whoo-ee!" **Which set of motions fits this music? twos or threes?** Encourage the children to experiment and discover that this song moves in threes.

4. Listen again to the first verse. **Did you hear some words that were repeated?** (Whoo-ee) **Let's sing the song! You sing the repeated words, and I'll sing the rest.**

Closing the Lesson OPTIONAL

Play the recording of "Menuetto." **Listen! Which movements will fit this music? twos or threes? (threes) Let your body become a ball. Move down on the heavy beats and up-up on the light beats. Play the recording again and have the children move in threes.**

Whoo-ee! Whoo-ee!

Words by Edith Lovell Thomas

German Folk Melody

LESSON 25

Lesson Focus
Melody: A series of pitches may move up, down, or remain the same. *(P–I)*

Materials
○ **Piano Accompaniment:** page 209
○ **Record Information:**
  • Whoo-ee! Whoo-ee!
    (Record 3 Side A Band 4)
  • *Hakof* (The Monkey)
    Record 3 Side A Band 6
    Voices: children's choir
    Accompaniment: flute, bassoon, trumpet, trombone, violin, cello, percussion
  • Hello **(Record 1 Side A Band 5)**
  • Menuetto **(Record 3 Side A Band 5)**
○ **Instruments:** resonator bells D, E, F, G, A, B♭, and D′; bell mallet
○ **Other:** stuffed toy monkey (optional); bell stairsteps for major and minor scales (See Binder, page A2, for instructions.)

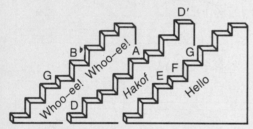

(continued on next page)

Hakof

18

Introducing the Lesson

Review "Whoo-ee! Whoo-ee!" (Lesson 24, page 50). Mirror the melodic contour as the class sings the first verse; encourage the children to imitate your movements.

Which words and melody did you repeat as you sang this song? (Whoo-ee) Put resonator bells G and B♭ on the major scale stairsteps. (See **Materials** for placement.) Give several children the opportunity to play the melodic pattern for the repeated word, "Whoo-ee." Listen to the recording and learn the remaining verses.

Developing the Lesson

1. Direct the children to turn to pages 18–19 in their books, or open the Jumbo Book to pages 18–19. **It looks like someone else is having a good time! A monkey is playing on a trampoline! How is the monkey moving?** (up-down)

2. **Follow the monkey as you listen to this song.** Play the recording of *"Hakof"* while pointing at the up-down picture in the Jumbo Book. **Can you follow the up-down picture in your books?** Play the recording again and have the children follow the melodic contour picture with their fingertips.

3. Choose two children to hold the ends of an imaginary trampoline. Choose another child to move a toy monkey (or form a fist with one hand to suggest an imaginary monkey) to show the up-down movement of the music. **Where will the monkey begin?** (in mid-air over the trampoline) Sing the song as the child moves the monkey. Other children may imitate and move their imaginary monkeys at the same time.

4. Put resonator bells D, A, and D′ on the minor scale stairsteps. **Can you play the picture in**

52

Materials *(continued)*

o **Teacher's Resource Binder:**
 • Optional —
  Curriculum Correlation 2, page C2
  Enrichment Activity 8, page E9
  Mainstreaming 15, page M15
  Orff Activity 18, page O23
o **For additional experience with melody:**
 Describe 9, page 174

Hakof (The Monkey)
Hebrew Folk Song
Words by Judith Eisenstein

Ha - kof goes up, ha - kof goes down,
Ha - kof o - leh, ha - kof yo - red

Oh, he is so gay! Ha -
al ha - nad ne - dah, Ha -

kof jumps up, ha - kof sits down when he's
kof a - yef, ha - kof yo - shev, ve - o -

all tired out from play.
hel ag - va - ni - yah.

your books? One child should play the basic melodic outline while others follow the picture on the pupil pages and decide if the performance was correct.

Can you sing the song while the bell player accompanies us?

5. **Listen! Can your monkey follow my music?**
Play various sequences of high-middle-low patterns on bells D, A, and D′ while the children move their "monkeys" appropriately.

Closing the Lesson *OPTIONAL*

Review the song, "Hello" (Lesson 4, page 8). **Can you sing and play this song?** Put out bells G, F, and E on the major scale stairsteps. **Which of these bells will you need in order to play the first "hellos"?** As one child experiments, help the class conclude that the "top" (G) and "bottom" (E) bells must be played. **We have to skip a bell, don't we?**

End the class by reviewing "Menuetto." The children may show the melodic contour as they listen.

LESSON 26

Lesson Focus

Melody: A series of pitches may move up, down, or remain the same.
Form: A musical whole is a combination of smaller segments. **(D–I)**

Materials

o **Record Information:**
  • *Hakof* (**Record 3 Side A Band 6**)
  • Goodnight
    Record 3 Side A Band 7
    Voice: woman
    Accompaniment: string quartet
  • Bath of Graces from *Les Aventures de Mercure*
    (The Adventures of Mercury)
    by Erik Satie (sah-**tee**), 1866–1925
    Record 3 Side A Band 8
    Utah Symphony Orchestra
    Maurice Abravanel, conductor

o **Instruments:** resonator bells D, A, and D′; bell mallet

o **Other:** bell stairsteps for minor scale (See Binder, page A2, for instructions.)

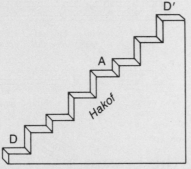

o **Teacher's Resource Binder:**
  Activity Sheets
  • **Activity Sheets 6a–b,** page A17 (Prepare one set of cards for each child; cut apart the eight pictures on each activity sheet and place each group of eight cards in a separate envelope.)
  • Optional —
    Biography 4, pages B7–B8
    Curriculum Correlation 11, page C19

o **For additional experience with form:** Perform 8, page 143

For Your Information

Form of "Bath of Graces":
  The same rhythmic pattern is repeated throughout this brief composition.

The basic melodic contours are as follows and are stated four times.

54

Countermelodies played by the violas and basses move stepwise.

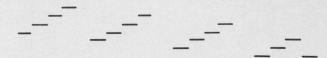

Introducing the Lesson

Place resonator bells D, A, and D′ on the stairsteps. (See **Materials** for placement.) Establish the tonality for *"Hakof"* by playing up and down patterns on these bells. **Show me which direction the melody is moving, up or down!** Begin to sing *"Hakof"* and invite the children to join in. Choose one child to point to the melody contour shown on Jumbo Book pages 18–19 while the rest of the class sings the song.

Play a game. One child plays patterns on the D, A, and D′ bells. The rest of the class must close their eyes and move their arms up or down to show the movement of each melody pattern.

Developing the Lesson

1. Hand out packets of picture cards prepared from Activity Sheet 6a (*Goodnight*). **We followed the picture of *"Hakof."* Can you make a picture of this song?** Play the recording of "Goodnight" as many times as necessary until the children have arranged their picture cards in the correct order to tell the story. **How many pictures did you use?** (eight) **That is because there are eight musical parts in this song!**

2. Play the recording again. Ask the children to make a picture of the melody with their hands. Replay the recording as necessary until the children seem sure of the melody contour. Then invite them to sing the song for you.

3. **Can you make a different kind of picture of our song?** Hand out a packet of cards prepared from Activity Sheet 6b (*Eight Melodic Direction Cards*) to each child. Play the recording of "Goodnight" or sing the song and have the children arrange the eight melodic direction cards in the correct order. When all the cards are in order, sing the song with the class one final time.

Closing the Lesson

End the class by listening quietly to "Bath of Graces." Mirror the melodic contour as the music plays. (See **For Your Information**.) **Does this music have a feeling that is the same as or different from "Goodnight"?** (very similar—sleepy, quiet, smooth)

Goodnight

Words by Lucy Sprague Mitchell

Music by Edna G. Buttolph

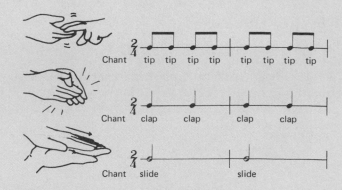

Chant tip tip tip tip | tip tip tip tip

Chant clap | clap | clap | clap

Chant slide | slide

Repeat the patterns at random; the children should continue to imitate immediately.

Developing the Lesson

1. Begin to sing "Chatter With the Angels" (Lesson 11, page 22). Tip and clap the rhythm of the first four measures.

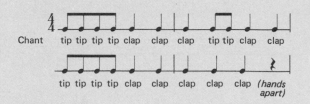

Chant tip tip tip tip clap clap clap tip tip clap clap

tip tip tip tip clap clap clap clap clap *(hands apart)*

2. **You can tip, clap, and slide short and long sounds. Can you hear short and long sounds?** Tip and clap this pattern:

Chant tip tip clap tip tip clap

Listen! What words in this song match the pattern I just tapped? Play the recording of "This Old Man." Replay the recording as necessary until the class identifies the correct words, "This old man, he played one."

3. **We've made pictures of melody. Do you think we could make a picture of rhythm?** Display two short melodic rhythm bars. (See **Materials.**)

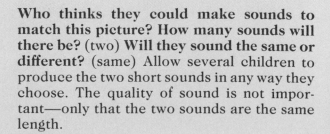

Who thinks they could make sounds to match this picture? How many sounds will there be? (two) **Will they sound the same or different?** (same) Allow several children to produce the two short sounds in any way they choose. The quality of sound is not important—only that the two sounds are the same length.

4. **What if I added a sound?** Add a long melodic rhythm bar after the two short bars.

LESSON 27

Lesson Focus

Rhythm: Individual sounds and silences within a rhythmic line may be longer than, shorter than, or the same as other sounds within the line. *(P–I)*

Materials

○ Record Information:
  • Goodnight **(Record 3 Side A Band 7)**
  • *Hakof* **(Record 3 Side A Band 6)**
  • Step in Time **(Record 1 Side B Band 1)**
  • Whoo-ee! Whoo-ee! **(Record 3 Side A Band 4)**
  • Chatter With the Angels
    (Record 2 Side A Band 1)
  • This Old Man
    Record 3 Side A Band 9
    Voices: children's choir
    Accompaniment: flute, bassoon, trumpet, trombone, violin, cello, percussion
  • Bath of Graces **(Record 3 Side A Band 8)**

○ **Instruments:** autoharp

○ Teacher's Resource Binder:

[Activity Sheets]
  • **Activity Sheet 7,** page A18 (Prepare set of rhythm bars—see instructions in Binder, page A1. Use the following bars for this lesson—melodic rhythm: 2 short bars, 1 long bar.)
  • Optional —
    Biography 4, pages B7–B8
    Kodaly Activity 9, page K14
    Orff Activities 3, 9, pages O3, O11

○ **For additional experience with rhythm:** Perform 17, page 155

Introducing the Lesson

Be my shadow! Mirror the melody for "Goodnight" (Lesson 26, page 54). **My hand is "singing" a song. Do you know what song it is?** As the children suggest songs, sing the lyrics of each song to the tune of "Goodnight" until the correct song is named.

Repeat the same activity with other familiar songs such as *"Hakof,"* "Step in Time," and "Whoo-ee! Whoo-ee!". After each song is correctly identified, establish the tonality on the autoharp and ask the class to sing the song for you.

You were good melody shadows. Can you shadow my rhythm patterns? Perform the following patterns; the children should imitate immediately without interrupting the rhythmic flow. (Remember to tip, clap, and slide by moving only one hand — the other hand remains still.)

Now how many sounds will there be? (three) **Will all the sounds be the same?** (no) **Which one is different?** (the last) **How will it sound?** (longer) Choose children to perform this pattern; ask the class to decide if the pattern as performed matches the picture. As various children clap, tap, or use vocal or body sounds to perform the pattern, begin to chant "short-short-long." Be sure to stretch out the word "long" so that it is twice as long as the word "short."

5. **You've just performed part of our song, "This Old Man." Let's listen to the recording again. Can you tap our pattern each time you hear it in the song?** Play the complete song; observe which children tap at the appropriate times.

6. Challenge the children to perform the song without the recording, while adding the following motions.

OPTIONAL

Measures 1–2: Tip and clap hands.
Measures 3–6: Pat appropriate part of body or make motions to depict words of song.
Measures 7–8: Move hands around each other in a rolling motion.

Closing the Lesson

Without comment, begin to play the recording of "Bath of Graces." As the music continues, begin to point to the short-short-long pattern of rhythm bars displayed. Indicate to the children that they may softly tap and chant the pattern with you. Play the complete recording. **How interesting! This whole piece of music uses our rhythm pattern all the way through!** Invite the children to leave music class stepping the short-short-long pattern as they hear "Bath of Graces" once again.

This Old Man

Traditional

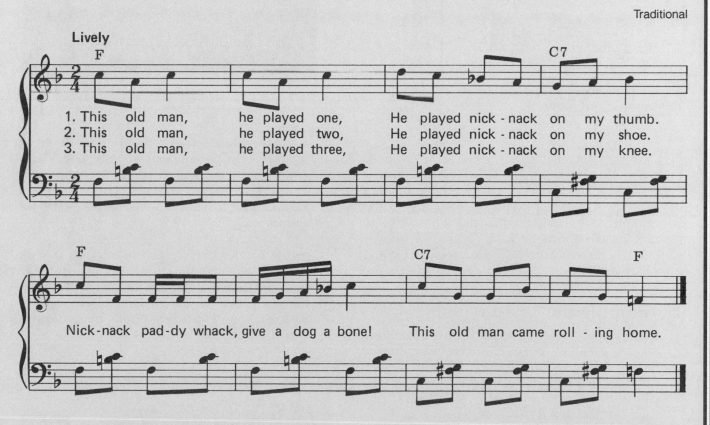

Lively

F

C7

1. This old man, he played one, He played nick-nack on my thumb.
2. This old man, he played two, He played nick-nack on my shoe.
3. This old man, he played three, He played nick-nack on my knee.

F

C7

F

Nick-nack pad-dy whack, give a dog a bone! This old man came roll-ing home.

4. . . . He played nick-nack on my door.
5. . . . He played nick-nack on my hive.
6. . . . He played nick-nack on my sticks.
7. . . . He played nick-nack up to heaven.

8. . . . He played nick-nack on my pate.
9. . . . He played nick-nack on my spine.
10. . . . He played nick-nack back again.

57

At the Circus

Lesson Focus

Melody: A series of pitches may move up, down, or remain the same. *(C–I)*

Materials

o **Piano Accompaniment:** page 210
o **Record Information:**
  • *The Man on the Flying Trapeze* (excerpt)
    Record 3 Side B Band 1
  • The Merry-go-round
    Record 3 Side B Band 2
    Voices: children's choir
    Accompaniment: barrel organ, percussion
  • Circus Music **(Record 1 Side A Band 4)**
o **Instruments:** resonator bells for E♭ chromatic scale (E♭, E, F, G♭, G, A♭, A, B♭, B, C, D♭, D, E♭'); bell mallet
o **Other:** bell stairsteps for chromatic scale (See Binder, page A2, for instructions.)

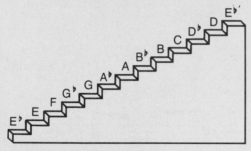

(continued on next page)

20

Introducing the Lesson

Play the recording of *The Man on the Flying Trapeze*. **What does this music make you think of?** (the circus) It is played on a strange-looking machine called a calliope. The calliope always used to appear in a circus parade. It seems to be saying, "Come on, everyone, come to the circus!" Are you ready? Let's go!

Developing the Lesson

1. Have the children open their books to pages 20–21, or show pages 20–21 of the Jumbo Book. Discuss the pictures. **Which performers are moving up?** (the tigers) **down?** (the horses) **up and down?** (the bears) **neither up nor down?** (the clown)

2. **Can you make up a melody on the bells that shows how these circus performers move?**

Choose several children in turn to create melodies on the resonator bells. (See **Materials** for placement of bells on stairsteps.) **Don't tell whose melody you're playing! Class, can you guess by listening to the way the melody moves?**

3. Sometimes when we go to the circus we can go on rides. **Can you make up a melody that sounds like a roller coaster? a merry-go-round?** As a child plays a melody for each ride, draw an appropriate melody contour on the chalkboard.

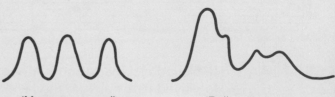

(Merry-go-round)   (Roller coaster)

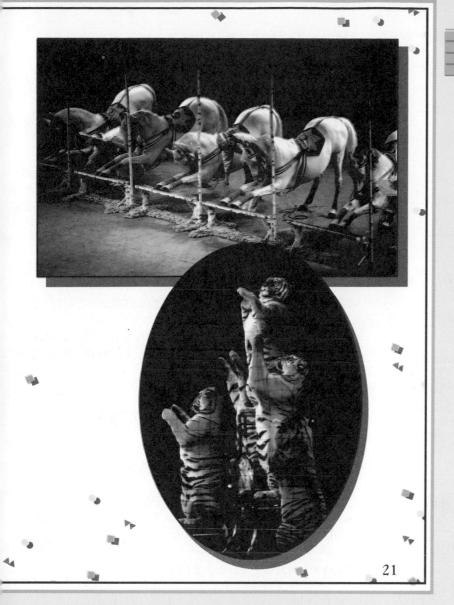

21

Materials *(continued)*

o **Teacher's Resource Binder:**
  • Optional —
    Biography 1, pages B1–B2
    Orff Activity 18, page O25
o **For additional experience with melody:**
  Create 3, page 184; Special Times 3, page 189

The Merry-go-round
Traditional Melody
Words by J. W. Beattie

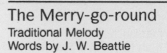

1. Far down the street I can hear a gay
2. Po - nies and ze - bras and el - e - phants

sound, Mer - ry - go - round! Mer - ry - go -
too, Mer - ry - go - round! Mer - ry - go -

round! Or - gan and an - i - mals
round! An - i - mals just like the

whirl - ing a - round, Rid - ing the
ones in the zoo, Ride on the

mer - ry - go - round.
mer - ry - go - round,

4. **I know a song about a merry-go-round. Listen! Does it move in the same way that (Susie's) merry-go-round melody moved?** Play the recording of "The Merry-go-round." As the music proceeds, draw its contour below the contour representing the child's made-up merry-go-round melody.

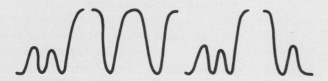

Discuss similarities and differences between the two pictures.

5. **Pretend your hand is riding on this merry-go-round. Show how you will move. Be sure you match the up-down shape of the mel-** ody! Trace the melody contour on the chalkboard as you play the recording again.

6. **How many different animals were on this merry-go-round?** Replay the recording until the children can name the animals. (ponies, zebras, elephants) Ask the class to sing the song without the recording. If the children have any problems singing the song, listen to the recording again.

Closing the Lesson   OPTIONAL

Review "Circus Music" (Lesson 3, page 6). Play the recording and have the children choose various circus acts to pantomime.

Lesson Focus

Rhythm: Individual sounds and silences within a rhythmic line may be longer than, shorter than, or the same as the underlying shortest pulse.
Melody: A series of pitches may move up, down, or remain the same. *(P–I)*

Materials

o **Record Information:**
  • The Happy Train **(Record 1 Side B Band 7)**
  • Chatter With the Angels
    (Record 2 Side A Band 1)
  • Miss Mary Jane
    Record 3 Side B Band 3
    Voices: children's choir
    Accompaniment: bass clarinet, trumpet, viola, piano, percussion

o **Instruments:** resonator bells C, D, E, and F; bell mallet

o **Other:** rhythm bars (as prepared for Lesson 27, page 56) —melodic rhythm: 6 short bars, 5 long bars, 2 lo-ong bars; rests: 1 short bar, 1 long bar; accents: 4 short bars; pulses: 14 short bars; bell stairsteps for major scales (See Binder, page A1, for instructions.)

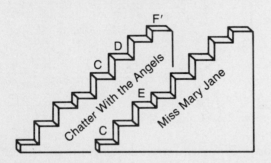

o **For additional experience with rhythm:** Perform 16, page 154

Introducing the Lesson

Play the recording of "The Happy Train." Have the class move with the underlying shortest sound. **Can you step in place to that shortest sound? Now try to tip, clap, and slide the short and long sounds of the words of our song.** Demonstrate for the class.

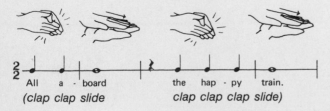

Here's a picture of what we just stepped and tapped. Display the following rhythm patterns. (See **Materials.**)

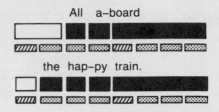

Point to the lower line of rhythm bars. **Here is a picture of the short sounds we heard and put in our feet.**

Point to the upper line of rhythm bars. **Here is a picture of the short and long sounds of the words of our song.**

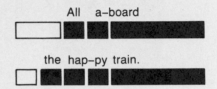

Have the class sing the song. Point to the rhythm bars each time the words "All aboard the happy train" are repeated. (three times)

Developing the Lesson

1. **Can you figure out the name of this song? It's one you already know!** Replace the rhythm patterns for "The Happy Train" with rhythm bars that represent the first two measures of "Chatter With the Angels."

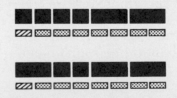

Establish the shortest sound. Then guide the children to tip and clap the displayed pattern while saying the words "short" and "long" as appropriate. Repeat the activity without saying the words. If the children are still unsure of the song name, hum the melody while continuing to tap the shortest sound.

2. When the children have identified the song, ask one child to play resonator bells F, D, and C (in that order) to establish the tonality. Then ask the class to sing the song.

3. You've done a good job of following the long-short picture of songs you know. I believe you can learn a new song by following its picture. Display rhythm patterns for "Miss Mary Jane":

4. Follow the same procedure with "Miss Mary Jane" as with the previous songs. First set the speed of the shortest sound and then ask the class to tip and clap while you chant "short-long." Repeat, using a neutral syllable such as "doo."

5. Rearrange the rhythm bar display as shown below. **What do you think our picture shows now?** (the up and down of the melody) Put bells C and E on the stairsteps. **Who can play our picture?** As one child experiments, the class should decide if the bell sounds match the picture.

6. Play the complete recording of "Miss Mary Jane" or sing the song for the class. **Which words match the tune you played?** ("Ridin' in the buggy, Miss Mary Jane") Play the recording again while the children make the sound of the horses' hooves (the shortest sound) on their knees.

7. **Can you sing Miss Mary Jane's song?** If the class is unsure of the melody, play the recording again.

Closing the Lesson OPTIONAL

End the class by asking a child to choose a favorite song for the class to sing. **Before we begin to sing we must find the starting sound.** Put the bell for the starting pitch on the stairsteps; ask a child to play the bell. Then ask the class to sing the pitch on "loo." **Now we must set up the short sounds so we know how fast to sing.** Sing the words "ready, sing" on the previously established starting pitch and signal the children to sing the song.

Miss Mary Jane

American Folk Song

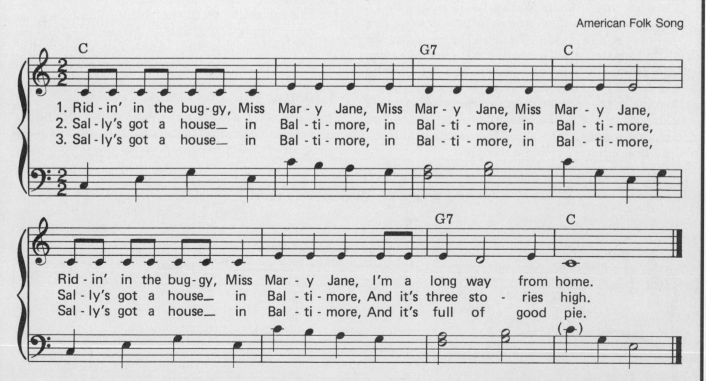

LESSON 30

Lesson Focus

Evaluation: Review concepts and skills studied in the Second Quarter.

Materials

○ **Record Information:**
- Wishy Washy Wee
- **Record 3 Side B Band 4**
  Voices: children's choir
  Accompaniment: piccolo, bassoon, French horn, guitar, accordion, double bass, percussion.
- Reuben and Rachel
- **Record 3 Side B Band 5**
  Voices: girl, boy
  Accompaniment: trumpet, trombone, tuba, violin, mandolin, accordion, cimbalom

○ **Other:** overhead projector

○ **Teacher's Resource Binder:**

Activity Sheets • **Activity Sheet 8,** page A19 (Prepare one copy for each child or make a transparency for use with the class as a whole.)

Evaluation • **Evaluation 2,** pages Ev4–Ev5
- **Musical Progress Report 2,** page Ev6
- Optional—
  Curriculum Correlation 13, page C21

Introducing the Lesson

Learn to sing "Wishy Washy Wee" by playing a song game. The class forms a circle with two "sailors" in the middle. The children forming the circle bend over with hands on knees and sway back and forth to imitate the motion of a boat on the sea. This swaying movement is continued throughout the song except on the words "come along with me." On these words, hands are thrown up toward the sky. The "circle children" then immediately resume swaying.

The sailors assume a sailor's jig position (one hand in front at waist, the other in back at waist). The sailors move around the circle during the verse and select new sailors, as indicated by the song lyrics, to enter the middle. The sailors are to make up a funny dance on each refrain.

Developing the Lesson

1. Discover how the melody for the verse of "Wishy Washy Wee" moves. Ask the children to show with their hands if the melody remains the same, goes up, or down.

Where did the melody skip up very high? ("come along with me") Remind the children that when playing the game, this was where they threw their arms up high.

2. Distribute a copy of Activity Sheet 8 *(Wishy Washy Wee)* to each child or display the sheet as a transparency. Ask the children to sing the song while following the pictures of the melody.

3. Learn to sing "Reuben and Rachel." Listen to the recording until the children can sing the song readily, without assistance. Use both "Wishy Washy Wee" and "Reuben and Rachel" as part of the quarterly evaluation.

Closing the Lesson

Administer *Evaluation 2* to check the children's understanding of ideas studied in the Second Quarter. The evaluation may be conducted with

Wishy Washy Wee

American Folk Song

Verse   C   G7

Oh, we are   1. two   2. four   3. six   4. eight   sail - ors   come from o'er   the sea.   If   you

62

the children individually or in small groups. If the evaluation is conducted as a small group activity, make sure to observe the progress of individual children as they participate in each part.

Complete the *Musical Progress Report 2* for each child. This report may be sent home as a report to parents or simply retained by the teacher as a record of each child's progress.

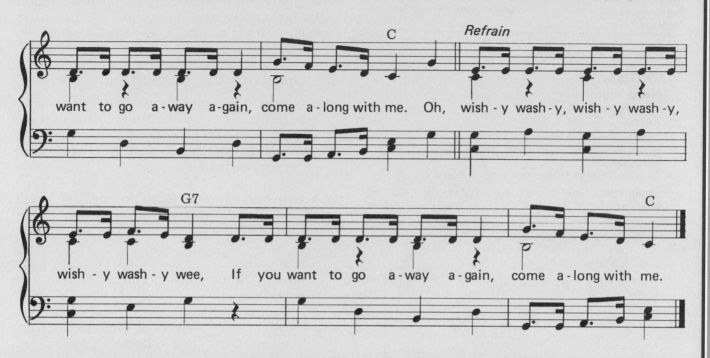

Reuben and Rachel

Words by B.A.

Traditional Melody

Lesson Focus

Melody: A melody may be relatively high or low.
Form: A musical whole is a combination of smaller segments. *(P–E)*

Materials

o **Record Information:**
  • Little Arabella Miller
  ▱ **Record 3 Side B Band 6**
    Voices: children's choir
    Accompaniment: two violins, viola, cello, harpsichord
  • Jack-in-the-Box **(Record 3 Side A Band 2)**

o **Instruments:** sand blocks; alto xylophone (C–C', see **Other**) or resonator bells (C–C'); xylophone or bell mallets

o **Other:** alto xylophone with C major bars; bell stairsteps for major scale (See Binder, page A2, for instructions.)

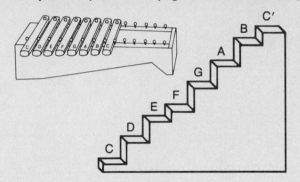

o **Teacher's Resource Binder:**
  • Optional—
    Curriculum Correlation 7, page C9
    Enrichment Activity 12, page E18
    Orff Activities 6, 10, pages O6, O12

o **For additional experience with melody:**
    Perform 5, page 138

For Your Information

CATERPILLAR, BUTTERFLY
by Sharon Beth Falk

Caterpillar, butterfly,
One will crawl, one will fly.
Which moves low? Which moves high?
Caterpillar, butterfly.

Introducing the Lesson

Sing or play the recording of "Little Arabella Miller." Some children may recognize that the melody is the same as "Twinkle, Twinkle, Little Star." Listen to the song several times and discuss the words until the children can sing the song without help.

As they sing, the children may add the sounds of a crawling caterpillar by swishing their hands back and forth rhythmically. Give some children sand blocks and have them make additional caterpillar sounds to accompany their singing.

Developing the Lesson

1. Introduce a poem about a caterpillar and a butterfly. (See **For Your Information.**) Speak the poem using vocal inflections—low sounds for caterpillar ideas and high sounds for butterfly ideas.

2. Help the children learn to say the poem. Have them imitate your high-low vocal inflections.

3. Add motions: Pat knees on the caterpillar parts of the poem; snap fingers in the air on butterfly parts.

4. Transfer the motions to an alto xylophone or resonator bells. (See **Materials.**) As the class speaks the poem, one child may play the low C for the caterpillar parts and the high C' for the butterfly parts, in the rhythm of the words.

5. Invite the children to sing the poem by moving between the two C's (in imitation of the instrument sounds).

6. After the poem has been played and sung several times, ask a child to use the sounds of the xylophone or bells to show how the caterpillar turns into a butterfly. (The child might play a *glissando*—moving the mallet rapidly across the bars or bells without lifting it—or one pitch at a time.)

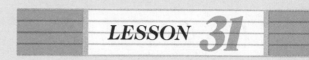

7. After the child has demonstrated his or her sound ideas, add a special ending to the children's poem-song:

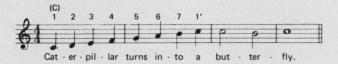

8. Perform the entire song with its special ending.

9. Create a "long song" by beginning with the version of the poem developed in Steps 4–5; then sing "Little Arabella Miller," followed by the special ending. (See Step 7.) **How many parts were there in our long song?** (three)

Closing the Lesson

Return to "Jack-in-the-Box" (Lesson 22, page 46). As the children sing the song, ask them to show with their bodies when the sound is high and when it is low.

Little Arabella Miller

Traditional Song

LESSON 32

Lesson Focus

Expression: Musical elements are combined into a whole to express a musical or extramusical idea. *(C–I)*

Materials

o **Teacher's Resource Binder:**

Activity Sheets
- **Activity Sheet 9**, page A20 (Prepare a set of four cards for each child—see instructions on activity sheet.)
- Optional—
Curriculum Correlation 13, page C21
Enrichment Activity 9, page E12

o **For additional experience with expression:**
Perform 9, page 144

Introducing the Lesson

Begin by reading the following nonsense poem to the children. Speak as expressively as possible.

PICKLE JACKS

by David Woods

There was an old woman who lived in the dell;
She would catch pickle jacks out of her well.
And how she would catch them, nobody knew
'Cause she never, no never, no never would tell!

Ask the children questions about the story told in the poem, line by line, until they can remember and recite the poem without your assistance.

Developing the Lesson

1. Use the poem "Pickle Jacks" as the basis for vocal-inflection play. Create a story line that involves the old woman in the poem, a giant, a snow elf, and a cat. Speak each part of the following poem, using voices as indicated.

   Once upon a time I met an old woman, and she said: *(Speak in a high, quavering voice.)*

(The class repeats the poem, imitating your high, quavering vocal quality.)
Then I met a very large giant, and he said: *(Use a low, ponderous voice.)*
(The class now says the poem in a "giant" voice.)
I walked through the forest and met a snow elf who said: *(Speak with a flowing, dance-like quality.)*
(The class repeats the poem, imitating your "snow elf" voice.)
Then I came upon a tattered old cat with one ear torn and drooping. The cat said: *(Speak with abrupt high and low vocal changes.)*
(The class then repeats the poem in a "cat" voice.)

2. After the children have enjoyed speaking the poem, ask them to dramatize the story. Repeat the expanded poem. This time the children are to move like each of the characters as they speak.

   Old Woman: move as though leaning on a cane
   Giant: heavy, long, ponderous steps
   Snow Elf: smooth, flowing, dance-like movements
   Cat: bouncing up-down movements, to follow vocal inflection

3. Add a new character to the story.

   I walked through the forest and met a bird who talked to a flower.

   Distribute the card packets prepared from Activity Sheet 9 *(Bird Songs)*. **Can you follow the pictures and be the bird talking to the flower?** Guide the children to improvise melodies that follow the up-down contour shown on each card. Give various children an opportunity to sing the bird's song in response to the four cards.

4. Choose a child to sing one of the bird's songs. The child whispers to you the picture he or she will "sing." After completing the song the class must identify the picture that matches the melody they just heard.

OPTIONAL

Closing the Lesson

Introduce the following riddle by speaking the first two lines.

GOING TO ST. IVES

From Mother Goose

> As I was going to St. Ives,
> I met a man with seven wives.

Choose seven children to play the wives. Each child must create a response to the first lines of the riddle. Their responses might be similar to the following:

I am the number one wife, and I am the prettiest of all.

I am the number two wife, and I am mean and cranky.

I am the number three wife, and I am scared of the dark.

I am the number four wife, and I am very, very tiny.

The children should use their voices to express the characteristics suggested by the words, for example, loud, high, low, soft, abrupt, or smooth.

Recite the second part of the riddle.

> Each wife had seven sacks,
> Each sack had seven cats.

Ask the rest of the class to be the cats. These children may create their own special "meows."

End the riddle.

> Kits, cats, sacks, and wives,
> How many were going to St. Ives?

Perform the entire riddle. Have the whole class recite the lines of the riddle, interspersed with the solo performances of wives and cats. End by having everyone say, "I don't know," several times (begin in a whisper and become gradually louder); then make an abrupt stop. After a short silence one child may give the answer to the riddle: "Only one." (Why only one? Because the man was the only one going to St. Ives.)

A Picture of Rhythm

22

Materials

o **Piano Accompaniment:** page 211
o **Record Information:**
  • Walking Song
    from *Acadian Songs and Dances*
    by Virgil Thomson, 1896–
    Record 3 Side B Band 7
    Little Orchestra Society
    Thomas K. Scherman, conductor
  • Loopidee Loo
    Record 3 Side B Band 8
    Voices: man, children's choir
    Accompaniment: flute, oboe, clarinet,
    bassoon, guitar, double bass, percussion
o **Instruments:** hand drum; cymbal; mallet
o **Other:** pencil and paper for each child
o **For additional experience with rhythm:**
  Describe 6, page 170

Introducing the Lesson OPTIONAL

Play the recording of "Walking Song." **Show me
the way the music moves by the way you move.**
Play a hand drum as the children move to the
recording.

Section A: steady drum beat
Section B: rub drum head
Section C: shorter drum taps

Comment on the different ways the children
moved in response to the long and short sounds.

Developing the Lesson

1. Ask the children to open their books to page
   22, or show page 22 of the Jumbo Book. **You
   moved to show long and short sounds. Can
   you make long and short sounds with your
   voices?** Point to each picture on the pupil
   page and ask the children to make appropriate sounds. (For the pictures of singers,

the children could make any long and short
funny sounds that follow the pattern shown.)

2. **All of these things make long and short
   sounds. The melodies we sing use long and
   short sounds too! Listen to this song! Slide
   your palms together each time you hear a
   long sound.** Sing the refrain of "Loopidee
   Loo," or play the recording.

3. **Here is a picture of the long and short
   sounds in "Loopidee Loo."** Sing the refrain
   while the class follows the picture on pupil
   page 23. **Can you sing the song for me?**

   Play the entire recording. **Can you now sing
   the whole song?**

Closing the Lesson

Give each child a pencil and a sheet of paper.
Explain what they are to do. **I will play a pattern**

Loopidee Loo

23

For Your Information

Structure of "Walking Song": rondo

A Consists of two phrases; each is two measures long and stated twice (**a a b b**). The main melody is played on clarinet; strings accompany in a "walking" rhythm.

A Repeated with flute now playing main melody.

B Strings introduce a new idea, in a slower tempo with sustained tones.

A Now played on wind instruments.

C Strings play a more vigorous melody at a slightly faster tempo.

A The final statement is performed on the oboe. Strings still perform the "walking" rhythm accompaniment.

---

on my instrument. Listen carefully. When I play the pattern again, draw long and short lines on your paper to match the sounds you hear. Play the following patterns on a hand drum or cymbal. After you play each pattern, discuss what the children's pictures should include (the number of lines and the length of each line).

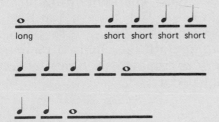

long   short short short short

Loopidee Loo

English Singing Game
Adapted by B.A.

Refrain

Here we go loo-pi-dee   loo,___ Here we go loo-pi-dee

lie,___ Here we go loo-pi-dee loo,

All on a Sat-ur-day night. 1. You night.___

Verse

put   your   left   hand   in,   You

take your left hand out,   You give your hand a

shake, shake, shake, and turn your-self a-bout.

2. right hand   3. left foot
4. right foot   5. whole self

69

LESSON 34

Lesson Focus

Rhythm: Individual sounds and silences within a rhythmic line may be longer than, shorter than, or the same as the shortest pulse. *(P–I)*

Materials

o **Record Information:**
  • What Have You Seen?
  ▭ **Record 4 Side A Band 1**
    Voices: child solo, children's choir
    Accompaniment: panpipes, crumhorn, sackbut, guitar, double bass, harmonium, percussion

o **Other:** overhead projector; rhythm bars (as prepared for Lesson 27, page 56)—melodic rhythm: 10 short bars, 2 lo-ong bars; accents: 2 short bars; pulses: 6 short bars

o **Teacher's Resource Binder:**
  | Activity Sheets | • **Activity Sheets 10a–b,** pages A21–A22 (Prepare a transparency from each activity sheet.) |

    • Optional—
    Mainstreaming Suggestion 16, page M15

o **For additional experience with rhythm:** Describe 3, page 166

Introducing the Lesson

Have the children open their books to page 22, or show page 22 of the Jumbo Book. Divide the class into two groups. Have one group perform the long sounds and the second group perform the short sounds on the pupil page. **Can you perform your sounds at the same time?** Point at the two "truck" lines simultaneously as the two groups perform the sounds. **How many short sounds did Group 2 make while Group 1 made one long sound?** (eight)

Remind the children of the pictures of sound they drew during the previous lesson. **Listen! Can you draw the sounds of this poem?** Perform the following chant; make the long sounds four times as long as the short ones.

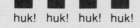

I cough!   huk! huk! huk! huk!

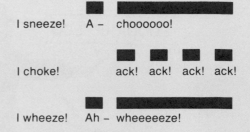

I sneeze!   A –   choooooo!

I choke!   ack! ack! ack! ack!

I wheeze!   Ah – wheeeeeze!

All of that makes me wiggle my knees!
(Wiggle knees for length of four short sounds.)

After the children have enjoyed hearing and saying the poem, ask one child to show a picture of the cough at the chalkboard with rhythm bars. (See **Materials.**) Repeat the activity with other children until all the sounds have been shown.

Developing the Lesson

1. Show page 23 of the Jumbo Book. Ask one child to point to the short and long sounds on the page as the children sing the refrain of "Loopidee Loo."

2. **Do you think you could learn the rhythm of a new song by following a picture of long and short sounds? Let's try!** Display the following pattern:

Establish the tempo of the short sounds by lightly tapping against your thigh. Ask the children to chant the rhythm, using the words "short" and "long." (Be sure the children say "lo-ong" so that the word lasts for four short sounds.) Next have the class perform the pattern (tip the short sounds and slide palms together on the long sound) while "thinking" the words short and lo-ong.

3. **Listen to this silly song. Can you find the pattern you chanted?** Sing or play the recording of "What Have You Seen?" (first verse only). Sing the verse or replay the recording until the children realize that the pattern is repeated six times, once for each word pattern.

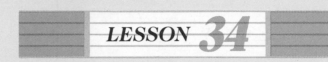

Closing the Lesson OPTIONAL

Can you sing the song while we follow its short and long pictures? Display the transparency prepared from Activity Sheet 10a *(What Have You Seen?)*. Enjoy the silly pictures of the short (upright) and long (stretched-out) pigs and sing Verse 1 of the song. Help the children sing the remaining verses by following the short and long rhythm bars shown on the transparency prepared from Activity Sheet 10b. (Be sure to keep sounding the short pulse by lightly tapping your thigh or palm.)

What Have You Seen?

French Folk Song

Tell us what you saw on the way to town.

Tell us what you saw walk - ing up and down.

1. I have seen a pig   dance an I - rish jig.
2. I have seen a hen   writ - ing with a pen.
3. I have seen a bear   dust - ing off a chair.

LESSON 35

Lesson Focus
Rhythm: Music may move in relation to the underlying shortest pulse.
Melody: A series of pitches may move up or down by steps or skips. *(P–I)*

Materials
o **Piano Accompaniment:** page 212
o **Record Information:**
  • Have You Seen My Honey Bears?
    Record 4 Side A Band 2
    Voices: child, woman
    Accompaniment: flute, oboe, clarinet, bassoon, guitar, double bass, percussion
o **Instruments:** tambourine; resonator bells D, E, F#, G, and A; bell mallet; autoharp
(continued on next page)

Have You Seen My Honey Bears?

Verse 1

Have   you   seen   my

hon - ey   bears,

hon - ey   bears,

Sit - ting   up - on

wood - en   chairs,

wood - en   chairs?

24

Introducing the Lesson

As the children enter the classroom, set up a steady short pulse on a tambourine.(See Pattern A at right.) Direct each child to find a space where he or she can step about without invading someone else's space.

Change from short sounds to a sound that is twice as long by shaking the tambourine. (See Pattern B at right.) **What must you do to show the sounds I'm making now on the tambourine?** (take longer steps)

Shift between short and long sounds every eight pulses. When the children can comfortably change the size of their steps as you change patterns, play Pattern C. **Can you step this pattern?** Repeat the pattern several times.

Continue the activity with various other combinations of short and long sounds. Remind the children to listen at least one time before trying to step each pattern.

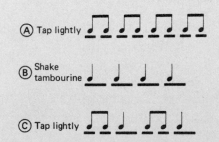

Developing the Lesson

1. **You can hear short and long sounds. You can step short and long sounds. Can you**

72

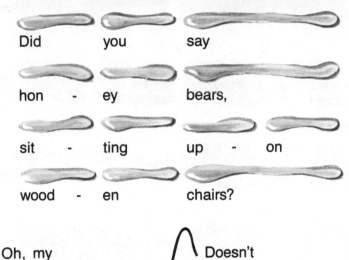

Did   you   say

hon - ey   bears,

sit - ting   up - on

wood - en   chairs?

Oh, my
        darling   Doesn't
                dear,   it seem
                                queer?

25

Materials *(continued)*
o **Other:** overhead projector; bell mat (See
Binder, page A3, for instructions.)

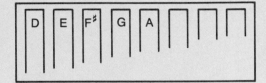

o **Teacher's Resource Binder:**

Activity Sheets
• **Activity Sheet 11**, page A23
(Prepare a transparency from
the activity sheet.)

o **For additional experience with rhythm
and melody:** Special Times 6, page 191;
Special Times 11, page 200

read the short and long sounds for a new
song? Tell the children to open their books to
page 24, or show page 24 of the Jumbo Book.
Discuss the picture; notice that the bear is
dripping honey from a honey pot. **What do
you notice about the drips of honey?** (Some
are short; some are long.)

Ask the class to describe the length of the
honey drips by chanting "short" or "long."
Establish the tempo and have the children
chant the pattern shown on the pupil page.
**Can you now tip and clap the picture while
you *think* the short and long sounds?**

2. Draw attention to the words below the honey
drips. **Here are the words of our new song.
Can you read the words and make each**

word short or long to match the length of
the honey drip? Help the class to first read
the words, including those that are hyphen-
ated. Then have the children chant the
words, correctly lengthening the words
"bears" and "chairs."

3. Listen to the recording of "Have You Seen My
Honey Bears?" (first verse only). **Did we
chant the words in the right rhythm?** The
children should slide their fingertips along
the pictures on pupil pages 24–25 as they
listen.

4. **Turn the page! Here is more of our song!** As
the children listen to Verse 2, help them follow the words and ikons on pupil pages
26–27.

LESSON 35

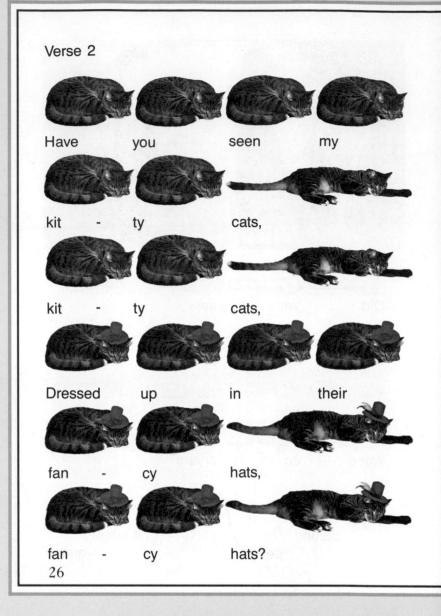

Verse 2

Have you seen my

kit - ty cats,

kit - ty cats,

Dressed up in their

fan - cy hats,

fan - cy hats?

26

5. Ask the children to turn to page 28. **This picture is different! What makes it different?** (shows melody as well as rhythm) Listen to Verses 3 and 4 while the children follow the up-down and short-long pictures on page 28.

6. Return to the beginning of the song and allow the children to listen to all four verses. Help them to follow the pictures in their books from page 24 through page 28 and to turn each page at the correct time.

7. **Can you sing the song for me?** Establish the tonality by playing the chord sequence **D-A7-D.** Challenge the children to sing without your assistance.

8. Draw attention to the pictures of resonator bells on pupil page 29. Ask one child to ar-range the bells on the bell mat as shown in the picture at the top of the pupil page. Tell the children that one can find the correct bells by looking for the alphabet letter on each bell.

When the bells are arranged correctly, one child may play the first two phrases of the song ("Have you seen my honey bears, honey bears, Sitting upon wooden chairs, wooden chairs?"). The class can help by telling the bell player whether to go up or down.

9. **Can you play the next part of the song?** (no, not enough bells) Add the E and G bells as shown in the picture at the bottom of the page and help a child play Phrase 3 ("Did you say honey bears, Sitting upon wooden chairs?"). Some children may also be able to figure out the melody for the final phrase.

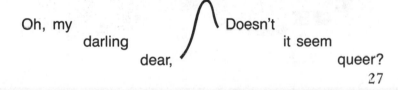
Did you say

kit - ty cats,

dressed up in their

fan - cy hats?

Oh, my
darling Doesn't
dear, it seem
queer?

27

Closing the Lesson OPTIONAL

Show the transparency prepared from Activity Sheet 11 (*Miss Mary Jane*). **Can you name this song by looking at its picture? Can you play it on the bells? It starts on the same bell as "Honey Bears."** End the class by singing "Miss Mary Jane" while everyone keeps the short pulse in their feet. One child can play the melody on the resonator bells already in place for "Have You Seen My Honey Bears?"

Have You Seen My Honey Bears?

Original English Text by Ruth Rubin
Traditional Yiddish Tune

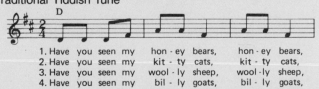

1. Have you seen my hon - ey bears, hon - ey bears,
2. Have you seen my kit - ty cats, kit - ty cats,
3. Have you seen my wool - ly sheep, wool - ly sheep,
4. Have you seen my bil - ly goats, bil - ly goats,

Sit - ting up - on wood - en chairs, wood - en chairs?
Dressed up in their fan - cy hats, fan - cy hats?
Rock - ing ba - bies fast a - sleep, fast a - sleep?
Sail - ing down on riv - er - boats, riv - er - boats?

Did you say hon - ey bears, sit - ting up - on wood - en chairs?
Did you say kit - ty cats, dressed up in their fan - cy hats?
Did you say wool - ly sheep, rock - ing ba - bies fast a - sleep?
Did you say bil - ly goats, sail - ing down on riv - er - boats?

Oh, my dar - ling dear, Does - n't it seem queer?
Oh, my dar - ling dear, Does - n't it seem queer?
Oh, my dar - ling dear, Does - n't it seem queer?
Oh, my dar - ling dear, Does - n't it seem queer?

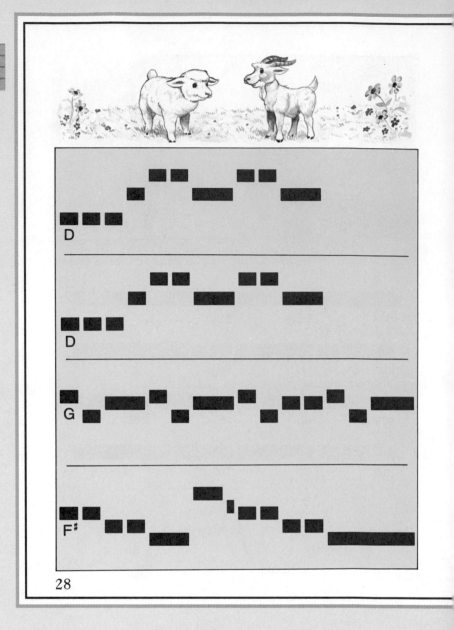

Play "Have You Seen My Honey Bears?".
Use these bells.

29

Lesson Focus

Melody: A series of pitches may move up or down by steps or skips.
Melody: A series of pitches bounded by the octave "belong together," forming a tonal set. *(P–I)*

Materials

o **Record Information:**
  • Have You Seen My Honey Bears?
    (Record 4 Side A Band 2)
  • Five Angels
    Record 4 Side A Band 3
    Voices: solo children's voices, children's choir
    Accompaniment: synthesizer, harp, celesta, percussion

o **Instruments:** resonator bells for C major scale (C, D, E, F, G, A, B, C'); bell mallet

o **Other:** bell stairsteps for major scale (See Lessons 22 and 31, pages 46 and 64, regarding placement of C major bells on stairsteps.)

o **Teacher's Resource Binder:**
  [Activity Sheets]
  • **Activity Sheet 12**, page A24 (Prepare one set of melodic direction cards for each child.)
  • Optional—
    Curriculum Correlations 3, 13, pages C4, C21
    Enrichment Activity 10, page E12

o **For additional experience with melody:** Describe 13, page 178

For Your Information

Body Scale (See bottom of page.)

Introducing the Lesson

Distribute a set of melodic direction cards prepared from Activity Sheet 12 *(Melodic Direction Cards)* to each child. **Find the cards that say "up" and "down." I'm going to play a melody pattern. Hold up the card that describes the sound I'm playing.** Play several patterns, each made up of at least three pitches. Randomly alternate between patterns that move up and patterns that move down; end with a pattern that moves in both directions.

Find the cards that say "steps" and "skips." Listen carefully! Can you decide whether I'm moving up and down by steps or by skips? Play several patterns and have the children hold up a card to identify each pattern.

Developing the Lesson

1. **Listen to a song you know. How does it begin? Show me with your cards.** Sing the first six pitches of "Have You Seen My Honey Bears?" The children might show either the "up" card or the "skip" card.

2. **Listen to a new song. Parts of the melody move by steps. When you hear those parts, hold up your "step" card!** Sing or play the recording of "Five Angels." (Six patterns move by steps, starting in Measure 5.)

3. **Listen again. Who is the song about?** Play the recording. Agree that the song is about angels. **What does each angel do?** Listen to the recording until the children have identified each angel's task.

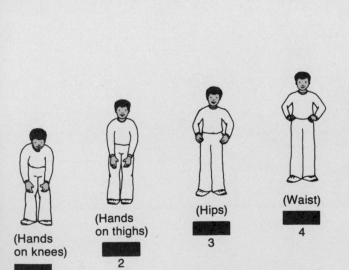
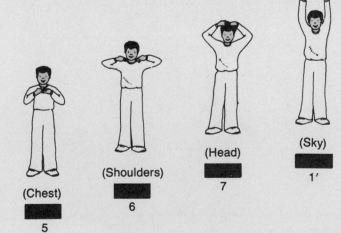

(Hands on knees) 1
(Hands on thighs) 2
(Hips) 3
(Waist) 4
(Chest) 5
(Shoulders) 6
(Head) 7
(Sky) 1'

4. Ask the class to sing the parts of the first four angels; you sing the other sections of the song.

5. Place resonator bells for the C major scale on the bell stairsteps. (See **Materials.**) Ask a child to find the pattern for the words, "The first one lights the fire." **How many different bells did we need to play this pattern? Let's count them while (Kenja) plays the pattern again.** Sing:

We played five bells. There are five steps in that melody pattern! Find the two cards that show how that melody pattern moved. ("up" and "step")

6. **I have another way to show how a melody moves. Watch!** Perform the first angel's phrase, using body scale motions for scale steps 1–1–2–3–4–5. (See **For Your Information.**) Ask the children to imitate your motions as you sing the pattern again. When

they can perform the first five steps of the body scale with reasonable accuracy, sing "Five Angels" again; add the body scale motions when singing about the five angels.

Closing the Lesson

Watch carefully! I'm going to use our body scale motions to show a song you know very well. Can you name the song I'm "singing"? Do body scale motions for Phrase 1 of "Have You Seen My Honey Bears?" (scale steps 1–1–1–3–5–5–3–5–5–3). Repeat the motions while singing the scale numbers. When the children identify the song, ask them to sing the first verse.

Repeat the activity with initial phrases of other familiar songs. The songs should use only the first five scale steps, such as those shown below.

Whoo-ee! Whoo-ee!: 5–3–5–3–2–1–2–3
The Merry-go-round: 1–2–3–1–2–3–1–2–3–5
Miss Mary Jane: 1–1–1–1–1–1–1–3–3–3

Five Angels

English Words by Adina Williamson

German Folk Song

Five an-gels ring a-round my bed. "Get up," they sing, "you sleep-y-head."

The first one lights the fire, The sec-ond one but-ters the bread,
The third one pours the milk, The fourth one sets the ta-ble,

The fifth one whis-pers soft - ly, "Come, sleep-y-head, hop out of bed."

LESSON 37

○ Teacher's Resource Binder:
• Optional—
Kodaly Activity 13, 14, page K20

Lesson Focus
Melody: A series of pitches bounded by the octave "belong together," forming a tonal set. *(P–I)*

Materials
○ **Record Information:**
• Miss Mary Jane **(Record 3 Side B Band 3)**
• Such a Getting Downstairs
  Record 4 Side A Band 4
  Voices: children's choir
  Accompaniment: fiddle, banjo, guitar, double bass, percussion
• Jack-in-the-Box **(Record 3 Side A Band 2)**
○ **Instruments:** woodblock and mallet; resonator bells D, E, F#, G, A, B, C#, D'; bell mallet; autoharp
○ **Other:** bell stairsteps for major scale
(See Binder, page A2, for instructions.)

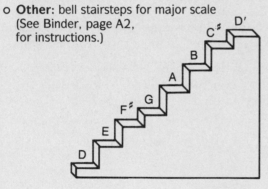

Introducing the Lesson
Begin class by doing the body scale for "Miss Mary Jane" (or any other song the children know well that uses only the first five scale steps). (Refer to the body scale motions shown in **For Your Information**, Lesson 36, page 78.) Pantomime the melody using body scale motions in the correct rhythm. Challenge the children to name the song. If they are unsure, perform the song again, this time singing the scale numbers while doing the body scale.

When the children have identified the song, sing it together. One child may play the underlying short pulse on a woodblock to suggest the sound of the horses' hooves.

Developing the Lesson
1. Ask a child to locate resonator bells D, E, F#, G, and A in the bell box and place each bell on the bell stairsteps. **Are they in the right order? Does the sound go up by steps?** As the bell player plays up the steps, the class should decide if the bells are in the right order. (See **Materials** for correct bell positions.)

Such a Getting Downstairs

Words Adapted

Oklahoma Play–Party Song

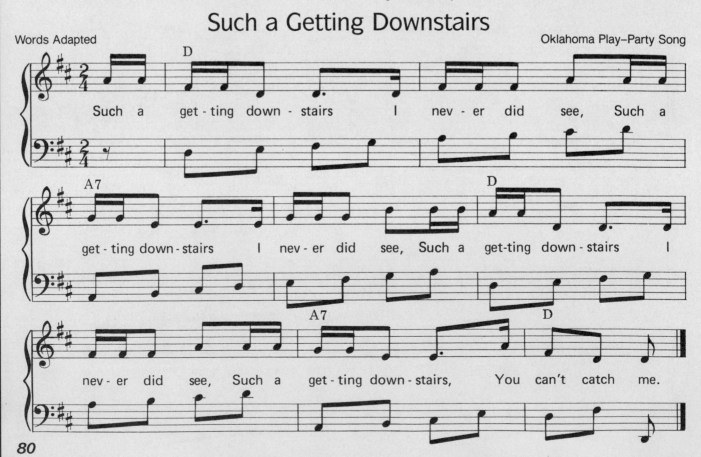

Such a get-ting down-stairs I nev-er did see, Such a get-ting down-stairs I nev-er did see, Such a get-ting down-stairs I nev-er did see, Such a get-ting down-stairs, You can't catch me.

2. Sing or play the recording of "Such a Getting Downstairs" (Phrase 1 only—"Such a getting downstairs I never did see"). Ask the children to sing the phrase. Help them by showing the melody pattern with body scale motions. Play the recording of the complete song. After listening again and discussing the words, challenge the class to sing the complete song. Assist by playing an accompaniment on autoharp.

3. Place bells for the rest of the D major scale on the bell stairsteps. One child may add a special ending for the song:

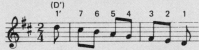

Perform the song with its special ending.

4. **How many steps are there in our musical stairs? Let's count them, beginning with the bottom step.** As a child plays each bell, have the class sing a number (1 2 3 4 5 6 7 8).

Draw attention to the fact that the lowest and highest bells have the same letter name—D. **So let's use the same number! Sing again. This time let's add our body scale motions.**

5. Choose another child to be bell player. Ask the class to sing "Such a Getting Downstairs"; the bell player plays either up or down the stairsteps. The class must then sing scale numbers to imitate the "up" or "down" scale played, while doing the appropriate body motions.

OPTIONAL

Closing the Lesson

I know another song that goes down our musical stairs by steps. Can you figure out its name? Pantomime, in correct rhythm, the body-scale motions for "Jack-in-the-Box" (Lesson 22, page 46). When the children have identified the song, sing it together with the motions.

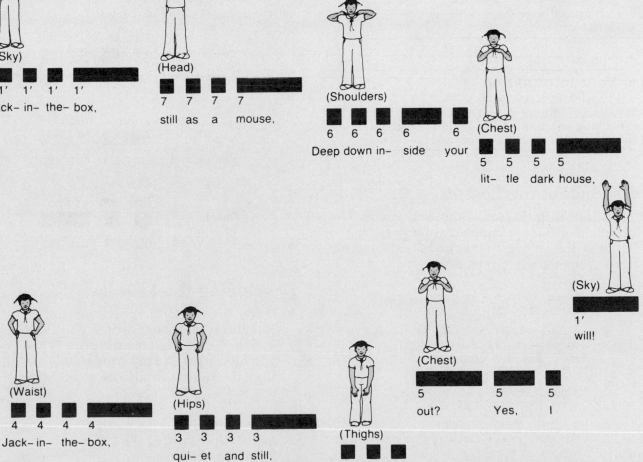

(Sky)

1' 1' 1' 1'
Jack- in- the- box,

(Head)

7 7 7 7
still as a mouse,

(Shoulders)

6 6 6 6 6
Deep down in- side your

(Chest)

5 5 5 5
lit- tle dark house,

(Waist)

4 4 4 4
Jack- in- the- box,

(Hips)

3 3 3 3
qui- et and still,

(Thighs)

2 2 2
Will you come

(Chest)

5 5 5
out? Yes, I

(Sky)

1'
will!

Lesson Focus

Rhythm: Individual sounds and silences within a rhythmic line may be longer than, shorter than, or the same as the underlying shortest pulse. *(D–I)*

Materials

o **Record Information:**
  • Cat in a Plum Tree
  Record 4 Side A Band 5
  Voices: children's choir
  Accompaniment: hammered dulcimer, autoharp, guitars, double bass, percussion
  • *Staines Morris Dance*
  Anonymous
  Record 4 Side A Band 6
  The Jaye Consort
o **Instruments:** finger cymbals
o **Other:** pencil and paper for each child
o **Teacher's Resource Binder:**
  Activity Sheets • **Activity Sheet 13**, page A25 (Prepare one copy for each child.)
  • Optional—
  Enrichment Activity 12, page E20
  Orff Activity 18, page O24
o **For additional experience with rhythm:** Describe 4, page 167

For Your Information

Structure of *Staines Morris Dance:*
  This dance consists of six parts (each in **A B** form) with the same **long short short** rhythm in the accompaniment throughout (low-sounding strings and tambourine).

Introducing the Lesson

Begin class by playing a "copy cat" game. The children pat their hands on their legs in the rhythm of the shortest sound while making the short mouth sounds shown below.

Sounds ch   ch   ch   ch (echo)
Pat   ▨   ▨   ▨   ▨

Sounds click click click click (echo)
Pat   ▨   ▨   ▨   ▨

Sounds buzz buzz buzz buzz (echo)
Pat   ▨   ▨   ▨   ▨

Add longer sounds while patting the same short pulse.

Sounds chhhhhhh   chhhhhhh (echo)
Pat   ▨   ▨   ▨   ▨

Sounds buzzzzzz   buzzzzzz (echo)
Pat   ▨   ▨   ▨   ▨

Combine long and short sounds with the same patting pulse.

Sounds ch   ch   chhhhhhh (echo)
Pat   ▨   ▨   ▨   ▨

Sounds buzzzzzz   buzz buzz (echo)
Pat   ▨   ▨   ▨   ▨

Continue the game. Randomly mix up mouth-sound patterns that are the same length as the underlying pulse with those that include longer sounds.

Distribute a pencil and a sheet of paper to each child. **Can you draw a picture of the patterns you've been patting and chanting? First draw a line of four short sounds to show the pulse you were patting. Now listen to my chant. Draw its picture above your short sounds.** Chant each of the following patterns in the order shown. Repeat each pattern as needed; discuss the relationship between your chant and the short sounds—same or longer.

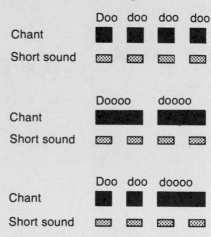

Developing the Lesson

1. Have the children continue to pat short sounds on their knees while you sing "Cat in a Plum Tree." **Listen carefully! When could you hear words in my song that were longer than the short sounds you were patting?** (at the end—"plum tree")

2. When the children can sing the song accurately while patting the short sound, add the following chant:

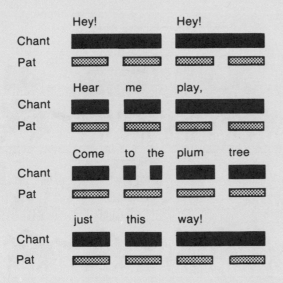

Chant — Hey!

Pat

Chant — Hear me play,

Pat

Chant — Come to the plum tree

Pat

Chant — just this way!

Pat

3. Ask one or more children to "come to the plum tree." Dictate the length of their steps with finger cymbals. Repeat the song and the chant several times. Each time accompany the chant with a different finger cymbal pattern to show how the child should "come to the plum tree." (The children should continue to pat the pulse throughout the song, chant, and finger cymbal pattern.)

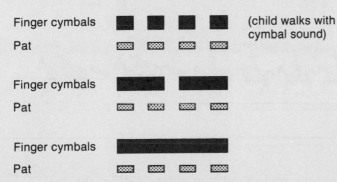

Finger cymbals

Pat — (child walks with cymbal sound)

Finger cymbals

Pat

Finger cymbals

Pat

4. Give each child a picture of the song, as prepared from Activity Sheet 13 (*Cat in a Plum Tree*). Ask them to perform the song again while following its picture.

OPTIONAL

Closing the Lesson

End the class by playing *Staines Morris Dance*. Quietly maintain the short sound while the children listen and imitate your gestures. **I heard a pattern that sounded like this.** Demonstrate the pattern as you speak:

long short short

Play the recording again while maintaining this pattern. (See **For Your Information** regarding instrumentation.)

Cat in a Plum Tree

Traditional Song

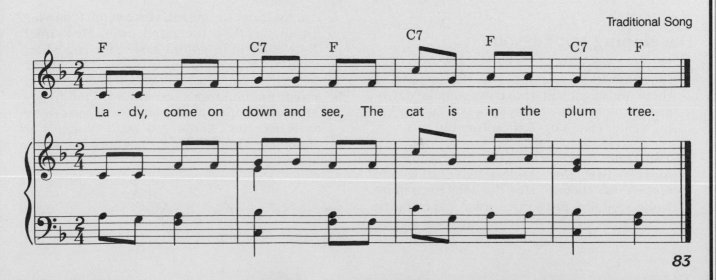

La - dy, come on down and see, The cat is in the plum tree.

Lesson Focus

Rhythm: Individual sounds within a rhythmic line may be longer than, shorter than, or the same as the underlying shortest pulse. *(P–I)*

Materials

○ **Piano Accompaniment:** page 213
○ **Record Information:**
  • Little Arabella Miller
    (Record 3 Side B Band 6)
  • Yankee Doodle
    Record 4 Side A Band 7
    Voices: children's choir
    Accompaniment: piccolo, snare drum, bass drum
  • *Semper Fidelis* by John Philip Sousa
    (**soo**-zuh), 1854–1932
    Record 4 Side A Band 8
    The Incredible Columbia All-Star Band
    Gunther Schuller, conductor
○ **Instruments:** several drums
○ **Teacher's Resource Binder:**
  • Optional—
    Biography 5, pages B9–B10
    Curriculum Correlation 15, page C24
    Kodaly Activity 2, page K2
    Mainstreaming Suggestion 19,
    page M18
    Orff Activity 1, page O1
○ **For additional experience with rhythm:**
  Perform 18, page 156; Describe 11, page 176

Yankee Doodle

30

Introducing the Lesson

Review "Little Arabella Miller" (Lesson 31, page 64). Ask the children to step the underlying short pulse and tap the rhythm of the melody as they sing. Help them discover that the pulse and the rhythm of the melody are the same.

Developing the Lesson

1. Play the recording of "Yankee Doodle." Ask the class to step in place to the underlying short pulse. Teach the class simple movements to perform as they listen to the recording again. (See **For Your Information.**)

2. **This time, can you sing the song while you move?** After the children have sung and moved, ask them to sing the song once more while stepping the short sound and clapping the rhythm of the words. Help them realize that the underlying pulse and the rhythm of

the melody are sometimes different.

3. Ask the children to look at pupil page 30, or show page 30 of the Jumbo Book. **Can you find pictures of long sounds?** (the pictures of the longer horses)

4. Ask the class to sing the verse while following the pictures on the pupil page. **How long does each long sound last?** (for two short sounds)

5. Direct the children's attention to pupil page 31. Ask them to read each drum pattern by chanting the words "short," "long," or "lo-ong," while patting the short sound on their legs.

Closing the Lesson `OPTIONAL`

Play the recording of *Semper Fidelis*. Ask the

84

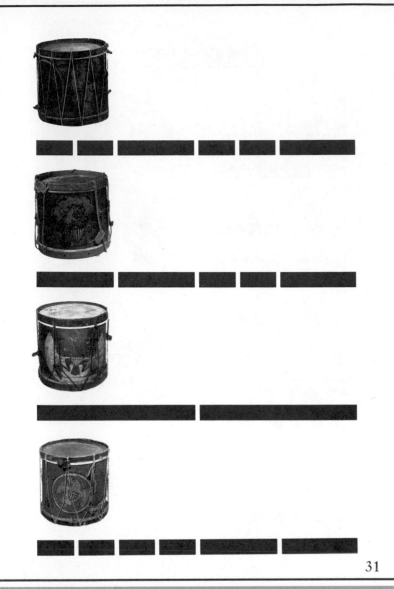

For Your Information

Dance movements for Yankee Doodle: Form a circle.

VERSE **Measures 1–4**: Step with short sound (four to a measure); walk clockwise around circle.

Measures 5–8: Stop; pretend to place feather in cap. Bow on final measure.

REFRAIN Measures 9–16: Stand in place in circle; clap the underlying short pulse.

Structure of *Semper Fidelis:* The piece is scored for marching band (brass, winds, and percussion).

Introduction: Brief; in duple meter

A Lively melody (full band); **A** repeated

B New melody (full band); **B** repeated

Bridge: Drum solo

C Cornet solo accompanied by percussion and low brass; **C** repeated twice with added melody in winds; more instruments added each time

D New melody (similar to **B**); **D** repeated

31

children to be your "copycats" as they listen and imitate a short-long pattern immediately after you perform it. Pat the following patterns:

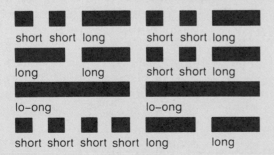

short short long   short short long

long   long   short short long

lo–ong   lo–ong

short short short short long   long

Change patterns frequently; rest during the drum "bridge." (See **For Your Information**.)

Yankee Doodle

Traditional American Song

Yan - kee Doo - dle came to town,

Rid - ing on a po - ny; Stuck a feath - er

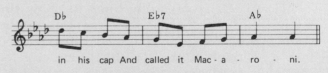

in his cap And called it Mac - a - ro - ni.

Refrain

Yan - kee Doo - dle, keep it up,

Yan - kee Doo - dle dan - dy, Mind the mu - sic

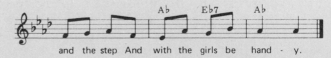

and the step And with the girls be hand - y.

85

Lesson Focus

Form: A musical whole is a combination of smaller segments. *(D–I)*

Materials

o **Piano Accompaniment:** page 214

o **Record Information:**
  • Little Cabin in the Wood
    (Record 2 Side A Band 7)
  • Clapping Land
    Record 4 Side B Band 1
    Voices: man, children's choir
    Accompaniment: fiddle, banjo, guitar, piano, double bass, percussion
  • *Song of the Narobi Trio*
    by Robert Maxwell, 1921–
    Record 4 Side B Band 2
    Hot Butter

o **Other:** pencil and paper for each child; rhythm bars (as prepared for Lesson 27, page 56)—melodic rhythm: 4 short bars, 20 long bars, 3 lo-ong bars, 2 loo-oong! bars; to construct ukuleles—heavy cardboard, saber saw with knife blade (or sharp knife), fine sandpaper, glue, tempera or acrylic paints, *or* large paper grocery bags, rubber bands

(continued on next page)

Clapping Land

32

Introducing the Lesson OPTIONAL

Review "Little Cabin in the Wood" (Lesson 16, page 32). Give a pencil and a sheet of paper to each child. **Can you draw lines to show the rhythm for the words, "little cabin in the wood"?** Sing the phrase and have the children draw a rhythm picture. Repeat the process for Phrase 2, "little man by the window stood." Then show the patterns with rhythm bars.

Continue the process with the remaining phrases. (Note: Phrases 1, 3, 5, and 6 use the same rhythm pattern; Phrases 4 and 8 also use a similar rhythm pattern. You can display each of these patterns with rhythm bars once, and then point out the repeated pattern on each occurrence.) **How many parts are there in the whole song?** (eight)

Developing the Lesson

1. Ask the children to open their books to page 32, or show page 32 of the Jumbo Book. **Some songs have many parts. Look at the pictures in your book. How many parts are in this song?** Listen to "Clapping Land." Conclude that there are 10 parts. (Each part consists of two phrases.) Replay the recording; invite the children to do the motion described in each verse. Then sing the entire song with the class.

2. **Here's another piece that has many parts. You can "accompany" this music while you listen.** Hand out the ukuleles prepared from Activity Sheet 14 *(Cardboard Ukuleles)* or have the children use "pretend" ukuleles. Ask the children to look at pupil page 33 and try pantomiming each way of playing.

3. Play the entire recording of *Song of the Narobi Trio*. The children may "accompany" the

Song of the Narobi Trio

Play your ukulele as you listen to the music.
Can you play a different way for each part?

| Strum | Tap with your fingers | Play like a violin |

| Play like a cello | Shake | Tap with your hand |

Find other ways to play!

33

Materials *(continued)*

○ Teacher's Resource Binder:

Activity Sheets • **Activity Sheet 14**, page A26 (Prepare one ukulele for each child. See activity sheet for instructions.)

For Your Information

Form of *Song of the Narobi Trio:*

Introduction: 16 pulses; accompaniment only—no melody

Parts 1–4: each part made up of two 16-pulse segments; woodblock pattern marks end of first segment; finger cymbals mark end of second segment

Interlude: 16 pulses; accompaniment only

Parts 5–8: (same as Parts 1–4)

Coda

Form picture: *Song of the Narobi Trio*

| Intro. | Part 1 | Pt. 2 | Pt. 3 | Pt. 4 |

| Interlude | Pt. 5 | Pt. 6 | Pt. 7 | Pt. 8 | Coda |

music and change "playing styles" as the music continues. Guide the children to "play" with the underlying pulse.

Closing the Lesson

Listen again. When you think that a new part has begun, change the way you are playing. As the children play, draw a geometric shape on the chalkboard each time a new part begins. (See form picture in **For Your Information**.)

How many parts were there? (11, including the introduction, interlude, and coda) **What helped you know that a main part had ended?** (A finger cymbal was played.)

Clapping Land
Danish Folk Song

I trav - eled far a - cross the sea, I

met a man and old was he. "Old man," I said, "where

do you live?" And this is what he told me:

1. "Come with me to clap - ping land,

clap - ping land, clap - ping land. All who want to

live with me, Fol - low me to clap - ping land."

2. stamping land   3. nodding land
4. dancing land   5. skipping land

87

LESSON 41

Lesson Focus

Form: A musical whole begins, continues, and ends. *(D–I)*

Materials

o **Record Information:**
- *Prelude in A Major* from Op. 28 by Frédéric Chopin (**show**-pan), 1810–1849
  Record 4 Side B Band 3
  Alexander Brailowsky, piano
- *Hush, Little Baby*
  Record 4 Side B Band 4
  Voice: woman
  Accompaniment: string quartet

o **Instruments:** hand drum

o **Other:** crayon and paper for each child

o **Teacher's Resource Binder:**

Activity Sheets • **Activity Sheet 15,** page A27 (Prepare one copy for each child.)
- Optional—
  Biography 6, pages B11–B12
  Orff Activity 18, page O26

o **For additional experience with form:** Describe 1, page 164

Introducing the Lesson

Play a counting game. Tell the children to walk to your beat as you count to "8." Accompany the count with a drum. Repeat the counting sequence several times without interrupting the steady pulse.

Next ask the children to walk as you count to "7" and to stop when you say "8":

1	2	3	4	5	6	7	8
step	step	step	step	step	step	step	pause

Repeat this sequence several times.

Complete the activity by asking the children to place their hands in a different spot "in the sky" each time they pause on the count of "8." **How many different places can you find? high? low? in front? behind?** Repeat the counting sequence several times.

Developing the Lesson

1. Play the recording of *Prelude in A Major.* Ask the children to stand in one place while listening but to continue moving their hands from spot to spot, as in the last part of **Introducing the Lesson.** Guide the children to fit their hand movements to the phrase structure of the music by modeling as you listen to the recording. (Each phrase ends with a long tone.)

2. Play the recording again. This time suggest to the children that they gracefully make wavy lines or circles as they move their hands from one spot to the next. **Be sure your hand always reaches a pausing spot at the end of each part of the music.**

3. Ask the children to listen to a song that has the same peaceful feeling as *Prelude in A Major.* Play the recording of "Hush, Little Baby." Discuss the way the music conveys the feeling of a lullaby. Play the recording a second time. This time ask the children to move their hands through the air to show the "smooth" melody; they should pause when the melody seems to pause.

4. Distribute a copy of Activity Sheet 15 *(Hush, Little Baby)* to each child. Before listening to the recording again, ask the children to put a finger on the "Begin" dot. While listening, they should follow the lines with their fingers and pause on each dot as that phrase comes to an end. The children must move their fingers slowly in order to match the phrase length and sense the 16 phrases of the song.

5. Invite the children to sing the song while following the lines and dots on the activity sheet to help them recall the words. **Sit up straight and begin by taking a good deep breath. Can you make your voices move smoothly from one tone to the next, just like your hands moved smoothly through the air?**

Closing the Lesson

End the class by returning to *Prelude in A Major.* Invite the children to create a picture that shows how they moved to this music. (See Steps 1 and 2.) Distribute a crayon and a sheet of paper to each child. (Some children might draw at the chalkboard.) Tell the children to begin with their crayon tip on the paper. Play the recording. The children should move their crayons in a continuous line as the music continues and make a large dot when the music seems to come to a rest. Have them repeat the two types of drawing as the music continues.

Their pictures might look like this:

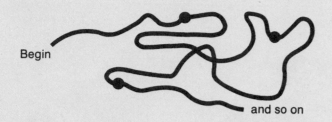

Hush, Little Baby

American Folk Song

1. Hush, lit - tle ba - by, don't say a word,
2. If that____ dia - mond ring turns____ brass,
3. If that____ bill - y goat don't____ pull,
4. If that____ dog named Rov - er don't____ bark,

Pa - pa's gon - na buy you a mock - ing - bird. If that mock - ing -
Pa - pa's gon - na buy you a look - ing glass. If that look - ing
Pa - pa's gon - na buy you a cart and bull. If that cart and
Pa - pa's gon - na buy you a po - ny cart. If that po - ny

bird won't sing, Pa - pa's gon - na buy you a dia - mond ring.
glass gets broke, Pa - pa's gon - na buy you a bill - y goat.
bull turns o - ver, Pa - pa's gon - na buy you a dog named Rov - er.
cart falls down, You'll__ be the sad - dest____ child in town.

LESSON 42

Whole and Parts

Lesson Focus
Form: A musical whole is a combination of smaller segments. *(D–I)*

Materials
o **Piano Accompaniment:** page 215
o **Record Information:**
  • Hush, Little Baby
    (Record 4 Side B Band 4)
  • Riding in My Car
  Record 4 Side B Band 5
    Voices: solo children's voices, children's choir
    Accompaniment: tenor banjo, guitars, double bass, sound effects, percussion
  • *Song of the Narobi Trio*
    (Record 4 Side B Band 2)
o **Instruments:** resonator bells D, E, F#, G, A, and B; bell mallet; finger cymbals; woodblock and mallet
o **Teacher's Resource Binder:**
  • Optional—
    Enrichment Activity 13, page E21
    Mainstreaming Suggestion 18, page M17

34

Introducing the Lesson

Review "Hush, Little Baby." Ask the children to sing and move as they did during the previous lesson. **How many parts are in this song? You can decide by counting the number of times you paused on count "8."** (four)

Developing the Lesson

1. **Many whole things are made up of parts. What wholes and parts can you find in this picture?** Ask the children to open their books to page 34, or show page 34 of the Jumbo Book. Discuss the pictures. **A whole car has many parts! A whole scale of bells is made up of eight parts.**

2. **Look at a picture of a song on page 35. How many parts do you think there are in this song?** After the children have offered suggestions, listen to the recording and decide

that the song has four parts. (Each part ends with one or two long sounds.)

3. Study each part (phrase) and guide the class to read the rhythm by saying "short," "long," "lo-ong," or "loo-oong!" in the correct order (as shown by the length of each rhythm bar).

($\flat$)($\downarrow$)	($\downarrow$)	($\circ$)
Rhythm bar		
Chant short long	lo–ong	loo–oong!

Then have a child play the melody on resonator bells. (The necessary pitches are shown on the pupil page at the beginning of each phrase.) **Can we sing the song?** Listen again to the recording to correct any singing errors.

Closing the Lesson ^{OPTIONAL}

Return to *Song of the Narobi Trio* (Lesson 40, page 86). Ask the children to step around the

90

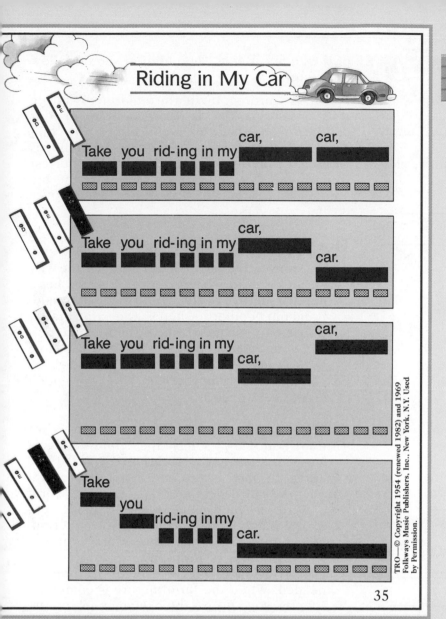

Riding in My Car

For Your Information

Additional verses for "Riding in My Car":

3. Click, clack, open up a door, girls,
   Click, clack, open up a door, boys,
   Front door, back door, clickety clack,
   Take you riding in my car.

4. Trees and houses walk along, long,
   Trees and houses walk along, long,
   Truck and a car and a garbage can,
   Take you riding in my car.

5. Climb, climb, rattle on a front seat,
   Spree I spraddle on a back seat,
   Turn my key, step on my starter,
   Take you riding in my car.

6. I'm-a gonna roll you home again, gain,
   I'm-a gonna roll you home again, gain,
   Brrm, brrm, chrrka, chrrka, rolly home,
   Take you riding in my car.

7. I'm-a gonna let you blow the horn, horn
   I'm-a gonna let you blow the horn, horn
   Oorah, oorahh, oogah, oogahh,
   Take you riding in my car.

8. Brrm, brrm, chrrka, chrrka, brrm, brrm,
   Brrm, brrm, chrrka, chrrka, brrm, brrm,
   Brrm, brrm, chrrka, chrrka, brrm, brrm,
   Take you riding In my car.

35

room and show the parts of this music. **Turn and go in a different direction each time you think a new part begins.** The children should stand still during the introduction (16 pulses) and begin to step as Part 1 begins.

Comment on the children who turned at the beginning of each new part of the music. (Since each part consists of two segments, some children may turn after 16 pulses and some after 32.) **What sounds did we hear that helped us know a part was ending?** (special instruments— woodblock or finger cymbals) **This time clap your hands lightly in front of you when you hear the woodblock end a part. Clap above your head when you hear the finger cymbals. Play the recording again.**

Give a woodblock and mallet to one child and finger cymbals to another. These children may play along with the recording to show the 16- and 32-beat segments, while the rest of the class continues to do the clapping motions.

Riding in My Car
Words and Music by Woody Guthrie

1. Take you rid-ing in my car, car,
2. En - gine it goes brrm, brrm,

Take you rid-ing in my car, car,
En - gine it goes brrm, brrm,

Take you rid-ing in my car, car,
En - gine it goes brrm, brrm,

Take you rid-ing in my car.
Take you rid-ing in my car.

(See **For Your Information** for additional verses.)

LESSON 43

Lesson Focus

Form: A musical whole may include an introduction, interludes, and an ending segment.
Form: A musical whole is a combination of smaller segments. *(D–I)*

Materials

o **Record Information:**
  • Riding in My Car **(Record 4 Side B Band 5)**
  • A-Hunting We Will Go
    (Record 1 Side A Band 3)
  • Step in Time **(Record 1 Side B Band 1)**
  • *Hakof* **(Record 3 Side A Band 6)**
  • Have You Seen My Honey Bears?
    (Record 4 Side A Band 2)
  • Signs of the Zodiac
    from *Les Aventures de Mercure*
    (The Adventures of Mercury)
    by Erik Satie (sah-**tee**), 1866–1925
    Record 4 Side B Band 6
    Utah Symphony Orchestra
    Maurice Abravanel, conductor.
o **Other:** geometric shapes as prepared for Lesson 20 (page 42)—cut out five examples of each shape
o **Teacher's Resource Binder:**
  • Optional—
    Biography 4, pages B7–B8
o **For additional experience with form:** Special Times 1, page 187

For Your Information

Structure of "Signs of the Zodiac":
1. Low tuba plays melody that descends by octave skips; rhythm of the melody moves in 2-to-1 relationship to the beat.
2. High wind instruments play a similar descending melody.
3. Low tuba plays ascending scalar melody; rhythm of the melody now moves in 3-to-1 relationship to the beat.
4. High trumpet plays up and down melody that outlines a major chord; rhythm of the melody returns to 2-to-1 relationship with the beat.
5. Low tuba plays same melody as Section 1.
6. High oboe plays same melody as Section 2.
7. Middle strings play same melody as Section 3.
8. Low tuba plays same melody as Section 4.

Introducing the Lesson

Review "Riding in My Car." Have the children turn to page 35 in their books, or show page 35 of the Jumbo Book. The children should follow the pictures as they sing the song.

Play the recording. Invite the children to "take a ride in the car." Form several circles of four children each. At the beginning of Verse 1, Child 1 in Circle 1 steps outside the circle and moves with light running steps (in time to the shortest sound). Another child joins the ride at the beginning of each phrase. A different circle moves during each verse.

Developing the Lesson

1. **We showed the parts of our song by the way we moved, but we left out some parts! Let's make a picture of the whole piece of music.** Hand out geometric shapes. (See **Materials**.) Choose one shape to show the introduction and coda, a second shape to show the song verses, and a third shape for interludes. (A possible picture of the recording is provided on the next page.)

2. **We can show the parts of other songs we know!** Review songs the children have learned, such as "A-Hunting We Will Go," "Step in Time," *"Hakof,"* and "Have You Seen My Honey Bears?". Develop a "form picture" of each piece of music, using geometric shapes to show the introduction, verses, interludes, and coda, as appropriate. (See examples of form pictures on the next page.) Listen to the recordings as often as needed. When the form picture is complete, sing the song. (Turn the balance knob on the record player so the children can sing with the recorded accompaniment but without the recorded voices.)

3. Continue the lesson by listening to "Signs of the Zodiac." As the children listen, guide them to determine the number of parts. Ask the first child in a row to stand as the music begins. Instruct the second child to stand when he or she thinks Part 2 begins, the third to stand at the beginning of Part 3, and so on. Then discuss the musical clues the children used to decide when a new section began. (See **For Your Information**.)

Closing the Lesson

End the class by making a form picture of "Signs of the Zodiac," using the geometric shapes. (See the last form picture on the next page.)

Form Pictures:

Riding in My Car

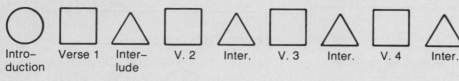

A–Hunting We Will Go

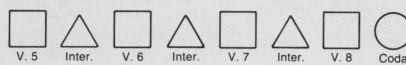

Step in Time

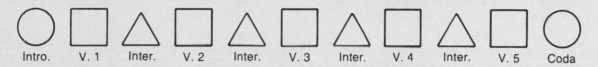

Hakof

Have You Seen My Honey Bears?

Signs of the Zodiac

o **Instruments:** resonator bells F, A, B♭, and C; bell mallet
o **Teacher's Resource Binder:**
  • Optional—
    Curriculum Correlations 3, 8, pages C4, C13
o **For additional experience with rhythm:** Perform 12, page 150, Perform 14, page 152

Lesson Focus

Form: A series of sounds may form a distinct musical idea within the musical whole.
Rhythm: Music may move in relation to the underlying steady beat. *(D-I)*

Materials

o **Record Information:**
  • Three Little Fishies
    Record 4 Side B Band 7
    Voices: woman, children's choir
    Accompaniment: electric guitar, acoustic guitar, electric bass, electric piano, synthesizer, percussion

Introducing the Lesson

Tell the children that they are going to hear a new song. Challenge them to show and tell you as much as they can about this music they have never heard before!

Play the recording of "Three Little Fishies." Begin a discussion of the song by talking about the silly words. Pay particular attention to the nonsense words of the refrain. Replay the recording as necessary until the children know the story.

Three Little Fishies

Words and Music by Saxie Dowell

94

Developing the Lesson

1. **This time, can you show me the steady beat?** Play the recording through Verse 1. The children may choose to show the beat by patting knees, tapping hands, and so on.

2. On the next hearing, guide the children to mirror the melodic shape. Discover that the song includes only two melodic shapes and draw them on the chalkboard:

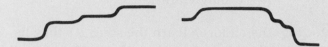

3. Show the general shape of the first melodic pattern with body scale motions while singing the scale numbers (1–1–3–3–4–4–5). (See Lesson 36, page 78, for body scale motions.)

Put out resonator bells and invite a child to play the pattern.

4. Experiment by playing the melodic pattern from Step 3 with each upward moving part of the song. Discover that the pattern works for measures 1–2, 3–4, 9–10, and 11–12.

Closing the Lesson

Help the children learn to sing the complete song. Replay the recording as necessary until the children can sing the entire story.

swam and they swam all o - ver the dam.
swam and they swam right out to the sea.

Refrain
Boop boop dit - tem dat - tem what - tem Chu! Boop boop dit - tem dat - tem

what - tem Chu!
1. And they swam and they swam all o - ver the dam.
2. And they swam and they swam right out to the sea.

3. "Whee!" yelled the little fishies, "Here's a lot of fun. We'll swim in the sea 'til the day is done." They swam and they swam, and it was a lark 'Til all of a sudden they met a shark!

4. "Help!" cried the little fishies, "Look at all the whales!" And quick as they could they turned on their tails. And back to the pool in the meadow they swam, And they swam and they swam back over the dam.

LESSON 45

Lesson Focus:

Evaluation: Review concepts and skills studied in the Third Quarter.

Materials

o **Record Information:**
  • Needle Sing
    Record 5 Side A Band 1
    Voices: solo child, children's choir
    Accompaniment: harmonica, guitars, double bass, percussion
o **Instruments:** triangle and striker, or finger cymbals; sand blocks; resonator bells C, D, F, G, and A; bell mallets
o **Other:** pencil and paper for each child
o **Teacher's Resource Binder:**
  Evaluation • **Evaluation 3,** pages Ev7–Ev8
    • **Musical Progress Report 3,** page Ev9
    • Optional—
      Curriculum Correlation 7, page C9

Introducing the Lesson

Help the children learn the following game. As the children stand in a line, begin to chant and move:

Chant: Wind and wind the thread,
Movement: *(Roll hands one over the other, away from the body.)*
Oh, wind and wind the thread,
(Roll hands; reverse direction.)
And pull and pull,
(Mimic pulling a rope, as in tug-o-war.)
And turn yourself about.
(Turn fully around.)
In and out we sew and sew,
(Join hands and form one long line. The person at one end is the "needle" and pulls the group in a "sewing" motion, going in and out between each pair of children in the line while finishing the chant.)
In and out the thread does go,
In and out we sew and sew,
See how quickly the needle goes.
(All stop; begin to "wind the thread" again as the game is repeated.)

Developing the Lesson

1. Listen to the song, "Needle Sing." Entertain the idea that a needle probably could sing, by reading the composer's poem:

    I guess a needle could sing,
    If you stitched it fast enough,
    And knitted as fast as lightning,
    And sewed as fast as a racehorse.

    (by Woody Guthrie)

2. Help the children learn the song. As they listen before singing, keep their attention by having them move differently each time they hear the words "sing, Zing!" (clap hands, snap fingers, stamp feet).

3. When the children can readily sing the song, add the sounds of a triangle or finger cymbals on the word, "Zing!". **Can you remember to be silent on the word "Zing!" and to listen for the instrument's sound?**

Closing the Lesson

Administer *Evaluation 3* to check the children's understanding of ideas studied in the Third Quarter. The evaluation may be conducted with the children individually or in small groups. If the evaluation is conducted as a small group activity, make sure to observe the progress of individual children as they participate in each part.

Complete the *Musical Progress Report 3* for each child. This report may be sent home as a report to parents or simply retained by the teacher as a record of each child's progress.

Needle Sing

Words and Music by Woody Guthrie

Lesson Focus

Expression: Musical elements are combined into a whole to express a musical or extramusical idea. *(C–E)*

Materials

o **Record Information:**
  • Old King Cole
  Record 5 Side A Band 2
  Voices: children's choir
  Accompaniment: bass clarinet, trumpet, viola, harpsichord, percussion

o **Other:** overhead projector

o **Teacher's Resource Binder:**
  Activity Sheets • **Activity Sheet 16,** page A28 (Prepare a transparency from the activity sheet.)
  • Optional—
  Enrichment Activity 11, page E14

o **For additional experience with expression:**
  Perform 1, page 134

Introducing the Lesson

Chant the nursery rhyme "Jack, Jump Over the Candlestick" (Lesson 1, page 1). Invite the children to join in. After rhythmically chanting the rhyme several times, have the children use vocal inflections to depict Jack jumping over the candlestick.

Give several children an opportunity to improvise.

Draw melody contours on the chalkboard to show as closely as possible the vocal inflections of the children as they "make Jack jump." Some possibilities are shown below.

Developing the Lesson

1. Learn the nursery rhyme "Old King Cole" by listening to and then singing along with the recording.

2. Invite the children to act out Old King Cole's story. First, assign the role of King Cole. Have this child act out the story while the rest of the class sings the rhyme they have just learned. To turn the rhyme into a play, the king can insert spoken dialogue such as the following:

Singers: Old King Cole was a merry old soul
    And a merry old soul was he.
    He called for his pipe...
King: Bring me my pipe!
Singers: And he called for his bowl...
King: Bring me my bowl!
Singers: And he called for his fiddlers three...
King: Bring me my fiddlers three—I want to hear music!

3. Repeat the drama, this time assigning the roles of several servants and the three fiddlers. These characters can speak to the king as they respond to his requests:

Servants: Here is your pipe (bowl), your Majesty.
Fiddlers: We'll play music for you, your Majesty.

4. **We have just acted in a play, but now we are going to change our story to an opera. In an opera, people sing their words instead of speaking them.**

5. Choose new children to play each of the characters; the rest of the class will again act as a chorus and sing the rhyme. When each character has dialogue, it should be sung improvisationally instead of spoken.

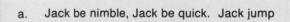

a.   Jack be nimble, Jack be quick. Jack jump   the candlestick.

Other ideas: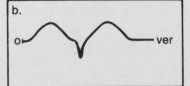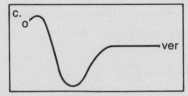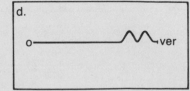

6. Encourage the children to expand the opera dialogue by introducing "conflict" into the story. A servant has brought the bowl to the king, but the bowl is chipped. What will the servant say? How will the king answer? A servant brings the pipe but trips! What might happen to the pipe?

Closing the Lesson OPTIONAL

Return to the original nursery rhyme. Help the children sense how the pitches of the melody move by "playing" the rhyme on the body scale. Display the transparency prepared from Activity Sheet 16 *(Old King Cole)* and demonstrate the body scale motions while the children sing the rhyme. The children will notice your use of a new motion—touching toes for the low 5. Have the children join you and "play" the melody using body scale motions.

Old King Cole

Traditional

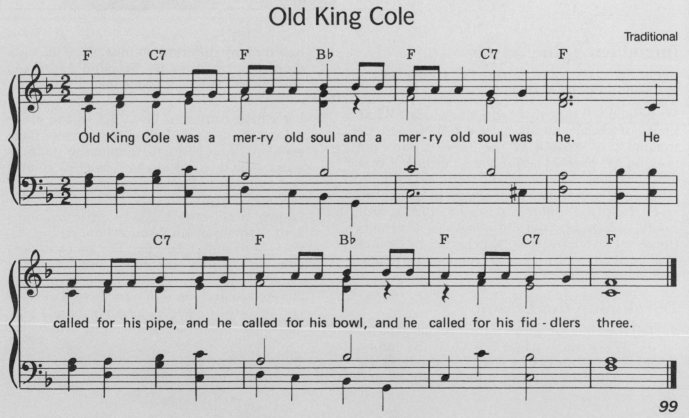

Lesson Focus

Expression: The expressiveness of music is affected by the way timbre, dynamics, articulation, and tempo contribute to the musical whole. *(C–I)*

Materials

o **Record Information:**
   • Old King Cole
     (Record 5 Side A Band 2)
   • *The Three Little Pigs*
     (Record 2 Side B Band 1)
   • *Sounds of the Kitchen*
     Record 5 Side A Band 3
     Accompaniment: sound effects

o **Instruments:** one instrument for each child, from a selection that could include maracas, drums of various sizes and mallets, claves, guiro and scratcher, woodblock and mallet, triangle and striker, finger cymbals, whistle, sand blocks, xylophone, and so on; "environmental-sound" instruments, such as a washboard, washtub bass, kitchen utensils, and so on

o **Other:** a pencil for each child

(continued on next page)

A Walk in the Zoo

Amy and Greg went for a walk in the zoo.
What did they see?
What did they hear?

36

Introducing the Lesson

Begin the class by reviewing "Old King Cole." Perform the nursery rhyme as an opera.

We helped tell that story with our voices! What kinds of vocal sounds helped tell the story? Remind the children of *The Three Little Pigs* (Lesson 17, page 34). Play the recording of that music drama. Discuss the different ways the instrumental accompaniment assists in telling the story. Help the children describe, with appropriate vocabulary, the differences in dynamics (loud–soft), tempo (fast–slow), timbre (sound quality, such as rasping or ringing), and articulation (smooth–jumpy).

Developing the Lesson

1. Tell the children to open their books to pages 36–37, or show pages 36–37 of the Jumbo Book. **Amy and Greg went for a walk in the zoo. They saw many different sights and heard many different sounds.** Give the children time to examine the pupil pages and identify the different sights and sounds.

2. **Let's help Amy and Greg get to the other side of the zoo by playing the story of their walk!** As the children examine the pictures again, ask them to suggest musical sounds that could describe each event.

3. Display a variety of classroom instruments and "environmental-sound" instruments. (See **Materials.**) Discuss the pictures and possible "sound events" again. As each sound event is mentioned, assign two or more children to prepare that part. Give them several minutes to select instruments and plan more specifically the sounds they will make.

4. To be sure the groups have planned their parts and that the children can remember

Tell the story of the walk with your own music.

37

Materials (continued)

o **Teacher's Resource Binder:**

[Activity Sheets] • **Activity Sheet 17,** page A29 (Prepare one copy for each child.)
   • Optional—
     Curriculum Correlation 5, page C8

o **For additional experience with timbre and expression:** Perform 7, page 142; Describe 7, page 171

For Your Information

Order of events in *Sounds of the Kitchen:*

1. water running
2. refrigerator door being slammed
3. milk being poured into a mixing bowl
4. blender running
5. telephone ringing
6. pans being banged against each other
7. oven timer ringing
8. voice saying ''dinner's ready''
9. voices of people as they begin to come to dinner

them, ask each group to demonstrate its part as you point to each event on the page.

5. Have the children perform the walk without stopping while you trace the path through the zoo on the Jumbo Book pages. Each group plays its part as you arrive at the appropriate point in the walk.

6. Discuss the performance of each group and how each sound event might be altered or added to in order to make the sound story more interesting. Repeat the walk.

7. Invite one child to be the ''conductor.'' Instruct the conductor to show how long an event is to last (and the amount of time between events) by moving his or her hand slowly or quickly along the path in the Jumbo Book.

[OPTIONAL]

Closing the Lesson

You just told a story of a walk using sound. Now we're going to hear the sounds that belong to another walk. Listen! Where do you think this walk takes place? Play the recording of *Sounds of the Kitchen.* Determine that the walk takes place in the kitchen.

Distribute a copy of Activity Sheet 17 *(Sounds of the Kitchen)* and a pencil to each child. **Can you draw the path of the story as the person moves about the kitchen? Listen to the beginning once more. Where does the walk begin?** Play the first part of the recording. Help the class decide that the walk begins at the sink because the first sound heard is running water. (See order of events in **For Your Information.**)

Direct attention to the activity sheet. **Begin with your pencil at the sink. As you hear the sounds of the walk, draw a path around the kitchen.** Play the recording several times.

 LESSON **48**

Lesson Focus

Expression: Musical elements are combined into a whole to express a musical or extramusical idea. *(P–I)*

Materials

o **Record Information:**
  • Goin' to the Zoo
    Record 5 Side A Band 4
    Voices: children's choir
    Accompaniment: woodwind quartet, percussion

o **Instruments:** autoharp; resonator bells E and B'; bell mallet

o **Other:** overhead projector

o **Teacher's Resource Binder:**

  Activity Sheets
  • **Activity Sheets 18a-c,** pages A30–A32 (Prepare one copy of Activity Sheet 18a for each child, with pictures cut apart; prepare six copies and a transparency from Activity Sheet 18b; prepare a transparency from Activity Sheet 18c.)
  • Optional—
    Curriculum Correlation 5, page C8

o **For additional experience with expression:** Perform 3, page 136

Introducing the Lesson

Invite the children to perform their composition, "A Walk in the Zoo," from Lesson 47 (page 100). Choose a child to be the conductor.

Developing the Lesson

1. **Listen! Here is a song about going to the zoo.** Play the recording of "Goin' to the Zoo" as the children pretend to walk (to the beat) while looking at the animals.

2. Give each child a set of picture cards prepared from Activity Sheet 18a *(Goin' to the Zoo—Verses)*. As the children listen to the recording again, they should put their pictures in the order that tells the story of the walk.

3. Display the transparency prepared from Activity Sheet 18b *(Goin' to the Zoo—Refrain)*. **Your pictures show the story part of the song. This picture shows the part of the song that keeps returning. Sing the refrain** for the children and with your finger, trace the melodic contour on the transparency.

Goin' to the Zoo

By Tom Paxton

102

Then ask the children to sing the repeated part (refrain) while you sing the story part (verses).

4. Choose six children to form a row in the front of the classroom. Give each child a different picture from the set distributed in Step 2. Ask the class to put the children in the correct order to show the story. Give six other children copies of Activity Sheet 18b. **Where should these children stand?** (One child should stand after each child holding a story picture.) **We've made a picture of the whole song. Can you sing the whole song?** Play an accompaniment on the autoharp while the children sing.

5. Choose a child to add an ostinato on resonator bells during the refrain.

Resonator bells

Closing the Lesson

Place the transparency prepared from Activity Sheet 18c *(Goin' to the Zoo—Bell Ostinato)* over the transparency of Activity Sheet 18b so that the class can observe how the two parts fit together. As one child plays the bell ostinato and the class sings the refrain, alternately trace each contour with your hand.

3. See all the monkeys scritch, scritch, scratchin',
   Jumpin' round scritch, scritch, scratchin',
   Hangin' by their long tails scritch, scritch, scratchin'.
   We can stay all day.

4. Big black bear all huff, a-puffin',
   Coat's too heavy, he's a-puffin',
   Don't get too near the huff, a-puffin'.
   You can't stay all day.

5. Seals in the pool all honk, honk, honkin',
   Catchin' fish and honk, honk, honkin',
   Little seals honk, honk, a-honkin'.
   We can stay all day.

6. We stayed all day, and I'm gettin' sleepy,
   Gettin' sleepy, gettin' sleepy,
   Home already, and I'm sleep, sleep, sleepy.
   We have stayed all day.

LESSON 49

Lesson Focus

Harmony: Two or more musical lines may occur simultaneously.
Timbre: The quality of a sound is determined by the sound source. *(D–I)*

Materials

o **Piano Accompaniment:** page 216
o **Record Information:**
  • The Cuckoo in the Woods
    from *The Carnival of the Animals*
    by Camille Saint-Saëns (san **sahns**),
    1835–1921
    Record 5 Side A Band 5
    Ernest Gold, conductor
  • Heigh-Ho
    Record 5 Side A Band 6
    Voices: children's choir
    Accompaniment: flute, double bass, whistler
o **Teacher's Resource Binder:**
  • Optional—
    Biography 7, pages B13–B14
o **For additional experience with harmony:** Perform 15, page 153; Create 4, page 185

The Cuckoo in the Woods

38

Introducing the Lesson

Play the recording of "The Cuckoo in the Woods" as the class begins. Invite the children to walk around the room and pause each time they hear the cuckoo. (See **For Your Information.**)

Tell the children to open their books to page 38, or show page 38 of the Jumbo Book. **Here is a picture of some of the music we heard.** Ask the children to follow the picture as they listen again; they should touch the green bars when the pianos are heard and the red curved line when the cuckoo (clarinet) joins in. (Play through only the first six "cuckoos"—16 measures.)

Developing the Lesson

1. **We could hear one sound pattern at a time or two at a time! Look at page 39. We're going to hear a new walking song. Can you tell by looking at the pictures at the top of**

the page when you will hear one sound? two sounds? three sounds? Guide the children to conclude that the number of sounds is shown by the number of people walking along the path.

2. Play the recording of "Heigh-Ho." As they listen, the children should point to the appropriate part of the picture at the top of the pupil page when they hear one, two, or three strands of sound at the same time. (See **For Your Information** for sequence.)

3. Draw attention to the pictures of instruments and singers at the bottom of the pupil page. **Which picture matches the sound you heard at the beginning when only one sound was heard? Was the sound high or low?** Help the children decide that the correct picture is that of the small instrument, the flute, because it could play the high sound.

104

Heigh-Ho

For Your Information

"The Cuckoo in the Woods" is performed by two pianos and a clarinet. The composition moves in a slow triple meter. The "cuckoo" is heard on the beats circled below.

123 1②3 123 1②3 123 123 123 1②3

(above sequence repeated)

123 12③ 123 12③

123 ①23 123 ①2③ 123 ①2③

12③ 12③ 123 123 123 123 ①23 123

12312③12312③12③12③123①2③123

Sequence of sounds in "Heigh-Ho":
  Introduction: one sound (flute)
  Verse: two sounds (flute and children)
  Interlude: one sound (flute)
  Verse: three sounds (double bass joins flute and children)
  Coda: three sounds (children now whistle throughout, with double bass and flute)

39

Which picture shows the second kind of sound you heard? (the singers) How would we know that the third picture on your page shows the last instrument to join in? (because the third sound was low—this instrument is big and can play low sounds) Introduce the name of the last instrument— the double bass.

4. Play the recording again and have the children point to each picture when its sound is heard. They will discover that sometimes they have to point to all three pictures at the same time!

Closing the Lesson OPTIONAL

Invite the children to sing the song first softly with the recording, then without accompaniment. Next, turn the balance on the record player so that only the accompaniment is heard and give the children the opportunity to perform with the accompaniment.

Heigh-Ho
Words and Music by Larry Morey and Frank Churchill

"Heigh - Ho, Heigh - Ho," To make your trou - bles
Ho, Heigh - Ho," It's home from work we

go. Just keep on sing - ing all day long "Heigh - Ho, Heigh-
go. *(whistle)* "Heigh-

Ho, Heigh - Ho, Heigh - Ho, Heigh-Ho," For if you're feel - ing
Ho, Heigh - Ho, Heigh - Ho, Heigh-Ho," All sev - en in a

low, You pos - i - tive - ly can't go wrong with a
row, *(whistle)* with a

"Heigh, Heigh - Ho, Heigh - Ho, Heigh-
"Heigh, Heigh - Ho."

105

Lesson Focus

Melody: A series of pitches may move up or down by steps or skips. *(D–I)*

Materials

o **Piano Accompaniment:** page 217
o **Record Information:**
  • This Old Man
    (Record 3 Side A Band 9)
  • It Rained a Mist
    Record 5 Side A Band 7
    Voices: children's choir
    Accompaniment: clarinet, trumpet, trombone, viola, percussion
o **Instruments:** resonator bells F, G, A, B♭, and C; bell mallet
o **Other:** bell stairsteps for major scale (See Binder, page A2, for instructions.)

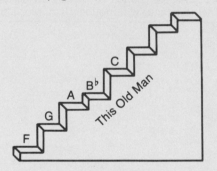

(continued on next page)

Find a Tune

40

Introducing the Lesson

Tell the children that you are looking for detectives to pick up clues and solve mysteries. **Can you pick up clues from me?** Chant the following rhyme:

· **Listen, listen for a clue; then you'll know just what to do.**
1–2–1–2–Clap your hands when I say "2."
1–2–1–2–1–2–1–2
Now that we have just begun, let's try clapping when I say "1."
1–2–1–2–1–2–1–2
Now that we have found the beat, walk the beat with your feet.
1–2–1–2–1–2–1–2
That seems very easy to do! Jump up high on the count of "2."
1–2–1–2–1–2–1–2
This is easy and lots of fun! Touch your toes on the count of "1."
1–2–1–2–1–2–1–2

You have done your very best; let's sit down and take a rest.
Whisper: **rest rest rest rest rest rest rest rest**
Chant: **If you're rested and ready to begin, let's repeat it all over again!**

Repeat the entire sequence except for the last direction, "If you're rested . . . ."

Developing the Lesson

1. Review "This Old Man" (Lesson 27, page 56). Tell the children to open their books to page 40, or show page 40 of the Jumbo Book. **Listen while you look at the first pattern in your book. What words from our song are sung to that tune?** Sing the pattern for the words "give a dog a bone" on a neutral syllable.

2. After the class has identified the words for Pattern 1, follow the same procedure for the four remaining examples on page 40 (2. This

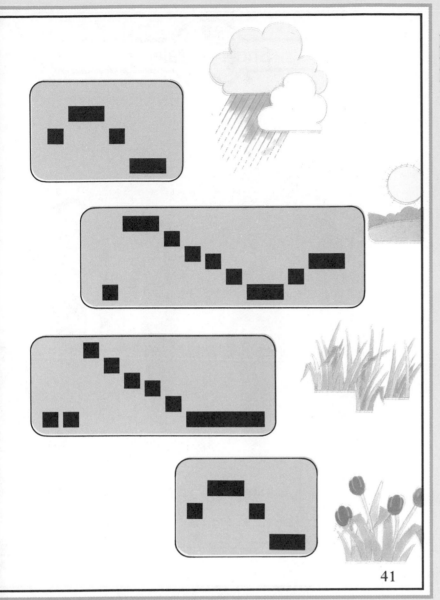

41

Materials *(continued)*
o **Teacher's Resource Binder:**
  • Optional—
    Enrichment Activity 12, page E19
    Kodaly Activity 15, page K23

It Rained a Mist

Virginia Folk Song

1. It rained a mist, it rained a
2. The sun came out, the sun came
3. And then the grass be-gan to
4. And then the flow-ers be-gan to

mist, It rained all o - ver the
out, It shone all o - ver the
grow, It grew all o - ver the
bloom, They bloomed all o - ver the

town, town, town, It rained___ all
town, town, town, It shone___ all
town, town, town, It grew___ all
town, town, town, They bloomed___ all

o - ver the town._____
o - ver the town._____
o - ver the town._____
o - ver the town._____

old man, he played one; 3. Nicknack, paddy whack; 4. He played nicknack on my thumb; 5. This old man came rolling home).

3. **Let's perform our song! We will sing everything except "This old man, he played one" and "give a dog a bone." Those parts will be played by a bell player.** Sing the song and choose a different child to play the two patterns for each verse. Have ten children (one for each verse) line up so that they will be ready to play when it is their turn.

4. **Can you use musical clues to match patterns for a new song with its words?** Play the recording of the first verse of "It Rained a Mist" while the children study the patterns on page 41.

Which picture matches this part of our song? Play or sing "It rained a mist." The

children may identify the pattern by pointing to the picture near the pattern. Then sing the rest of the song one pattern at a time until the children have matched each pattern with its words (cloud—"It rained a mist"; flower—"It rained a mist"; sun—"It rained all over the town, town, town"; grass—"It rained all over the town").

5. Ask the children to sing the first verse while pointing from one pattern to the next in the correct order.

OPTIONAL

Closing the Lesson

Play the complete recording of all the verses of "It Rained a Mist." Discover with the children that the little pictures near the patterns help to show the order of the song's "story." Sing the complete song.

107

LESSON 51

Lesson Focus

Melody: A series of pitches may move up or down by steps or skips.
Melody: A series of pitches bounded by the octave "belong together," forming a tonal set. *(P–I)*

Materials

o **Piano Accompaniment:** page 218
o **Record Information:**
 • Taffy
   Record 5 Side B Band 1
   Voices: children's choir
   Accompaniment: synthesizer, piano, celesta, harpsichord, electric organ, sound effects, percussion
o **Instruments:** resonator bells C, D, E, F, G, A, B, and C'; bell mallet
o **Other:** bell stairsteps for major scale (See Binder, page A2, for instructions.)

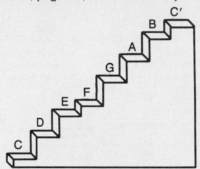

Show a Scale

4
waist

3
hips

2
thighs

1
knees

42

Introducing the Lesson

Tell the children to open their books to pages 42–43, or show pages 42–43 of the Jumbo Book. Examine the illustrations. Discuss the fact that the pictures show a child doing the body scale, which the class has already learned.

Can you sing the pattern that the child is showing? Can you sing the numbers as you do the motions? Establish the tonality: Play up and down the C major scale on the resonator bells while singing the scale numbers. Invite the children to sing the scale and then add the motions.

Developing the Lesson

1. Introduce the following game: The teacher sings a melodic pattern with numbers while doing the appropriate body motions. (Patterns might include the following: 1–2–3–4–5, 5–4–3–2–1, 1–3–5, 5–3–1, 1–3–5–1,

1–2–3–4–5–6–7–1'.) The children echo the pattern and the motions. Extend the game by dividing the class into teams. Give each team points for the exact reproduction of both pitches and motions.

2. **Here is a harder job! Watch carefully!** This time do the body scale motions for the song "Taffy." Perform the song measure by measure, singing the scale numbers in the rhythm of the song. Ask the children to echo each measure.

Pat Knees   Thighs   Hips   Waist

4/4 (Taf-fy was a hound dog, Taf-fy was a thief)

Sing 1 1 1 1 2 2 3 3 3 3 4

Complete the song in this manner.

3. **You've just performed the melody and**

108

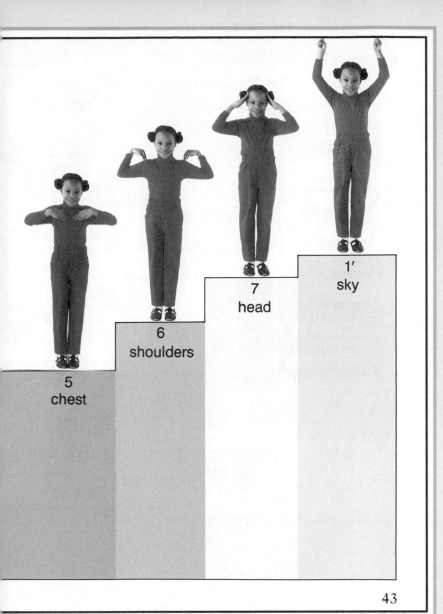

5
chest

6
shoulders

7
head

1'
sky

43

Taffy
Traditional

Taf-fy was a hound dog, Taf-fy was a thief,

Taf-fy came to our house and stole a leg of beef.

I went to Taf-fy's house, Taf-fy was in bed;

I took a feath-er and tick-led his head!

rhythm of a new song! Listen! Here are the words. Play the recording. Enjoy the amusing words of the song with the children. Ask the children questions about the lyrics until they are sure of the words. Then invite them to sing the song without the recording. Assist the children by continuing to do the body scale motions.

Closing the Lesson

Remind the children of the detective games they played in the previous lesson. **Can you figure out these clues?** Silently perform the body scale motions for the beginning of familiar songs. When the children suggest a possible song title, sing the words of the suggested song to the tune you were showing. The children should decide if their solution was correct. You might use the following well-known songs:

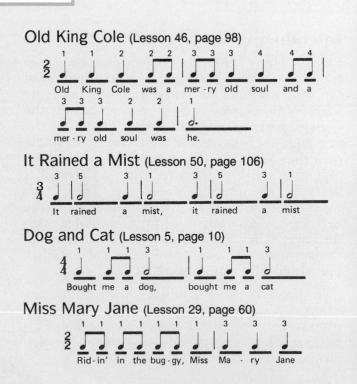

Old King Cole (Lesson 46, page 98)

Old King Cole was a mer-ry old soul and a mer-ry old soul was he.

It Rained a Mist (Lesson 50, page 106)

It rained a mist, it rained a mist

Dog and Cat (Lesson 5, page 10)

Bought me a dog, bought me a cat

Miss Mary Jane (Lesson 29, page 60)

Rid-in' in the bug-gy, Miss Ma-ry Jane

LESSON 52

Lesson Focus

Melody: A series of pitches bounded by the octave "belong together," forming a tonal set.

Rhythm: A series of beats may be organized into regular or irregular groupings by stressing certain beats. *(P–I)*

Materials

o **Piano Accompaniments:** page 219

o **Record Information:**
- Taffy **(Record 5 Side B Band 1)**
- To London Town
- 📷 **Record 5 Side B Band 2**
  Voices: children's choir, solo child
  Accompaniment: crumhorns, sackbuts, percussion
- Rain
  Record 5 Side B Band 3
  Voices: children's choir
  Accompaniment: synthesizer, electric piano, electric bass, percussion
- The Cuckoo in the Woods
  (Record 5 Side A Band 5)
- Signs of the Zodiac
  (Record 4 Side B Band 6)

o **Instruments:** resonator bells (C, D, E, F, G, A, B, and C') for C major scale; 8 bell mallets

(continued on next page)

To London Town

Rain

44

Introducing the Lesson

Review "Taffy" from the previous lesson. When the children have demonstrated that they recall the song and can sing it while doing the body scale motions, pass out resonator bells for the C major scale to a row of eight children. Give the first child the lower C bell; deliberately scramble the other bells. Ask the players to play the bells, one after another. Discover with the class that the sequence does not sound like "Taffy." **Can we put the bells in the right order?** Have the bell group experiment, always beginning with the lower C bell, until the entire scale is in order. Congratulate the class. **You have put together the sound of a *major scale*!**

Ask the bell players to play the melody for "Taffy." While they play, trace the melody on the transparency prepared from Activity Sheet 19 *(Taffy)*. Ask the rest of the class to show the melody by doing the body scale motions.

Developing the Lesson

1. Tell the children to open their books to pages 44–45, or show pages 44–45 of the Jumbo Book. Look at "To London Town." Discover that it uses all the steps of the scale (1–1').

2. Choose a new set of bell players. **Before we can begin playing, we must also think about the rhythm of our song.** Observe that the bars under each scale number in the first phrase are all the same length except for the high "1'," which shows a long sound. Draw attention to the pictures of the underlying beat (shown below the words). Help the children decide that the beats are grouped in threes (heavy–light–light) and that each melody sound is the same length as the beat except for the word "pray," which lasts for three beats.

3. Ask the class to pat and clap the underlying

110

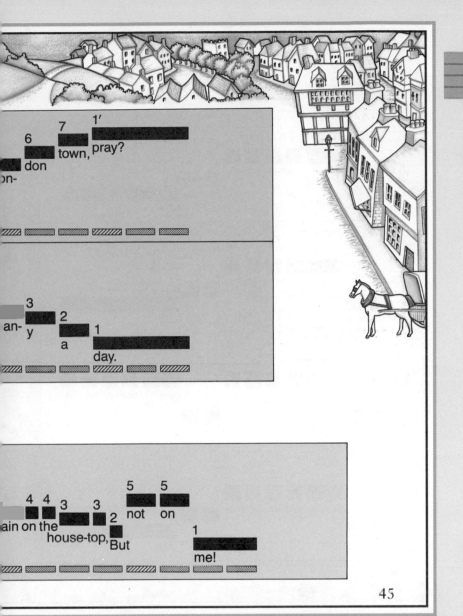

6 don-
on-
7 town,
1' pray?

3 an-
y 2
a 1
day.

4 4 3 3
2
ain on the house-top, But
5 not
5 on
1 me!

45

Materials *(continued)*

o **Other:** overhead projector
o **Teacher's Resource Binder:**

Activity Sheets
  • **Activity Sheet 19**, page A33 (Prepare a transparency from the activity sheet.)
  • Optional—
    Biographies 4, 7, pages B7–B8, B13–B14
    Curriculum Correlation 2, page C2
    Enrichment Activities 12, 13, pages E19–E20, E21

o **For additional experience with melody:** Create 2, page 182

beat (pat knees–clap–clap) while chanting the words of the entire song. Then ask the bell players to perform the first phrase while the class continues to tap out the beat. Next, ask the children to sing the first phrase while the bell players accompany them.

Follow a similar procedure to learn the second phrase. Then sing the whole song.

4. Direct the children's attention to "Rain." Choose new bell players and help the children learn this song, following the same procedure used to learn "To London Town."

Closing the Lesson

End the class by resting and listening to some favorite music. Play the recording of "The Cuckoo in the Woods" (Lesson 49, page 104) or "Signs of the Zodiac" (Lesson 43, page 92).

To London Town
Traditional English Song

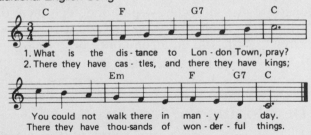

1. What is the dis-tance to Lon-don Town, pray?
2. There they have cas-tles, and there they have kings;

You could not walk there in man-y a day.
There they have thou-sands of won-der-ful things.

Rain
Traditional Rhyme
Music by Josephine Wolverton

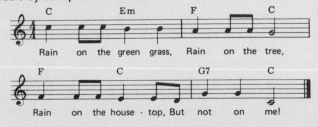

Rain on the green grass, Rain on the tree,

Rain on the house-top, But not on me!

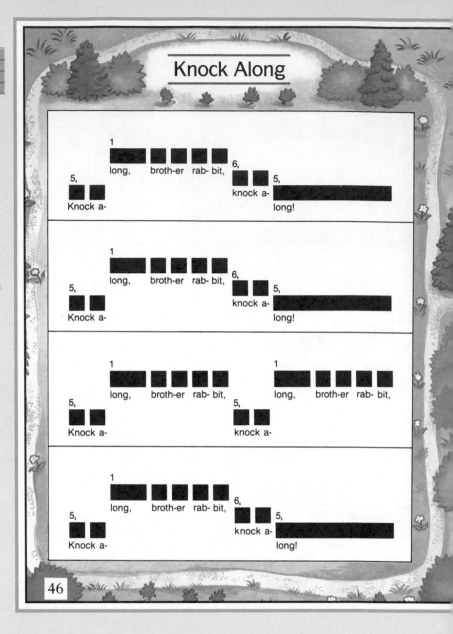

LESSON 53

Lesson Focus

Form: A musical whole may be made up of same, varied, or contrasting segments.
Form: A musical whole begins, continues, and ends. *(P–I)*

Materials

○ **Piano Accompaniment:** page 220
○ **Record Information:**
  • Knock Along
    Record 5 Side B Band 4
    Voices: children's choir
    Accompaniment: ocarina, psaltery, hammered dulcimer, autoharp, guitar, double bass
○ **Instruments:** resonator bells D, E, F#, and G; bell mallet; woodblock and mallet; xylophone with D, E, and G bars (see **Other**); xylophone mallet; autoharp

(continued on next page)

Introducing the Lesson

Ask the children to pat a "walking beat." Demonstrate for the class—pat one leg, then the other leg. Then play the recording of "Knock Along" while the children continue to pat.

Developing the Lesson

1. **This time, tap the rhythm of the words, "Knock along Brother Rabbit, knock along," each time you hear them.** Demonstrate how to tap two fingers against the palm. Then sing the refrain. Help the children realize that they had to tap through the whole refrain!

2. Tell the children to open their books to page 46, or show page 46 of the Jumbo Book. Direct the children's attention to the picture of the rhythm they tapped. Help them discover

that Lines 1, 2, and 4 are exactly the same but that Line 3 ends differently.

3. Draw attention to the scale numbers written above the rhythm bars. Establish a G-major tonality by playing resonator bells (G–D,–E,–F#,–G) and singing (1–5,–6,–7,–1). Help the children sing the refrain with scale numbers and then with the words.

4. Play the complete recording. Ask the children to listen to the verse and join the singing when they hear the refrain. *OPTIONAL*

5. Focus attention on the upper part of pupil page 47. **Here is a picture of the whole song. How many times will we sing the refrain that tells Brother Rabbit to "knock along"?** (twice) **How many times will we sing the story part?** (once) Sing the entire song with the class and ask the children to point to the appropriate picture when each section of the song begins.

47

Materials *(continued)*

o **Other:** bell stairsteps for major scale
(See Binder, page A2, for instructions.)

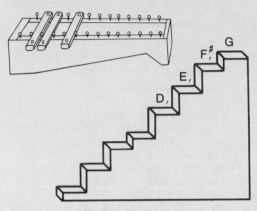

o **Teacher's Resource Binder:**
  • Optional—
    Orff Activity 7, page O7

o **For additional experience with form:**
  Describe 8, page 172

Closing the Lesson

Invite the children to add an accompaniment to the refrain. One child may play a repeated pattern on a woodblock, such as the following:

Choose another child to improvise a steady-beat melodic accompaniment on resonator bells or xylophone bars D♭, E♭, and G. The teacher may accompany the verse on an autoharp.

Knock Along
American Folk Song

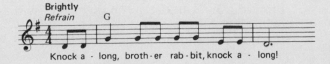

113

Lesson Focus
Form: A musical whole is a combination of smaller segments.
Form: A musical whole may include an introduction, interludes, and an ending segment. *(D–I)*

Materials
o **Record Information:**
- Knock Along
  (Record 5 Side B Band 4)
- *Children's Symphony,* Third Movement by Harl McDonald, 1899–1955
  Record 5 Side B Band 5
  Philadelphia Orchestra
  Harl McDonald, conductor
- *Children's Symphony,* First Movement
  (Record 1 Side A Band 2)

o **Other:** pencil and paper for each child

o **For additional experience with form:** Special Times 7, page 192

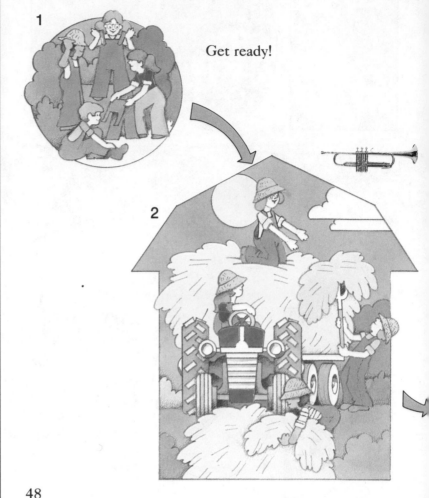

Children's Symphony
(Third Movement)

1

Get ready!

2

48

Introducing the Lesson [OPTIONAL]
Review "Knock Along" (Lesson 53, page 112). **How many parts does our song have?** (three) **Which parts sound alike?** (the first and last parts) **Which part is different?** (the middle part)

Developing the Lesson
1. **Listen to this music. Can you hear some parts that are the same and others that are different? The instruments play songs you know. Can you name the songs?** Play the recording of *Children's Symphony*, Third Movement. Help the children identify the songs played by the orchestra ("The Farmer in the Dell" and "Jingle Bells"). Review the two songs to be sure the children have both tunes well in mind.

2. Ask the children to open their books to page 48, or show page 48 of the Jumbo Book. Give the children time to examine all the pictures on pupil pages 48–51; draw their attention to the large pictures. **What are the children doing in Picture 2?** (farm chores) **Picture 4?** (riding in sleigh) **Can you find any pictures that are the same as either of these?** (Picture 6 is the same as Picture 2.) Decide that in the smaller pictures children are changing their costumes to get ready for the next activity.

3. Follow the illustrations from Picture 1 to Picture 7. Help the children discover the sequence of events.

   Picture 1: Children get ready to be farmers.
   Picture 2: Children do farm chores.
   Picture 3: Children change to winter clothing.
   Picture 4: Children go sleigh riding.

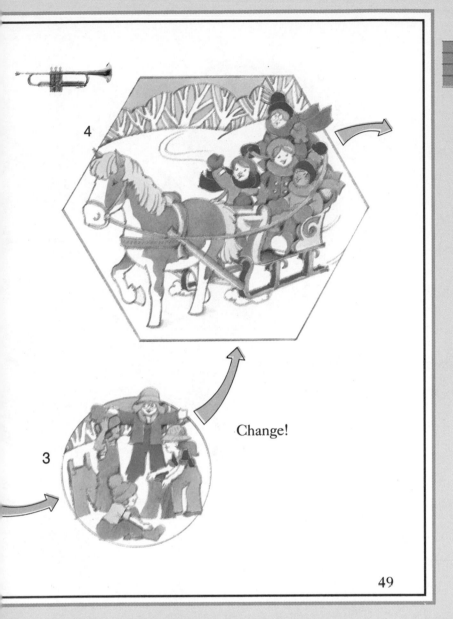

4

Change!

3

49

For Your Information

Structure of *Children's Symphony,* Third Movement:

Introduction: Hustling, bustling music

Section A: "The Farmer in the Dell"—played twice, with bugle calls

Interlude: Music slows down, then speeds up

Section B: "Jingle Bells"—with bugle calls

Interlude: Hustling, bustling music—similar to **Introduction**

Section A: "The Farmer in the Dell"—played twice, with bugle calls

Coda: Includes hustling, bustling sounds from **Introduction** and a tune borrowed from "The Farmer in the Dell"

Picture 5: Children change clothing to become farmers again.

Picture 6: Children do farm chores.

Picture 7: Children change back into everyday clothes.

4. **Let's listen to the music again and see if it matches the pictures. Each time you hear a number spoken look at the picture with that number.** Play the recording. The children may wish to move their fingers from picture to picture as they listen. You may need to remind them to turn the page after hearing Section B and looking at Picture 4.

5. **How many large pictures did you see as you followed the music?** (three—Pictures 2, 4, and 6) **What made the music that matched those pictures different from the music that matched the small pictures?** The children may have various answers (these sections are longer, more "important," have tunes they know, and so on).

6. **Which parts were alike?** (Parts 2 and 6—the ones with matching pictures) Play the recording again and ask the children to once again follow the pictures.

Closing the Lesson

Play the first movement of *Children's Symphony* (Lesson 1, page 1). Recall the two songs performed in this movement ("London Bridge Is Falling Down" and "Baa, Baa, Black Sheep"). Give each child a pencil and a sheet of paper. Ask the children to draw pictures showing the different parts of the music. They can begin by drawing big circles to show the "important"

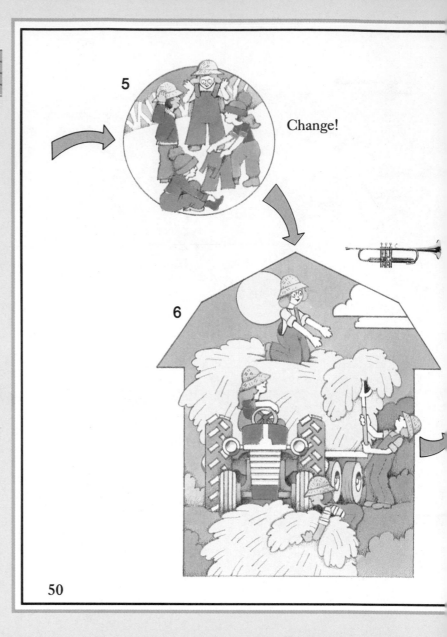

5

Change!

6

50

parts and little circles for the parts about "getting ready" or "changing." A child's page might look like the following:

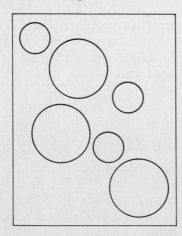

After the children have drawn circles for each part, ask them to listen to the recording again and to draw a picture inside each circle. Remind

them that the pictures should look the same for music that sounds the same. A completed picture might look like the following:

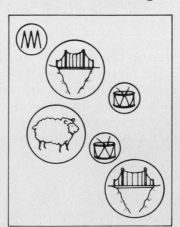

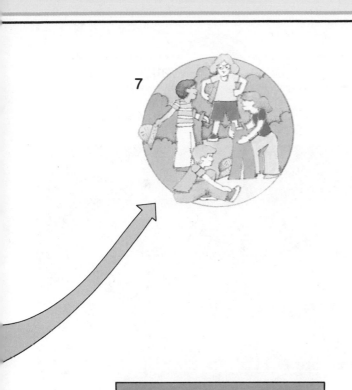

7

The End

51

The Farmer in the Dell
Singing Game

The farm - er in the dell,____ The farm - er in the dell,____ Heigh - o the mer - ry - o, The farm - er in the dell.____

Jingle Bells
Traditional

(Refrain only)

Jin - gle bells, jin - gle bells, jin - gle all the way! Oh, what fun it is to ride in a

1. one-horse o - pen sleigh!___ 2. one-horse o - pen sleigh!

LESSON 55

Lesson Focus

Expression: Musical elements are combined into a whole to express a musical or extra-musical idea. *(C–I)*

Materials

o **Piano Accompaniment:** page 222
o **Record Information:**
  • Loopidee Loo
    (Record 3 Side B Band 8)
  • Trot, Pony, Trot
    Record 5 Side B Band 6
    Voices: children's choir
    Accompaniment: percussion
  • It Rained a Mist
    (Record 5 Side A Band 7)
o **Instruments:** woodblock and mallet; finger cymbals; hand drum; xylophone and mallet; cymbals
o **Other:** overhead projector
o **Teacher's Resource Binder:**
  | Activity Sheets | • **Activity Sheet 20,** page A34 (Prepare one copy for each child and one transparency for use with the class as a whole. You might also prepare a cutout of the pony shown on the activity sheet for each child.) |

Going for a Walk

Picture 1

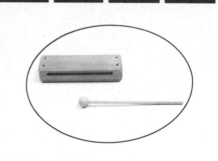

52

Introducing the Lesson

Review "Loopidee Loo" (Lesson 33, page 68). Ask the children to use their hands to show the longest sounds in the melody as they sing. Agree that these sounds occur on the syllables "loo" and "lie" (at the end of each phrase). Ask the children to sing the song again. This time invite them to make up a motion to show the longest sound (rubbing hands together, drawing a long line in the sky, and so on).

Developing the Lesson

1. Ask the children to open their books to page 52, or show page 52 of the Jumbo Book. Invite the children's responses to the works of art shown on pupil pages 52–55. Then read the following story and point to each picture in the Jumbo Book at the appropriate time.

(Picture 1) **Once, on the kind of bright day when little white clouds look like twirly mustaches up near the edge of the sky, a nice dappled horse used to take his family and his friends all dressed up for a walk to see the sights.**
(Picture 2) **And sometimes, all dressed up, it was fun to stroll, stopping to look this way or that way, or**
(Picture 3) **to scamper straight ahead like a proud little puppy.**
(Picture 4) **Sometimes, too, it was fun to imagine stepping right up into the sky, or better still,**
(Picture 5) **to think about running with a spinning hoop through an almost empty street.**

118

Picture 2

Picture 3

53

2. **The paintings in your book help us think about the ideas in our story. We can also use sounds to help us think about ideas in the story. We can show musical sounds with lines.** Draw attention to the picture of the instrument and the rhythm bars below Picture 1. **What do you think these musical lines are showing?** (the sound of the horse's hooves) Ask one child to perform this musical pattern on a woodblock.

3. Follow a similar procedure for the instruments and rhythm pictures shown near the paintings on pupil pages 53–55. The children may suggest other sound patterns to accompany each painting. For example, some children might add the sounds of voices talking over the noise of the horse's hooves for Picture 1.

4. Play the recording of "Trot, Pony, Trot." After the children have discussed the words of the song, display the transparency prepared from Activity Sheet 20 *(Trot, Pony, Trot)* and distribute a copy of the activity sheet to each child. As the children listen to the song again, invite them to follow the musical path. **Can you touch each part of the path as the pony trots along?** (The children could touch each section of the path with their fingers or use a cutout of the pony to move along the path.) Help the children realize that the sections of the path match the sequence of short and long sounds heard in the song.

5. After the children have demonstrated that they can move along the path in the rhythm of the words, ask them to sing the melody.

Picture 4

54

Closing the Lesson OPTIONAL

Review "It Rained a Mist" (Lesson 50, page 106). Ask one child to draw lines on the chalkboard to show the long–short rhythm of this melody while the class sings the song.

Trot, Pony, Trot
Chinese Folk Song

Trot, trot, po-ny trot, Trot to Grand-ma's gate - way.

She comes out and calls the dog, And then we ride on,

jog - a - jog. Trot, trot, trot, trot, trot, trot.

Picture 5

55

LESSON 56

Lesson Focus

Rhythm: Individual sounds and silences within a rhythmic line may be longer than, shorter than, or the same as other sounds within the line. *(P–I)*

Materials

o **Record Information:**
  • Rain **(Record 5 Side B Band 3)**
  • Bingo
    Record 5 Side B Band 7
    Voices: children's choir
    Accompaniment: guitar, double bass, banjo, percussion

o **Instruments:** resonator bells C, D, E, F, G, A, B, and C'; bell mallet; hand drum; sand blocks

o **Other:** one set of rhythm bars for each child (as prepared for Lesson 27, page 56)—melodic rhythm: 8 short bars, 8 long bars, 2 lo-ong bars; overhead projector and overhead pen (water soluble); bell stairsteps for major scale (See Binder, page A2, for instructions.)

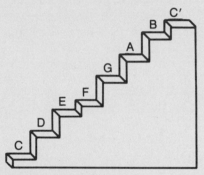

o **Teacher's Resource Binder:**
  Activity Sheets • **Activity Sheets 21a–c,** pages A35–A37 (Prepare a transparency from each activity sheet.)
  • **Activity Sheet 22,** page A38 (Prepare a transparency from the activity sheet.)

o **For additional experience with rhythm:** Perform 11, page 148; Perform 21 (activity/rest), page 160

Introducing the Lesson

Review "Rain" (Lesson 52, page 110). Tell the children to open their books to page 44, or show page 44 of the Jumbo Book. Ask a child to "get us started" by playing the resonator bells "backwards" down the C major scale (see **Materials**), while you tap the underlying short pulse (eight short sounds per measure). When the children demonstrate that they recall the song and can sing it without assistance, help them to develop an accompaniment.

Begin by adding the sound of raindrops. One child may choose a "raindrop instrument" (such

as a hand drum played with fingertips). Display the transparency prepared from Activity Sheet 21a *(Short Sounds)*. **Can you play a raindrop rhythm that sounds like this?** Help the child establish and maintain a steady sequence of short sounds.

Place the transparency prepared from Activity Sheet 21b *(Beat)* on top of the first transparency. **Who can add the sound of someone walking in the rain?** Choose a child to make this sound using sand blocks. Then invite the two children to play their sounds at the same time.

Place the transparency prepared from Activity Sheet 21c *(Long Sounds)* on top of the other two transparencies. **How long must each of these sounds last?** (as long as four short sounds or two beat sounds) Choose a third child to play a descending pattern on the C major resonator bells in this rhythm.

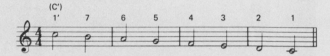

Invite the class to sing the song while the three accompanists play their parts.

Developing the Lesson

1. **You sang short sounds, sounds that lasted for two short sounds, and sounds that lasted for four short sounds. Can you make a picture of what you sang?**

   Give each child a set of rhythm bars. (See **Materials**.) Sing one measure of "Rain" at a time while tapping the underlying short sound. Repeat each measure several times until the children have arranged their rhythm bars. Then, leaving all three transparencies in place, draw the correct pattern on the transparency prepared from Activity Sheet 21c above the rows of long sounds. When completed your four patterns should look like this:

2. Divide the class into four groups and perform the complete score as shown on the overhead projector: Group 1 taps the short sounds on

122

their knees; Group 2 claps the beat; Group 3 softly whispers "sssh" for the long sounds; Group 4 chants the words of the song in rhythm.

3. Compliment the children on how well each group maintained its part. **I'm going to change the picture. Group 4, can you still perform your part?** Erase the first rhythm bar in each row and replace it with an "empty" (white) rhythm bar. The first row will look like this:

What do you think Group 4 will have to do at the beginning of each rhythm pattern? (be silent) **For how long?** (two short sounds) **Yes, whenever we see this kind of picture we must *rest*!**

Closing the Lesson

Play the recording of "Bingo." Place the transparency prepared from Activity Sheet 22 (*Bingo*) on top of the transparency prepared from Activity Sheet 21a and cover up all but the first box. **Can you clap this rhythm for me?**

Let's listen to the song again. How many times do you hear our pattern? Can you clap it each time it's repeated in the music? Play the recording. (The pattern is repeated three times.)

Invite the children to sing the refrain while you sing the verse. Sing the song a second time and help the class clap the rhythm of the refrain as they sing. Then uncover the second box. Challenge the children to chant the letters "B–I–N–G–O" while clapping the rhythm. **This time, you will need to "rest" instead of saying the letter "O."**

After they have practiced the pattern, invite them to sing the refrain; they should remember to remain silent on "O" each time that letter occurs. Then, in turn, uncover the third and fourth boxes and practice each new pattern. Finally, ask the class to perform the complete song (verse and refrain). They should sing the song four times, each time resting on one or more additional letters when they perform the refrain.

Bingo

American Folk Song

123

LESSON 57

How Long?

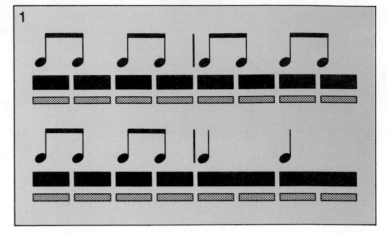

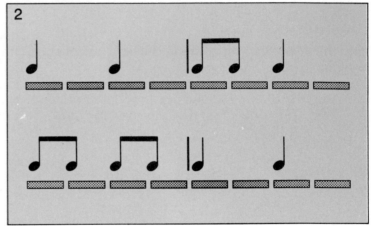

56

Lesson Focus

Rhythm: Individual sounds and silences within a rhythmic line may be longer than, shorter than, or the same as other sounds within the line. *(D–S)*

Materials

o **Piano Accompaniment:** page 223

o **Record Information:**
  • Chatter With the Angels
    (Record 2 Side A Band 1)
  • This Old Man
    (Record 3 Side A Band 9)
  • Cat in a Plum Tree
    (Record 4 Side A Band 5)
  • Trot, Pony, Trot
    (Record 5 Side B Band 6)
  • Little Tommy Tucker
    Record 5 Side B Band 8
    Voices: children's choir
    Accompaniment: recorders, harpsichord, percussion

o **Other:** transparency prepared for Lesson 56 (page 122, from Activity Sheet 21a, *Short Sounds*); overhead projector

(continued on next page)

Introducing the Lesson

Display the transparency prepared for Lesson 56. (See **Materials**.) Overlay it with the transparency prepared from Activity Sheet 23 (*Chatter With the Angels/This Old Man*). Cover Boxes 3 and 4. Ask the children to describe the length of each sound in Boxes 1 and 2 in comparison to the short sound: the "same" or "long." **Can you name the song that begins with this rhythm?** ("Chatter With the Angels" Lesson 11, page 22) Sing the song.

Uncover Boxes 3 and 4 of the transparency. Follow a similar procedure until the children recognize "This Old Man." (See Lesson 27, page 56.)

Developing the Lesson

1. **Here's another way to show a rhythm.** Place two single eighth notes prepared from Activity Sheet 24 (*Notes*) above the first two short rhythm bars in Box 1. **Each of these notes is**

the same length as a short sound. Ask the children to tell you when to use the same or a different note over each of the remaining rhythm bars in Boxes 1–2. The complete series of notes for "Chatter With the Angels" should look like this:

Cover the rhythm bars and ask the class to clap the rhythm by reading the notes.

2. Follow the same procedure for Boxes 3–4 on the transparency. This time, ask a child to place a note above each rhythm bar. The complete series should look like this:

124

Little Tommy Tucker

2/4

Lit - tle Tom - my Tuck - er,

Sing for your sup - per.

"What shall I be ask - ing for?"

White bread and but - ter.

57

3. Replace the first two eighth notes in Box 3 with paired eighth notes. **These notes have their "tails tied together," but they sound just like two single eighth notes.**

4. Tell the children to open their books to pages 56–57, or show pages 56–57 of the Jumbo Book. Ask the children to decide how long each note in Box 1 is in relation to the short sounds. Read the rhythm using the syllable, "bah." Guide the children to realize that the pattern they just read is the beginning of "Cat in a Plum Tree" (Lesson 38, page 82); sing the song.

5. **Look at Box 2. There are no rhythm bars to show the rhythm of the melody for this song. Can you still read the rhythm?** Help the children discover that this is also a familiar song, "Trot, Pony, Trot" (Lesson 55, page 118).

Closing the Lesson

End the class by learning the rhyme on page 57, "Little Tommy Tucker." Chant the rhythm using a "doo" sound while tapping the underlying short sound. Then chant the rhyme. Play the recording and help the children learn to sing the song.

Little Tommy Tucker
Traditional

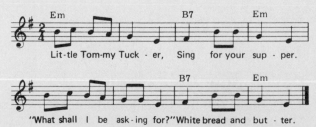

Lit-tle Tom-my Tuck - er, Sing for your sup - per.

"What shall I be ask-ing for?" White bread and but - ter.

125

Lesson Focus

Melody: A series of pitches may move up, down, or remain the same. *(P–I)*

Materials

o **Piano Accompaniment:** page 224

o **Record Information:**
- Redbird
  Record 5 Side B Band 9
  Voices: man, children's choir
  Accompaniment: harmonica, banjo, guitar, double bass

o **Instruments:** resonator bells G, A, and B; bell mallet

o **Other:** bell stairsteps for major scale (See Binder, page A2, for instructions.)

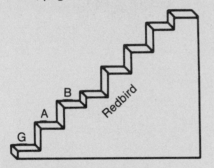

o **Teacher's Resource Binder:**
- Optional—
  Kodaly Activity 11, page K17

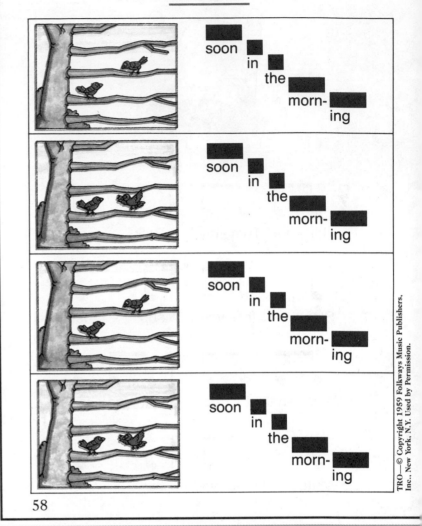

Redbird

58

Introducing the Lesson

Ask the children to open their books to page 58, or show page 58 of the Jumbo Book. Focus their attention on the pictures of the redbirds. **Look at the birds in the first box. One is on a low branch; the other is on a higher branch. Can we make up a song for these birds?** Place resonator bells G and B on the stairsteps. (See **Materials** for placement of bells on stairsteps.) Ask a child to play the two bells (from low to high) as the class sings "redbird":

Red-bird

Developing the Lesson

1. **Look at the next pair of birds. Are they sitting on the same branches as before?** (No,

the bird at the right is flying over a lower branch, closer to the bird at the left.) **Should we sing the same song for these redbirds as for the first pair of birds?** (No, the sounds should be closer together.) Add the A bell to the stairsteps and ask a child to play a pattern to match the second picture.

Red - bird

2. **Look at the two remaining pairs of birds. Decide that the first bell pattern (G–B) should be repeated for the third box; the second pattern (G–A) should be played for the fourth box.**

3. **How will we sing the words "soon in the morning"?** (begin high and move down) Play the recording or sing the refrain of "Redbird"

126

Verses:

Red-bird, red-bird,

What's the mat-ter with the red-bird?

Cat got the red-bird,

There goes the red-bird,

SOON IN THE MORN- ING.

59

Redbird

New words and new music arrangement by Huddie Ledbetter
Edited with new additional material by Alan Lomax
Additional verse by B.A.

Refrain

Red-bird, soon in the morn - ing,

Red - bird, soon in the morn - ing,

Red - bird, soon in the morn - ing,

1.3.4. *Fine*
Red-bird, soon in the morn - ing.

2.
soon in the morn - ing. 2. What's the

as the children follow the pictures on the pupil page. Then invite the class to sing the refrain for you.

4. Draw the children's attention to page 59. **Here is another part of our song! Listen! Can you hear whether the bird's song goes up, down, or stays the same?** Help the children follow the pictures on pupil pages 58 and 59 while they listen to the recording of the entire song.

Closing the Lesson OPTIONAL

Invite the children to sing "Redbird" with a res-onator-bell accompaniment. Choose one child to play the appropriate "redbird" pattern on bells at each occurrence of the word in the refrain. The rest of the class sings the song while following the pictures on the pupil pages.

Verse

1. Red - bird, red-bird,
   mat-ter with the red-bird?
3. Cat got the red-bird,
4. There goes the red-bird,
   } soon in the morn-ing, { What's the

Red - bird, red-bird,
mat-ter with the red-bird?
Cat got the red-bird,
There goes the red-bird,
} soon in the morn-ing, { What's the

Red - bird, red-bird,
mat-ter with the red-bird?
Cat got the red-bird,
There goes the red-bird,
} soon in the morn-ing, { What's the

Red - bird, red - bird,
mat-ter with the red - bird?
Cat got the red - bird,
There goes the red - bird,
} soon in the morn - ing.

127

LESSON 59

Lesson Focus

Rhythm: Individual sounds and silences within a rhythmic line may be longer than, shorter than, or the same as other sounds within the line.
Melody: A series of pitches may move up or down by steps or skips. *(P–S)*

Materials

o **Piano Accompaniment:** page 226
o **Record Information:**
  • Redbird
    (Record 5 Side B Band 9)
  • Who's That Tapping at the Window?
    Record 6 Side A Band 1
    Voices: children's choir
    Accompaniment: clarinet, trumpets, trombone, viola, percussion
  • This Old Man
    (Record 3 Side A Band 9)
  • Have You Seen My Honey Bears?
    (Record 4 Side A Band 2)
  • Little Tommy Tucker
    (Record 5 Side B Band 8)
  • Goodnight
    (Record 3 Side A Band 7)
o **Other:** overhead projector

(continued on next page)

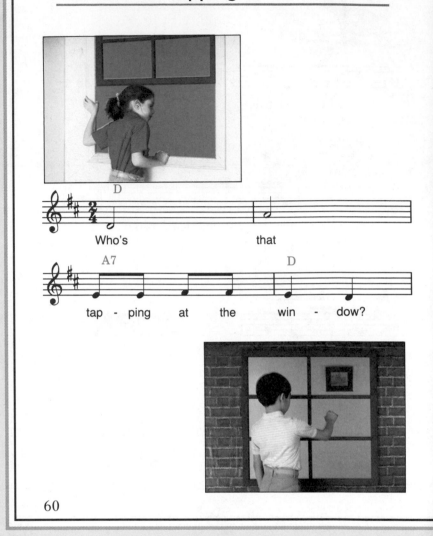

Chords not shown on pupil page

Who's That Tapping at the Window?

Who's that

tap - ping at the win - dow?

60

Introducing the Lesson *OPTIONAL*

Ask the children to open their books to pages 58–59, or show pages 58–59 of the Jumbo Book. Review "Redbird"; have the children follow the pictures on the pupil pages while they sing.

Developing the Lesson

1. Display the transparency prepared from Activity Sheet 25a *(Read a Song)*. **Can you learn to sing this new song all by yourselves, without my help?**

   Direct the children's attention to the first box; decide with the class that the rhythm is made up of two lo-ong sounds (each equal to four short sounds) and that the melody skips up from 1 to 5.

2. **Before we sing, let's "tune up."** Establish a D major tonality by performing body scale motions and singing 1–2–3–4–5 (D–E–F#–G–A). Then ask the children to sing the pattern shown in Box 1 with the words, "Who's that."

3. Look at the second box. Ask the class to chant the rhythm (short–short–short–short–long–long). Give them the starting pitch (E) and ask them to sing the melody with scale numbers (2–2–3–3–2——1——). **Now, can you sing the first two parts of our song with words?** Help the children sing the patterns in Boxes 1 and 2.

4. Look at Box 3. Ask the children to compare this pattern with the patterns in Boxes 1 and 2. They should discover that the pattern is the same as in Box 1. Then follow the same procedure as in Step 3 to learn the melody for the last box. The children should recognize that it is almost the same as the pattern in

128

Who's   that

A7   D

knock - ing   at   the   door?

61

Materials *(continued)*

o **Teacher's Resource Binder:**

Activity Sheets

• **Activity Sheets 25a–b**, pages A41–A42 (Prepare a transparency from the first activity sheet; from the second sheet prepare a set of cut-apart cards for each child.)
• **Activity Sheet 26**, page A43 (Prepare a set of cut-apart cards for each child.)
• Optional— **Orff Activity 17**, page O20

o **For additional experience with rhythm:** Describe 5, page 168

Box 2, except at the end. **Can you sing the whole song?**

5. Distribute a set of melody cards prepared from Activity Sheet 25b *(Show a Song)* to each child. Explain that these melody patterns show the song written in notes on a staff. **Can you put your cards in the order that shows the song we just learned? How can you decide which pattern goes first?** (by comparing each box on the transparency with the patterns shown on the cards)

Give the children a few minutes to arrange their cards. Then have them open their books to pages 60–61, or show pages 60–61 of the Jumbo Book. **Compare the song you made by arranging your cards with the song in the book. Does your song look the same?** Invite the class to sing the song again as they follow either their cards or the notes in the Jumbo Book.

Closing the Lesson

Give each child a set of Cards 1–4 from Activity Sheet 26 *(Test Your Eyes and Ears)*. **I'm going to sing the first part of a song you know. Can you find its picture?** Sing "This old man, he played one" (Lesson 27, page 56). The children should find the picture that matches the pattern (Card 1). Continue the game, singing the first pattern from each song.

Card 2: "Have you seen my honey bears" (Lesson 35, page 72)
Card 3: "Little Tommy Tucker" (Lesson 57, page 124)
Card 4: "Goodnight room; goodnight light" (Lesson 26, page 54)

When the children have correctly identified all four songs, hand out Cards 5–8. Challenge the class to match this set of cards with those they've already identified. Then sing each song.

Lesson Focus

Evaluation: Review concepts and skills studied in the Fourth Quarter.

Materials

o **Piano Accompaniment:** page 227
o **Record Information:**
  • One Day My Mother Went to the Market
    Record 6 Side A Band 2
    Voices: solo child, children's choir
    Accompaniment: panpipes, mandolin, guitar, double bass, accordion, percussion
o **Teacher's Resource Binder:**

[Evaluation]
  • **Evaluation 4,** pages Ev10–Ev11
  • **Musical Progress Report 4,** page Ev12

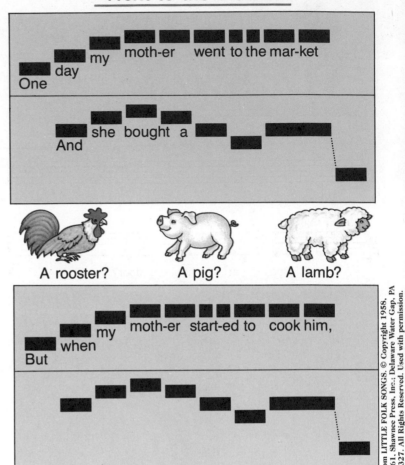

One Day My Mother Went to the Market

One day my moth-er went to the mar-ket

And she bought a

A rooster?   A pig?   A lamb?

But when my moth-er start-ed to cook him,

62

Introducing the Lesson

Play the recording of "One Day My Mother Went to the Market" and enjoy the amusing words. Play the recording again and invite the children to join in on the spoken question-and-answer parts (" 'A rooster?' 'A rooster!' " and so on).

Developing the Lesson

1. Explore with the class how the melody moves up, down, or stays the same. Ask the children to move their hands appropriately while listening to the recording again.

2. Ask the children to listen to the first two phrases of the song and decide when the melody moves by steps ("One day my moth-"; "And she bought a handsome roost-"), moves by skips ("rooster"), or stays the same ("mother went to the market").

3. Tell the children to open their books to pages 62–63, or show pages 62–63 of the Jumbo Book. **Look at the picture of the melody for the first two phrases. Were you right? Did you hear the places where the melody moved up and down by steps, by skips, or stayed the same?** After the children have checked their answers, focus attention on the rest of the song and guide the children to identify the same kinds of movement patterns. The children will notice that the last phrase has double lines. Listen again to the recording. **Can you decide why there are double lines for this part?** (two singers, one singing higher; one singing lower)

4. Ask the children to sing the song while following the pictures on the pupil pages. Point to the appropriate animal picture in the Jumbo Book as each animal's name is spoken.

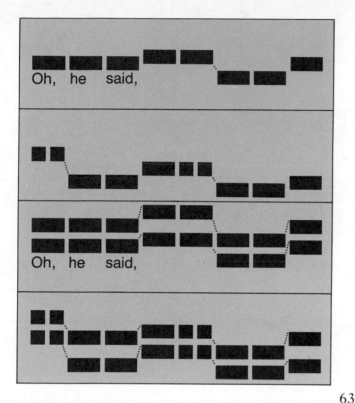

63

Closing the Lesson

Administer *Evaluation 4* to check the children's understanding of ideas studied in the Fourth Quarter. The evaluation may be conducted with the children individually or in small groups. If the evaluation is conducted as a small group activity, make sure to observe the progress of individual children as they participate in each part.

Complete the *Musical Progress Report 4* for each child. This report may be sent home as a report to parents or simply retained by the teacher as a record of each child's progress.

One Day My Mother Went to the Market

Words by Leo Israel
Music collected and adapted by Rudolph Goehr

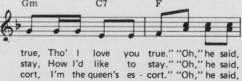

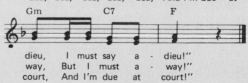

Unit Overview

Materials in Unit 2 provide the teacher with lessons that may be used to supplement, enrich, or replace core lessons. In **Perform Music** the children are guided through additional experiences in singing and in playing instruments. The activities in **Describe Music** help the children demonstrate what they hear and understand as they respond to music. In **Create Music** the children apply what they have learned in the core unit to create their own music. Finally in **Special Times,** musical learnings are integrated with the celebration of holidays and seasons.

Perform Music by Singing

For most children, singing is the first and most natural musical activity they experience. Many children will experiment with pitch variation before they begin to speak. In the first grade, children should be encouraged to continue vocal experimentation and to develop a repertoire of songs. Children whose earlier vocal experimentation has been met with approval will participate in the singing experience enthusiastically and will be quick to learn new melodies.

It will not be unusual to encounter a first grader who can sing familiar tunes accurately only if he or she chooses the beginning pitch and performs independently; such a child cannot sing accurately within a group when tonality is established by someone else. Learning to "match one's voice" to an outside model is an important goal for the first-grade singer.

Vocal Experimentation and Improvisation

The following activities may be used during music class and might also be incorporated into the daily class routine.

A. The spontaneous vocal improvisations of young children are often based on two or three pitches. Base classroom improvisations on these same two- or three-tone chants. Use these chants to carry on conversations, give instructions, or ask questions. The children may respond by imitating each chant exactly or by varying the melody.

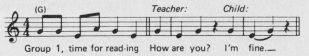

B. Encourage improvisation by means of dramatic play. A number of such activities are included in this book; the children might also enjoy creating brief "dramas" based on everyday situations in the classroom.

C. Use improvisation as a way to help children expand their vocal range. Ask a child to be:

Pitch Accuracy Through Imitation

As the children "discover" their singing voices (in contrast to their speaking voices), begin to focus on tone matching — the ability to sing back what has been heard at the identical pitch level.

A. Engage in "copycat" games in which the children are encouraged to imitate your words and melody exactly. Keep in mind that the most comfortable vocal range for the five- to seven-year-old is D to A.

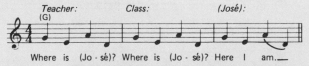

If a child responds with the correct contour at a different pitch level, help that child become aware of the "possibility" of matching by shifting your pitch level to match the child's.

B. Gradually expand the children's vocal range by singing the same melody pattern at a higher or lower pitch level:

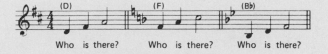

C. When the children sing in groups, focus their attention on the importance of "listening to each other" and matching pitches.

D. Many children are unaware that they are not singing the sounds they have heard. Instead of their actual voice, they "hear" an image in their head. One way to help children realize that their sound is not the same as that of the model is by using a microphone to project their voices so that they can hear themselves as others hear them. (You might use the microphone from a tape recorder.)

Singing Expressively

Even a very young child can begin to be sensitive to the expressive use of the voice. When engaged in vocal improvisation or dramatic play, help the children become aware that the quality of voice used is as important as the words or pitches used.

A. Play a game. Vary the quality of your voice as you sing a short melody on a neutral syllable. The children must choose one of two words to describe the feeling you are expressing, for example:

- anger (with a harsh vocal quality) or silliness (with a squeaky quality)
- tiredness (with a breathy voice) or excitement (with a full, open quality)

At another time engage in a similar activity, this time representing an animal that the children must identify, such as:

- a horse (descending pitch pattern, nasal vocal quality)
- a pig (low, "grunting" sounds)
- a bird (high, light vocal quality)
- a kitten (light, soft, "sweet" quality)

B. Sing fragments of familiar songs with an inappropriate vocal quality. The children must decide what is wrong. For example, sing:

- "Have You Seen My Honey Bears?" as though you were angry
- "Step in Time" as though it were a lullaby
- "Goodnight" as though it were a march

PERFORM 1

Lesson Focus

Expression: The expressiveness of music is affected by the way melody contributes to the musical whole. *(C–E)*

Materials

o **Other:** Create a structure or an area in the classroom to represent the Singer Machine. You might mark off a special place with masking tape or build a structure from a cardboard box.

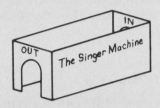

o **Extends Lesson 46,** page 98

The Lesson

1. Invite the children to visit Music Land. In Music Land all conversation is sung rather than spoken. To become a citizen of Music Land, the children have to walk through the Singer Machine to be turned into Singing People. Remind the children that until they walk back through the machine, they will continue to be Singing People.

2. Lead the class through the machine into Music Land. The children enter the machine one at a time, continuously speaking their names; when they come out the other side of the machine, they will be singing their names:

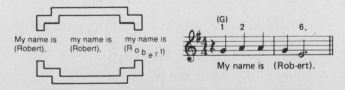

3. Walk back through the machine to once again become a "talker"; then tell the following story to motivate improvised song play.

Once upon a time there was a little boy (girl) who went through the Singer Machine, but something went wrong and he did not come out a singer. He came out a talker! He walked into Music Land and met an old man. The boy said, "Hello, I'm a new boy in town." But the old man just shook his head and turned his back because he could only understand words that were sung. The talking boy walked on down the street and met a police officer. The boy said, "Hello, I'm a new boy in town." But the police officer could not understand him either and shook her head and walked on down the street. (Repeat this idea as long as desired; each time, the boy should meet a different person.) Finally the little boy sat down and began to cry:

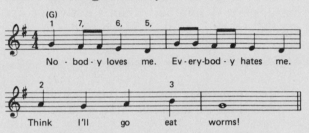

All the people turned around and sang:

The boy happily answered, using his speaking voice, "Hey, I'm a new boy in town." But because he had used his speaking voice once again, the people could not understand and they turned away. The little boy was so disappointed that he began to cry again:

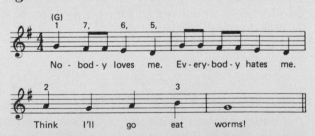

This time the people sang, "We don't hate you; we can't understand unless you sing to us." (Improvise a tune for the people's answer.) The little boy then understood that in

134

Music Land everyone sings to each other instead of talking. He very happily sang:

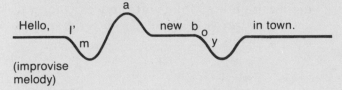

(improvise melody)

And all the people sang back:

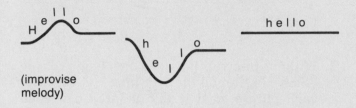

(improvise melody)

4. Invite the children to dramatize the story. Together plan who will be the boy or girl, who will be the townspeople, where the characters will stand, and how they will move. The children should follow the story and musical responses as previously indicated.

Lesson Focus

Expression: The expressiveness of music is affected by the way melody contributes to the musical whole. *(P–E)*

Materials

o **Record Information:**
  • Grandma Moses
    Record 6 Side A Band 3
    Voices: children's choir
    Accompaniment: tenor banjo, double bass, percussion
o **Teacher's Resource Binder:**
  • Optional—
    Kodaly Activity 18, page K26
o **Extends Lesson 12,** page 24

The Lesson

1. Perform "Grandma Moses." Exaggerate the difference in quality between the singing and speaking sections. **Show me! When am I singing? When am I talking? Open your mouth when I sing; close your mouth when I talk.**

2. Perform the song again. This time invite the children to add the motions implied by the words in the second part of the song ("Hands up" and so on). Have the children combine motions, singing, and talking to complete their performance.

Grandma Moses
Singing Game

135

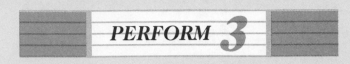

Lesson Focus

Expression: Musical elements are combined into a whole to express a musical or extramusical idea. *(P–E)*

Materials

o **Record Information:**
  • Sally Go 'Round the Sunshine
    Record 6 Side A Band 4
    Voices: children's choir
    Accompaniment: autoharp, percussion
o **Instrument:** autoharp and pick
o **Teacher's Resource Binder:**
  • Optional—
    Curriculum Correlation 11, page C19
    Orff Activity 14, page O17
o **Extends Lesson 48,** page 102

The Lesson

1. Present a sequence of movement and pitch ideas and ask the children to echo each idea.

(Pause between ideas only long enough for the children to imitate.) Ideas might include stretching, bending, and whirling movements; high-low, loud-soft, and exaggerated speech patterns; and melody patterns such as the following:

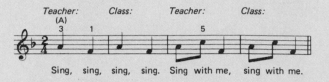

2. Without interrupting the game, begin to sing "Sally Go 'Round the Sunshine." Pause after each phrase so that the children can echo each pattern. After echo playing, sing the complete song with the children.

3. *OPTIONAL* Repeat the song, substituting the name of a child in the class for "Sally." That child then becomes the leader and may choose a favorite song to sing. The class "shadows" the leader by echoing the song back to that child, phrase by phrase.

Sally Go 'Round the Sunshine

American Singing Game

Lesson Focus

Form: A musical whole may be made up of same, varied, or contrasting segments. *(D–E)*

PERFORM 4

Materials

o **Record Information:**
  • The Muffin Man
    Record 6 Side A Band 5
    Voices: man, child
    Accompaniment: lute, percussion
o **Instruments:** miscellaneous percussion instruments; mallets and/or strikers
o **Other:** blindfold (optional)
o **Extends Lesson 20,** page 42

The Lesson

1. **Here is a song that is made up of a question and an answer. Listen!** Play the recording of "The Muffin Man." **What is the question?** ("Do you know the muffin man?") **What is the answer?** ("Yes, I know the muffin man.") **Where does the muffin man live? Listen again!** (Drury Lane)

2. *OPTIONAL* Sing "The Muffin Man." Substitute the names of other workers that the children suggest (firefighter, baker, mechanic, and so on).

3. **This time if I sing the question parts, can you sing the answer parts?** When the children can sing the answer parts easily, reverse roles. Continue until the children know the entire melody.

4. **Now we're going to play a game. Can you tell each other's voices without seeing each other? Let's find out!** One child is chosen to be "it." This child must either stand where he or she cannot see the other children or must be blindfolded. The class sings the question from the song; the teacher then points at a child to sing the answer. The child who is "it" tries to guess the name of the answer singer. (This activity can be repeated as desired.)

5. **This time instead of naming voices, can you name instruments? Close your eyes and listen.** Play rhythm patterns on various classroom percussion instruments and elicit answers from volunteers.

The Muffin Man

Traditional English Song

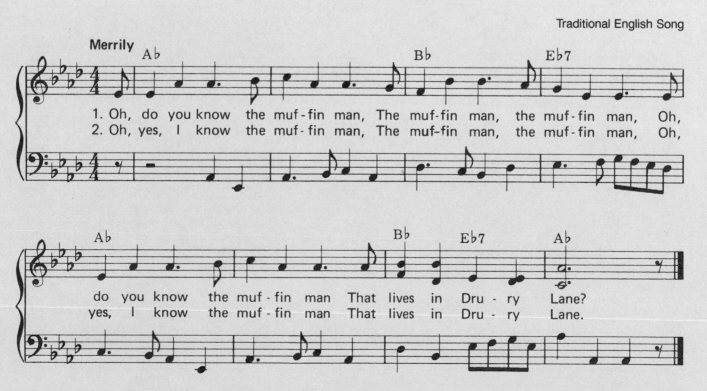

1. Oh, do you know the muf-fin man, The muf-fin man, the muf-fin man, Oh,
2. Oh, yes, I know the muf-fin man, The muf-fin man, the muf-fin man, Oh,

do you know the muf-fin man That lives in Dru-ry Lane?
yes, I know the muf-fin man That lives in Dru-ry Lane.

o **Teacher's Resource Binder:**
  • Optional—
    Curriculum Correlation 11,
    page C19
o **Extends Lesson 31,** page 64

Lesson Focus

Melody: A series of pitches may move up, down, or remain the same.
Melody: A melody may be relatively high or low. *(P–E)*

Materials

o **Record Information:**
  • Little Arabella Miller
    (Record 3 Side B Band 6)
  • Goodnight
    (Record 3 Side A Band 7)
  • Stay Awake
    Record 6 Side A Band 6
    Voices: children's choir
    Accompaniment: small show orchestra

The Lesson

1. Review "Little Arabella Miller" (Lesson 31, page 64). Agree with the class that it is a funny, silly song.

2. **Sometimes we sing silly songs and sometimes we sing very lovely, peaceful songs, full of feeling.** Ask the class to sing "Goodnight" (Lesson 26, page 54) as an example of a peaceful song.

Stay Awake

Words and Music by Richard M. Sherman
and Robert B. Sherman

© 1963 Wonderland Music Company. Used by permission.

138

3. **Listen to this song. Is this a silly song or a very lovely, peaceful song?** Play the recording of "Stay Awake." Replay the song as needed, until the children are sure of the words. Decide with the class that the music and words suggest a calm and soothing mood. Help the children realize that even though the words of the song suggest staying awake, the feeling is really that of a lullaby that is inviting them to go to sleep.

4. Play the recording again as the children mirror the melody. Discover that it seems to "rock" — up–down–up–down — as though someone were rocking a baby.

5. Ask the children to sing the song and continue to mirror the rocking contour of the melody. If the children have any problems singing the song, play the recording again.

6. When the children have become familiar with the melody, guide them to think about the way they are singing the song. **Can you sing**

the song so that your voice helps express its lovely, peaceful mood? Suggest that the children:

• Take a good, deep breath at the beginning of each phrase.
• Hold the long sounds at the ends of phrases so that the melody is very smooth.

7. **OPTIONAL** As the children work toward producing a lovely vocal quality, help them further refine their expressive singing by asking: **Will we sing the song loud or soft?** (soft)

8. **OPTIONAL** Return to the songs reviewed at the beginning of the class. **Which song will we sing with the same kind of vocal quality as "Stay Awake"?** ("Goodnight") Have the class sing "Goodnight" again and try to produce a lovely, smooth vocal quality.

Lesson Focus

Melody: A series of pitches may move up, down, or remain the same.

Expression: The expressiveness of music is affected by the way timbre contributes to the musical whole. *(P–E)*

Materials

o **Record Information:**
  • Hey, Lolly, Lolly
  Record 6 Side A Band 7
  Voices: children's choir
  Accompaniment: tin whistle, acoustic guitar, electric guitar, electric bass, steel drums, percussion
  • Shoheen Sho
  Record 6 Side A Band 8
  Voices: children's choir
  Accompaniment: oboe, French horn, cello, harp

o **Other:** paper and crayon for each child

o **Teacher's Resource Binder:**
  • Optional—
  Curriculum Correlations 2, 7, pages C2, C9
  Enrichment Activity 12, page E17
  Kodaly Activity 10, page K14

o **Extends Lesson 22,** page 46

The Lesson

1. **How many different voices do you have?** Children may suggest (and demonstrate) various voices — shouting, crying, whispering, and so on. **We also have a very special voice, a singing voice! Let's find our singing voice.**

2. Help the children find the "dent" in the middle of their collarbone. **Hold two fingers in this spot and match my sounds. A frog says: "grrrrumph, grrrrumph."** (Make a low, growly sound.) **A bird says "twee, twee, twee, twee."** (Use a high, light, "sing-song" voice.)

Discuss the different sensations the children had as they made the two sounds. **When you made the frog's sound, what did your fingers feel as you touched your throat?** (buzzing, a vibration) **When you made the bird's sound, what did your fingers feel?** (nothing, or very little vibration) Tell the children that when they felt a "buzz," they were using their talking voice; when they felt "no buzz," they were using their singing voice.

Hey, Lolly, Lolly

Words by B. A.

Traditional Melody

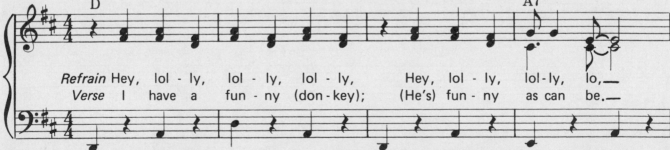

Refrain Hey, lol - ly, lol - ly, lol - ly, Hey, lol - ly, lol - ly, lo,___
Verse I have a fun - ny (don - key); (He's) fun - ny as can be.___

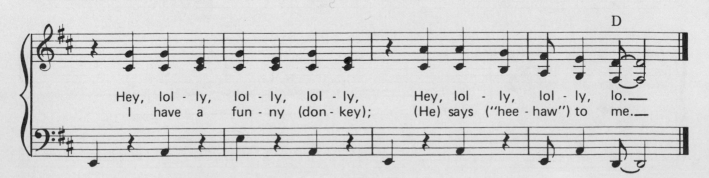

Hey, lol - ly, lol - ly, lol - ly, Hey, lol - ly, lol - ly, lo.___
I have a fun - ny (don - key); (He) says ("hee - haw") to me.___

3. Draw a picture of the melodic contour for the first pattern in "Hey, Lolly, Lolly."

How do you think this picture will sound? Will the melody go up? down? After the children offer their ideas, several children may take turns improvising a melody on "loo" to match the picture, using a "no-buzz" voice. Then sing the song refrain for the class.

4. Hand out a sheet of paper and a crayon to each child. **We have a picture of the first part of our song. Can you make a picture of the rest of it?** Sing the refrain phrase by phrase, repeating as necessary while the children draw an up-down picture. The completed picture should look like this:

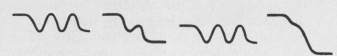

5. Ask the class to sing the melody first on "loo" and then with the refrain words, while following their pictures. Then invite the children to

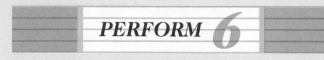

create silly verses about various animals, for example:

I have a funny donkey;
He's funny as can be.
I have a funny donkey;
He says "hee-haw" to me.

Urge the children to change the quality of their singing voice to suggest the different animal sounds.

6. *OPTIONAL* Follow the same procedure to learn "Shoheen Sho" as was used for "Hey, Lolly, Lolly." Sing each melodic pattern and ask the children to draw their own shapes; then invite them to sing the melody they have drawn, first using a neutral syllable and then singing the words.

7. *OPTIONAL* Discuss the different vocal qualities the children might use to perform "Shoheen Sho" (sweet, quiet quality) and the silly song, "Hey, Lolly, Lolly" (bright, open).

Shoheen Sho

Welsh Folk Song

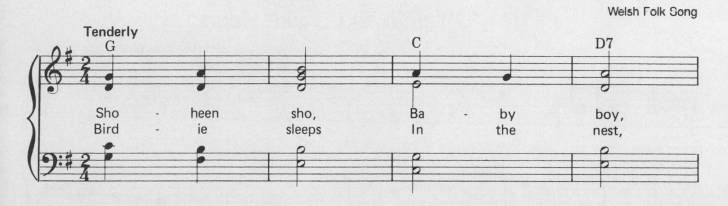

Tenderly

Sho - heen sho, Ba - by boy,
Bird - ie sleeps In the nest,

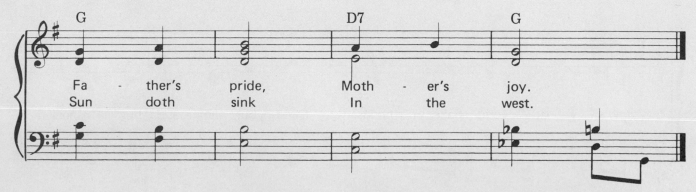

Fa - ther's pride, Moth - er's joy.
Sun doth sink In the west.

Lesson Focus

Timbre: The quality of a sound is affected by the way the sound is produced. *(P–E)*

Materials

o **Record Information:**
  • How D'ye Do and Shake Hands
    Record 6 Side A Band 9
    Voices: man, children's choir
    Accompaniment: guitar, double bass, accordion, percussion
o **Instrument:** autoharp
o **Extends Lesson 47,** page 100

The Lesson

1. **Let's learn a new song!** Sing or play the recording of "How D'ye Do and Shake Hands." Move about the room, shaking hands with a different child each time "shake hands" is mentioned.

2. *OPTIONAL* Repeat the song with each child facing a partner. **Shake hands with your partner each time you hear the words "shake hands."** Play the recording or sing the song

again; help the children sense the beat as they perform the motions.

3. Review with the children the difference between their singing and speaking voices. (See Perform 6, page 140.) **Let's now use our speaking voices!** Teach the children the following chant to add to the song:

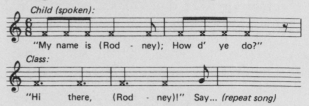

To begin, I'll be the singing voice; you'll be the speaking voice. Perform the song and chant. Give several children the opportunity to perform the solo part of the chant.

4. **This time, can you shift to your singing voices and also perform the singing part of the song?** When the children demonstrate that they can sing the melody, help them to perform the song with the chant. Give other children the opportunity to use their speaking voices during the chant solo.

5. Invite the children to now use their singing voices and improvise a melody as they "state their name and bus' ness." Play a C chord on the autoharp to accompany the improvisation. Then perform the improvised section with the song.

How D'ye Do and Shake Hands

Words and Music by Oliver Wallace and Cy Coben

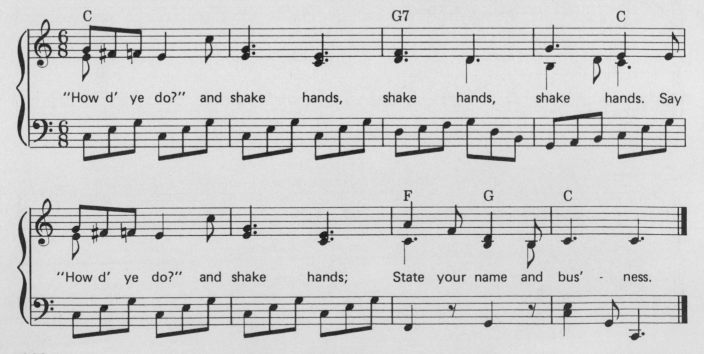

Lesson Focus

Form: A musical whole is a combination of smaller segments. *(D–I)*

Materials

o **Record Information:**
  • The Sleeping Princess
  Record 6 Side A Band 10
  Voices: solo children's voices, children's choir
  Accompaniment: recorder, shawm, racket, crumhorn, sackbut, lute, harpsichord, positive organ, percussion

o **Other:** overhead projector

o **Teacher's Resource Binder:**
  [Activity Sheets]
  • **Activity Sheets 27a–b**, pages A44–A45
  (Prepare a copy of Activity Sheet 27a for each child and cut the pictures apart; prepare a transparency from Activity Sheet 27b.)

o **Extends Lesson 21**, page 44; **Lesson 26**, page 54

The Lesson

1. Play the recording of "The Sleeping Prin-

cess." The children may recognize that this is a version of a favorite story. Distribute a set of picture cards prepared from Activity Sheet 27a *(Many Parts Make a Whole Song)* to each child. Play the recording as often as needed until the children have arranged the pictures in the correct order.

2. Display the transparency prepared from Activity Sheet 27b *(The Sleeping Princess)*. As the children sing each verse, trace the melodic contour on the transparency. Help them realize that the melody remains the same even though the words change.

3. Choose children to play the parts of the princess, the sorcerer, and the prince and then **OPTIONAL** dramatize the story.

The Sleeping Princess

German Folk Song

1. There was a pret-ty prin-cess, a prin-cess, a prin-cess; There was a pret-ty prin-cess,
2. A spell was cast up-on her, up-on her, up-on her; A spell was cast up-on her,
3. The cas-tle was en-chant-ed, en-chant-ed, en-chant-ed; The cas-tle was en-chant-ed,
4. A hun-dred years she slept there, she slept there, she slept there; A hun-dred years she slept there,

Long a-go.

5. The thorns grew thick around her...

6. A handsome prince came riding...

7. He woke the pretty princess...

8. They had a royal wedding...

143

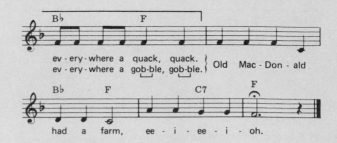

ev-ery-where a quack, quack.
ev-ery-where a gob-ble, gob-ble. } Old Mac-Don - ald

had a farm, ee - i - ee - i - oh.

3. ...sheep...baa 4. ...pigs...oink 5. ...cows...moo 6. ...horses...neigh

PERFORM 9

Lesson Focus

Expression: Musical elements are combined into a whole to express a musical or extramusical idea. *(P–E)*

Materials

o **Record Information:**
  • Little White Duck
    Record 6 Side B Band 1
    Voices: children's choir
    Accompaniment: oboe, French horn, cello, harp

o **Instruments:** guiro and scratcher; hand drum; tambourine or jingle tap; sand blocks; resonator bells E, F, and C'; bell mallet

o **Teacher's Resource Binder:**
  • Optional—
    Curriculum Correlation 3, page C4

o **Extends Lesson 32,** page 66

The Lesson

1. Sing a favorite song, "Old MacDonald," with the class. (The children probably learned this song at home or elsewhere.) Identify the various animals in the song (ducks, turkeys, sheep, pigs, cows, horses) and where they live (on a farm).

Old MacDonald
Traditional

1. Old Mac-Don-ald had a farm, ee - i - ee - i -
2. Old Mac-Don-ald had a farm, ee - i - ee - i -

oh, And on that farm he had some ducks,
oh, And on that farm he had some tur-keys,

animal noises accumulate

ee - i - ee - i - oh. With a quack, quack here and a
ee - i - ee - i - oh. With a gob-ble, gob-ble here and a

quack, quack there, Here a quack, there a quack,
gob-ble, gob-ble there, Here a gob-ble, there a gob-ble,

2. **Listen to a song about some other animals. Where do they live?** Play the recording of "Little White Duck" and decide that the animals probably live in a pond.

3. **Can you name the animals in this story? Listen again before you tell me.** Play the recording and discover that there are four animals in the story — a duck, a frog, a bug, and a snake.

4. Give the children ample opportunity to learn the melody before trying to sing the song. They may "act out" the story while they listen. **Who will be ducks? frogs? bugs? snakes?**

5. Invite the children to sing each animal's sound at the end of each verse. **Can you make your voice suggest the animal's sound?**

6. Sing the song as a dialogue. The children should sing Phrase 1 (Measures 1–4) and Phrase 3 (Measures 9–12) while you sing the more difficult middle phrase.

7. **Can we find instrument sounds that suggest each animal's voice?** Choices might include:

   quack — guiro
   glumph — hand drum
   chir — tambourine or jingle tap
   hiss — sand blocks
   boo hoo — resonator bells C', E, F

   Distribute the instruments to five children. As the class sings the song, these children may add the appropriate instrument sound when each animal's voice is heard.

144

Little White Duck

Music by Bernard Zaritsky

Words by Walt Barrows

1. There's a lit-tle white duck, sit-tin' in the wa-ter, Lit-tle white duck, do-in' what he ought-er. He took a bite of a lil-y pad, Flapped his wings, and he said, "I'm glad I'm a lit-tle white duck, sit-tin' in the wa-ter, Quack, *(quack) quack, (quack) quack (quack, quack)."

2. There's a lit-tle green frog, swim-min' in the wa-ter, Lit-tle green frog, do-in' what he ought-er. He jumped right off of the lil-y pad That the lit-tle duck bit, and he said, "I'm glad I'm a lit-tle green frog, swim-min' in the wa-ter, Glumph, (glumph) glumph, (glumph) glumph (glumph, glumph)."

3. There's a lit-tle black bug, float-in' in the wa-ter, Lit-tle black bug, do-in' what he ought-er. He tick-led the frog on the lil-y pad That the lit-tle duck bit, and he said, "I'm glad I'm a lit-tle black bug, float-in' in the wa-ter, Chir, (chir) chir, (chir) chir (chir, chir)."

4. There's a lit-tle red snake, fly-in' in the wa-ter, Lit-tle red snake, do-in' what he ought-er. He fright-ened the duck and the frog so bad, Ate the lit-tle bug, and he said, "I'm glad I'm a lit-tle red snake, fly-in' in the wa-ter, Hiss, (hiss) hiss, (hiss) hiss (hiss, hiss)."

5. Now there's no-bod-y left, sit-tin' in the wa-ter, No-bod-y left, do-in' what he ought-er. There's noth-ing left but the lil-y pad; The duck and the frog ran a-way, It's sad! Now there's no-bod-y left, sit-tin' in the wa-ter, Boo (boo) hoo, (hoo) hoo (hoo, hoo)!

* spoken

145

Perform Music by Playing

The first grader is gradually developing the ability to hear with discrimination and is gaining control over both large and small motor responses. Activities involving the use of simple classroom instruments will help to develop essential perceptual and psychomotor skills. Provide many opportunities for the children to experiment with different kinds of instruments, improvise instrumental melodies and rhythms, and perform accompaniments for classroom songs. Encourage the children to perform expressively by choosing instrument timbres and sound qualities appropriate to a song or idea.

Developing Basic Instrumental Skills

Give the children many opportunities to explore different ways of producing sounds on instruments. Then guide them to learn to hold and play each instrument in the way that will produce that instrument's traditional sound quality. The pictures below indicate the appropriate playing positions for some common instruments.

A. Non-pitched percussion instruments
- **Drums:** Young children may be able to control the sound more easily by using their hands instead of a mallet.
- **Woodblocks:** Hold the woodblock in one palm and strike the upper surface with a mallet. By striking different parts of the surface, the children can produce different pitch levels.
- **Triangles:** Suspend the triangle from a holder. Strike the closed side with a metal striker.

- **Tambourines:** With the head facing upward, hold the rim of the tambourine with one hand. Strike the center of the head with your knuckles, tap near the edge with the middle finger, strike the head against a knee or elbow, or shake the tambourine sideways.
- **Finger cymbals:** Hold one in each hand, by the straps. Strike the cymbal edges together with a downward motion.
- **Rhythm sticks:** Hold the sticks firmly; strike them together near their center. Help the children discover that different sounds may be produced by using sticks of different lengths and diameters.
- **Maracas:** Play both maracas by shaking up and down or tap one maraca against a palm.
- **Jingle taps:** Strike taps against a leg or palm.

B. Melodic percussion instruments
- **Resonator bells:** The mallet should strike the center of the bar and "bounce" away so the bar can vibrate freely. The children can experiment with wood and rubber mallets to explore differences in sound quality.
- **Mallet instruments** (xylophones, glockenspiels, metallophones): Show the children how to hold each mallet between the thumb and index finger, with the other fingers closed lightly around the mallet. Remind the children to quickly lift the mallet after striking each bar to allow the sound to resonate.
- **Autoharp:** Use the autoharp for sound exploration activities. Introduce different types of sound starters, such as rubber and wooden mallets, or plastic and metal picks.

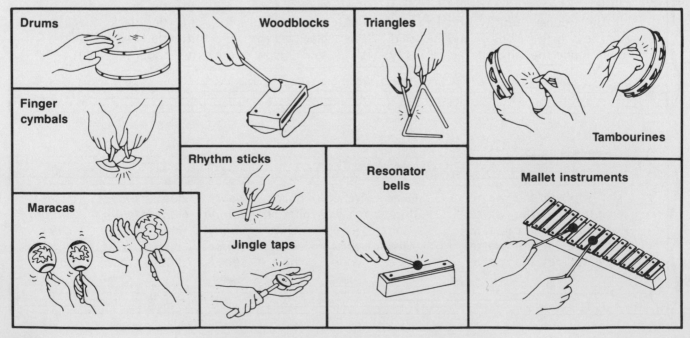

Drums · Woodblocks · Triangles · Finger cymbals · Rhythm sticks · Maracas · Jingle taps · Resonator bells · Tambourines · Mallet instruments

Lesson Focus

Expression: The expressiveness of music is affected by the way timbre contributes to the musical whole. *(P–E)*

Materials

o **Instruments:** drums; whistle; maracas; sand blocks; woodblock and mallet; xylophone or resonator bells for C chromatic scale (if available, see **Other**); xylophone mallet or bell mallet; finger cymbals

o **Other:** bell stairsteps for C chromatic scale (See Lesson 28, page 58, for illustration of chromatic stairsteps.)

o **Extends Lesson 9**, page 18

The Lesson

1. **Did you ever pretend that you were scared? that a lion, a tiger, or maybe even a ghost was chasing you? Was it fun to laugh when the "let's pretend" time was over? I have that kind of a "let's pretend" story for you, but to tell it I need your help.**

2. Ask the children to pat a steady beat on their thighs as you tell the story. Using pantomime, indicate to the children that they are to echo your words after each phrase and add body sounds when you do. Speak rhythmically and as expressively as possible.

   Let's go on a bear hunt. . . (echo)
   We're going to find a bear. . . (echo)
   Open the door, squeak. . . (echo)
   Slam the door, bang. . . (echo)
   Walk down the path. . . (echo)
   Open the gate, clickety clack. . . (echo)
   Coming to a wheat field. . . (echo)
   Can't go under it. . . (echo)
   Can't go over it. . . (echo)
   Have to walk through it. . . (echo)

   Interrupt the beat; rub your hands together to make swishing sounds.

   Got through the wheat field. . . (echo)
   Did you see a bear? . . . (echo)
   Noooooooooooo. . . (echo)

   Begin patting the beat again on your thighs.

   Coming to a bridge. . . (echo)
   Can't go under it. . . (echo)
   Have to walk over it. . . (echo)

   Interrupt the beat; pound your fists on your chest.

   We're over the bridge. . . (echo)
   Did you see a bear? . . . (echo)
   I didn't see a bear. . . (echo)

Resume patting the beat.

Coming to a river. . . (echo)
We can't go under it. . . (echo)
We can't fly over it. . . (echo)
We'll have to cross it. . . (echo)
Can you swim? . . . (echo)

Stop patting the beat; make up-down sounds with your voice.

We're across the river. . . (echo)
Did you see a bear? . . . (echo)
I didn't see a bear. . . (echo)

Resume patting the beat.

We're coming to a cave. . . (echo)
We can't go under it. . . (echo)
We can't go over it. . . (echo)
Let's tiptoe in. . . (echo)

Tap your palm with one finger, then stop and whisper.

It's very dark inside. . . (echo)
I can see two eyes. . . (echo)
And a big furry body. . . (echo)
(Yell) It's a bear! RUN!. . . (echo)

Patting your hands quickly, reverse the sound patterns for the story without speaking.

• Run back to the river (pat beat).
• Swim across the river (vocal sounds).
• Cross the bridge (chest-pounding sounds).
• Run through the wheat field (swishing sounds).
• Open the gate (clickety clack).
• Run up the path, open the door (squeak).
• Slam the door (clasp hands).

3. Retell the story using instruments to provide the special sounds. Ask players to stand in a row; indicate to them when each is to play. They may choose such instruments as:
   drums — walking sounds (beat)
   whistle — squeaking door
   maracas — gate opening
   sand blocks — swishing through the field
   woodblock — crossing the bridge
   xylophone or resonator bell glissandos — swimming the river
   finger cymbals — tiptoeing

   To tell the last part of the story (running away from the bear) the players should perform their sounds in reverse order.

147

Lesson Focus

Rhythm: Music may move in relation to the underlying shortest pulse. *(P–I)*

Materials

o **Record Information:**
  • What Time Do You Get Up?
    Record 6 Side B Band 2
    Voices: children's choir
    Accompaniment: synthesizer, sound effects, percussion

o **Instruments:** miscellaneous percussion instruments; woodblock and mallets; finger cymbals; cymbal and soft mallet; resonator bells E and G; bell mallet; triangle and striker

o **Other:** transparencies prepared for Lesson 56 (page 122, from Activity Sheets 21a–c, *Short Sounds, Beat,* and *Long Sounds*); overhead projector

o **Teacher's Resource Binder:**
  • Optional—
    Curriculum Correlations 11, 12, pages C19, C21

o **Extends Lesson 56,** page 122

For Your Information

Form of recording of "What Time Do You Get Up?": The song is repeated three times. On each repetition, a different kind of clock is suggested by the rhythm of the accompaniment — a tiny clock by an eighth-note rhythm, a larger mantel clock by a quarter-note rhythm, and a grandfather clock by a half-note rhythm.

The Lesson

1. Ask the children to name all the different kinds of clocks and watches they can think of: alarm clocks, travel clocks, mantel clocks, big grandfather clocks, wristwatches. **Do they all sound the same?** (No, some clocks tick very quickly, such as windup alarm clocks; some tick more slowly, like mantel clocks; some tick very slowly, like grandfather clocks. Some clocks make a chiming sound on the hour; alarm clocks make a buzzing sound to wake us up. Electric clocks may make a soft, whirring sound; quartz-or battery-run wristwatches make no sound at all.) As each different sound is described, ask someone to choose an instrument and produce that sound.

2. Play the recording of "What Time Do You Get Up?" Question the children about the words

of the song and replay the recording several times until they are sure of them.

Draw attention to the accompaniment. (See **For Your Information.**) Play the recording again and invite the children to lightly tap the three different clock rhythms. **How are they the same?** (They are all steady and even.) **How are they different?** (The first moves with short sounds, the second with long sounds, the third with lo-ong sounds.)

3. Invite the children to sing the song without assistance. They may decide what time they want to get up and insert that number in Measure 11.

4. Plan an introduction, an accompaniment, and a coda for the song. First display the three transparencies simultaneously. (See **Materials.**) Ask the children to identify the pattern that matches each clock (tiny clock — short sounds, Activity Sheet 21a; mantel clock — beat, Activity Sheet 21b; grandfather clock — lo-ong sounds, Activity Sheet 21c). Then ask each child to decide which clock he or she will describe for the performance and assign children to play the bell and triangle parts as described below.

The performance might be as follows:
Introduction:
Alarm clock: Play short sounds on woodblock. (Use two mallets and find high and low pitches — one child could hold a woodblock for another child.)

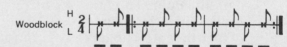

Mantel clock: Play beat on finger cymbals.

Grandfather clock: Play accented beats on a cymbal, using a soft mallet.

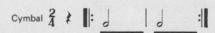

Song accompaniment: Continue patterns used for **Introduction.**
Coda: Play resonator bell pattern, repeating it enough times to signal the hour the children have chosen as the time to get up.

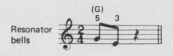

148

End with the sound of the alarm clock played on a triangle. (Place the triangle striker in the middle of the triangle and move it rapidly around, against all three sides.)

What Time Do You Get Up?

Traditional

There's a clock on the man-tel go-ing tick, tick, tock, And it

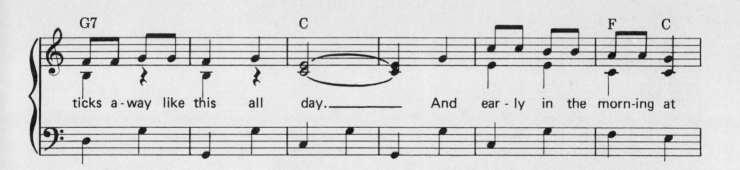

ticks a-way like this all day._____ And ear-ly in the morn-ing at

(___) o'-clock___ This is how it starts my day._____

o **Teacher's Resource Binder:**
  • Optional—
    Mainstreaming Suggestion 17, page M17
o **Extends Lesson 44**, page 94

Lesson Focus

Rhythm: Music may move in relation to the underlying shortest pulse. *(P–E)*

Materials

o **Record Information:**
  • Japanese Rain Song
    Record 6 Side B Band 3
    Voices: children's choir
    Accompaniment: shakuhachi, samisen, koto, percussion

o **Instruments:** xylophone or resonator bells C and G; two mallets; triangles and strikers, or finger cymbals

The Lesson

1. Ask the class to chant the following sounds of a rainy day with you. Then add the indicated body sounds to each chant.

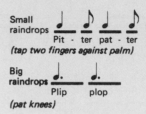

Japanese Rain Song

English Words by Roberta McLaughlin

If accompanying with autoharp, softly strum the C chord throughout.

A - me, a - me fur - e, fur - e, ka - a - san_____ ga,
1. Pit - ter pat - ter, fall - ing, fall - ing, rain is fall - ing down,
2. Un - der-neath the droop - ing wil - low stands a lit - tle child,

Jya - no me - de o mu kae_____ U - re - shi_____ na.
Moth - er comes to bring um - brel - la, Rain is fall - ing down.
No um - brel - la, child is weep - ing, Rain is fall - ing down.

Refrain

Pi chi, pi chi, cha pu, cha pu, ran, ran, ran.

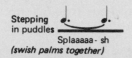

Stepping
in puddles
Splaaaaa- sh
(swish palms together)

2. Listen to the recording of "Japanese Rain Song." After discussing the words, add the sound of small raindrops from Step 1 (tapping fingers against palm) while listening again. Listen to the song a third time while the children add the sound of big raindrops by patting both knees. During a fourth hearing, the children might add the sound of stepping in puddles (swishing palms together).

3. Ask the children to sing the song independently. Then add an accompaniment. Choose a child to play pitches C and G on the xylophone or resonator bells. Tell the child to play the two pitches simultaneously, using the

OPTIONAL

Lesson Focus

Rhythm: Music may move in relation to the underlying steady beat or shortest pulse.
Expression: The expressiveness of music is affected by the way timbre contributes to the musical whole. *(C–E)*

Materials

o **Instruments:** hand drum; xylophone and mallet; rhythm sticks; woodblocks and mallets; resonator bell G and bell mallet
o **Extends Lesson 6**, page 12

The Lesson

1. Chant the rhyme, "Wee Willie Winkle." Ask the children to accompany you by patting short "running" sounds on their legs, alternating left and right. Repeat the activity and invite the children to chant the words with you.

2. When the children know the rhyme, add an instrumental accompaniment. Assign parts:

    resonator bell (G) — To start the performance, indicate the time by striking the bell eight times.
    drum — Play short sounds to suggest Willie running through the town.

PERFORM 12

same heavy, sustained gesture used when making big raindrop sounds.

4. Add an introduction and coda. The introduction could be a combination of the rainy-day chants from Step 1. Suggest that the children plan a coda with triangle or finger cymbal sounds; they could play fewer and fewer (and softer and softer) sounds to show the rain is ending. The final sound might be the sound of stepping in a puddle — the word "splaaaaash" and palms swished together.

PERFORM 13

xylophone — Play a glissando on the words "upstairs" and "downstairs."
rhythm sticks and woodblocks — Play the rhythm pattern of the words, "Rapping at the windows."

Choose one child to chant Willie's solo ("Are the children in their beds? . . ."). The rest of the class chants the first three lines of the rhyme.

Perform the rhyme, signaling to the players and "Willie" when to play or chant.

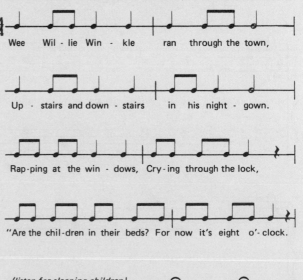

151

PERFORM 14

Lesson Focus

Rhythm: Individual sounds and silences within a rhythmic line may be longer than, shorter than, or the same as other sounds within the line. *(P–I)*

Materials

o **Record Information:**
  • Jingle at the Windows
   Record 6 Side B Band 4
   Voices: children's voices
   Accompaniment: tack piano, double bass, drums, rhythm guitar, spoons, tenor banjo
o **Instruments:** rhythm sticks; drums; jingle bells
o **Other:** rhythm bars (as prepared for Lesson 27, page 56) —melodic rhythm: 4 short bars, 8 long bars, 1 lo-ong bar
o **Extends Lesson 44,** page 94

The Lesson

1. Play the recording of "Jingle at the Windows." **How many different rhythm pat-** terns can you find? (three) Show each pattern with rhythm bars.

Ask the class to identify the words that match each pattern. (1. "Pass one window"; 2. "tideo"; 3. "Jingle at the windows")

2. Add movements to the song. Pat legs for "Pass one window," clap for "tideo," and turn around for "Jingle at the windows."

3. Ask the class to sing the song while a child points to the rhythm bar patterns.

4. Have the children play the rhythm patterns on instruments while they sing — rhythm sticks for "Pass one window," drums for "tideo," and jingle bells for "Jingle at the windows."

Jingle at the Windows

Singing Game

152

Lesson Focus

Harmony: Chords and melody may move simultaneously in relation to each other. *(P–I)*

Materials

o **Record Information:**
  • There Was a Crooked Man
  Record 6 Side B Band 5
  Voices: children's choir
  Accompaniment: synthesizer
o **Instruments:** resonator bells E, F, and G or bass xylophone with E, F, and G bars; mallet
o **Other:** overhead projector
o **Teacher's Resource Binder:**
  Activity Sheets • **Activity Sheet 28,** page A46 (Prepare a transparency from the activity sheet.)
  • Optional—
  Curriculum Correlation 1, page C1
o **Extends Lesson 49,** page 104

The Lesson

1. Help the children learn "There Was a

Crooked Man" by listening to the recording. Then display the transparency prepared from Activity Sheet 28 *(There Was a Crooked Man)*. Ask the children to follow the pictures and show when the crooked man is walking by patting both knees simultaneously and when the crooked cat is walking by patting their right knee with both hands.

2. Ask the children to alternate the man and cat movements as they listen to the song and follow the pictures on the transparency. Then put out the resonator bells or bass xylophone. (See **Materials.**) Choose a child to play E and G simultaneously when you point at the crooked man, and F and G when you point at the crooked cat. Perform the song with movements and accompaniment.

There Was a Crooked Man

Words from Mother Goose

Traditional Tune

PERFORM 16

Lesson Focus

Rhythm: Music may move in relation to the underlying steady beat. *(P–E)*

Materials

o **Record Information:**
  • Lirum, Larum
    Record 6 Side B Band 6
    Voices: children's choir
    Accompaniment: piccolo, oboe, clarinet, bassoon, French horn, guitar, double bass
o **Instruments:** several sets of resonator bells D and D' or several xylophones with D and D' bars; mallets; miscellaneous classroom instruments and mallets
o **Extends Lesson 29,** page 60

The Lesson

1. Sing "Lirum, Larum" for the children while they tap the steady beat on right and left thighs alternately. Sing the song again and ask the children to sing with you while continuing to tap the beat.

2. Choose children to add an accompaniment on resonator bells or xylophone. They should use the same motion used when tapping their thighs, now alternating between D and D' as the class sings the song again.

3. Invite individual children to improvise their own dances by singing:

   Lirum, larum, Little (Jason) dance!
   Other children quiet be,
   Waiting, waiting patiently,
   Little (Jason), dance!

4. The song may also be used to initiate instrumental play. Sing the following invitation:

   OPTIONAL

   Lirum, larum, Little (Kate) may play.
   Other children quiet must be. . .*(and so on)*

The chosen child may play the shortest sound or the steady beat on his or her favorite instrument.

Lirum, Larum

German Children's Game

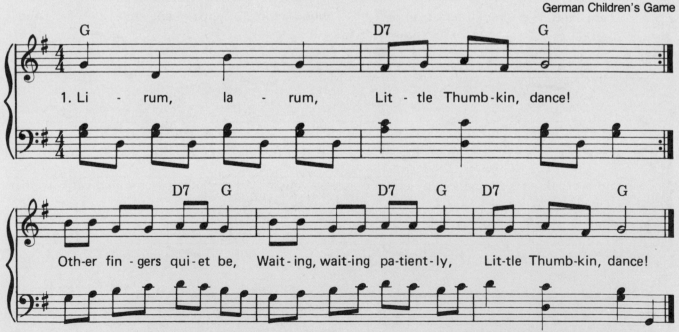

1. Li - rum, la - rum, Lit - tle Thumb-kin, dance!
Oth-er fin - gers qui-et be, Wait-ing, wait-ing pa-tient-ly, Lit-tle Thumb-kin, dance!

2. Lirum, larum, Little Pointer, dance!...

3. Lirum, larum, Tall Man, Tall Man, dance!...

4. Lirum, larum, Ring Man, Ring Man, dance!...

5. Lirum, larum, Little Finger, dance!...

6. Lirum, larum, Every Finger, dance!

No one has to quiet be,

No one waiting patiently,

Every Finger, dance!

Lesson Focus

Rhythm: Individual sounds and silences within a rhythmic line may be longer than, shorter than, or the same as other sounds within the line. *(D–E)*

Materials

o **Record Information:**
  • Johnny Works With One Hammer
    Record 6 Side B Band 7
    Voice: man
    Accompaniment: clarinet, trumpet, trombone, viola, percussion

o **Instruments:** drums; resonator bells C and C′ and/or xylophones with C and C′ bars for several children; bell and/or xylophone mallets (two for each child)

o **Teacher's Resource Binder:**
  • Optional—
    Kodaly Activity 1, page K2

o **Extends Lesson 27,** page 56

The Lesson

1. Listen to "Johnny Works With One Hammer." Ask the children to show that they know "a time to play and a time not to play." They are to pat their knees (or play a drum) with the beat when the hammers are being counted; they are to hold their hands in the air on all other words.

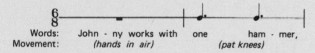

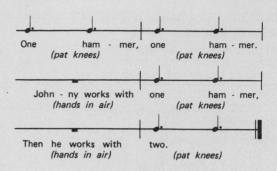

2. Replay the recording and repeat the activity several times. When the class can sing the song easily, give several children resonator bells or xylophones and two mallets each. (See **Materials.**) They are to hold the mallets in the air or play the two pitches simultaneously in the same manner as in Step 1. Other children may continue to sing and pat knees until they have a turn to play an instrument.

3. Return to the song at another time. This time the children may add a new movement for each verse as follows:

1. Tap floor with one fist
2. Tap floor with two fists
3. Tap floor with two fists and one foot
4. Tap floor with two fists and two feet (alternately)

Johnny Works With One Hammer

American Folk Song

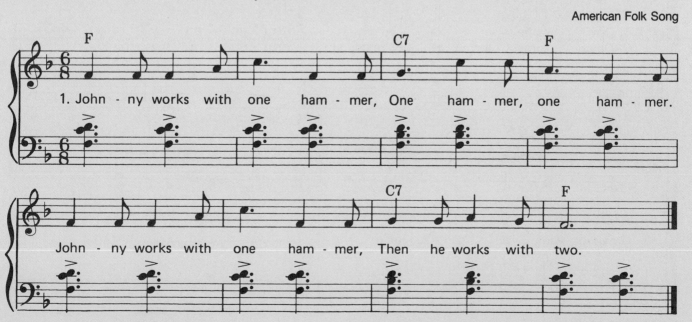

Verse 1: Stand in place while clapping the beat.
Interlude: The first child in Row 1 "struts" down between the rows and takes her place at the foot of the row.
Verse 2: Same as for Verse 1
Interlude: The first child in Row 2 "struts" down and takes his place at the foot of the row.

Lesson Focus

Rhythm: Individual sounds and silences within a rhythmic line may be longer than, shorter than, or the same as the underlying steady beat. *(P–E)*

Materials

o **Record Information:**
  • Struttin' on Through
    Record 6 Side B Band 8
    Voices: children's choir
    Accompaniment: percussion
o **Instruments:** xylophone with F and C bars or piano; xylophone mallet; glockenspiel with F, G, A, C, and D bars, or resonator bells F, G, A, C, and D; glockenspiel or bell mallet
o **Teacher's Resource Binder:**
  • Optional—
    Orff Activity 15, page O18
o **Extends Lesson 39,** page 84

For Your Information

Singing game for "Struttin' on Through":
The children form two lines facing each other (girls in Row 1; boys in Row 2). Allow enough space between the lines for children to walk down the middle. Repeat the following sequence as many times as desired.

The Lesson

1. Begin by tapping the underlying short sound (the eighth note) for "Struttin' on Through."

   Ask the children to join you in tapping while you sing the song. Discuss the words and sing the song again.

2. Ask a child to add a short-sound accompaniment on xylophone or piano (playing low F and C simultaneously).

3. Choose two children to improvise an interlude between verses. (The short-sound accompanist continues to play during the interlude.) These children may use glockenspiel or resonator bell pitches F, G, A, C, and D; their music should move with longer sounds to contrast with the short sounds played by the accompanist.

4. Play a singing game. (See **For Your Information.**) Include the instrument parts from Steps 2 and 3. *(OPTIONAL)*

Struttin' on Through

Traditional Singing Game

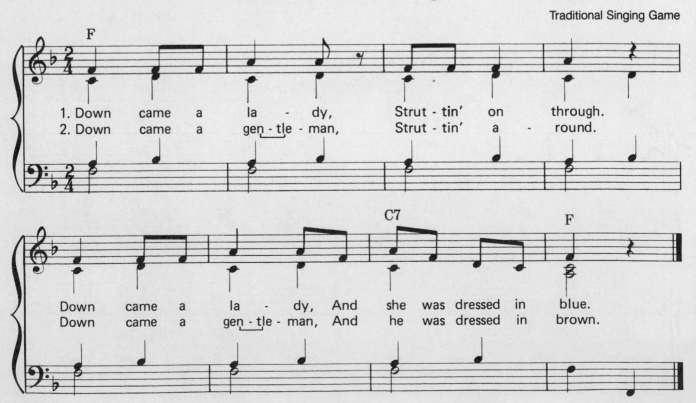

1. Down came a la - dy, Strut - tin' on through.
2. Down came a gen - tle - man, Strut - tin' a - round.

Down came a la - dy, And she was dressed in blue.
Down came a gen - tle - man, And he was dressed in brown.

156

Lesson Focus
Timbre: The quality of a sound is determined by the sound source. *(P–E)*

Materials
o **Record Information:**
  - Ally Bally Bee
    Record 6 Side B Band 9
    Voices: children's choir
    Accompaniment: oboe, English horn, harp, celesta
o **Instruments:** drum; jingle bells; rhythm sticks; tambourine
o **Teacher's Resource Binder:**
  - Optional—
    Curriculum Correlations 7, 9, pages C9, C16
o **Extends Lesson 8,** page 16

The Lesson
1. Help the children learn to sing the song by listening to the recording. Replay the recording as necessary.

2. Direct the children to form a circle and place a drum, jingle bells, rhythm sticks, and a tambourine in the center. As the children sing the song, they are to move as follows:

   Ally bally, ally bally bee, *(walk counter-clockwise)*

Sittin' on your daddy's knee, *(stop; panto-mime sitting in chair)*
Begging for a wee penny *(begging gesture)*
To buy a drum for you and me. *(select a child to go to the center and play drum through interlude)*

3. Repeat the game with different children choosing the instrument to be played. At first you may wish to choose each child who will play an instrument. Later, the children may choose the next player.

4. Help the children acquire the vocabulary associated with the sounds they have been playing. **Which of the sounds we played are ringing sounds?** (jingle bells) **clicking sounds?** (rhythm sticks) **thudding sounds?** (drum) **clattering sounds?** (tambourine)

5. The children may enjoy changing the words in the last phrase of the song to list other things to buy. For example, they might sing: "To buy a pretty dolly....a box of raisins....some fresh, green broccoli...."

Ally Bally Bee

Traditional

1. Al - ly bal - ly, al - ly bal - ly bee, sit - tin' on your dad - dy's knee, beg - ging for a wee pen - ny to buy a drum for you and me.

2. ...buy some bells for you and me.   3. ...buy some sticks for you and me.
4. ...buy a tambourine for you and me.

157

Lesson Focus

Expression: The expressiveness of music is affected by the way timbre contributes to the musical whole. *(P–E)*

Materials

o **Record Information:**
 • Dr. Knickerbocker
  Record 7 Side A Band 1
  Voices: man, children's choir
  Accompaniment: bass clarinet, tenor saxophone, trumpet, electric guitar, double bass, percussion

o **Instruments:** several of each of the following—rhythm sticks; drums; slide whistles; bicycle horns (or other horns)

o **Teacher's Resource Binder:**
 • Optional—
  Curriculum Correlation 13, page C21
  Enrichment Activity 13, page E21

o **Extends Lesson 3,** page 6

The Lesson

1. Introduce the song game "Dr. Knickerbocker" by playing the recording. Invite the children to do the body movements as instructed in the song while they listen.

2. When the children know the song, substitute instrument sounds for the body movements. On the chalkboard write the name (or draw a picture) of each instrument to be played next

Dr. Knickerbocker

Playground Game

to the words for which each sound is to be
substituted:

hands; one, two   rhythm sticks
feet; three, four   drums
eyes; five, six   slide whistle
hips; seven, eight   bicycle horn
nine (last measure only)   all instruments

3. Give four groups of children as many instruments as are available from the instrument
groups listed on the chalkboard. They are to
play at the appropriate times in Verse 2—on
the rests after the instrument name is sung
and in place of the numbers at the end of the
song.

4. Give other children an opportunity to play
the instruments while the rest of the class
sings the song.

Verse 2: Substitute the following for hands,
feet, eyes, hips—sticks (click), drum (tap),
whistle (whee), horn (toot).

Last three measures: Substitute instrument sounds.

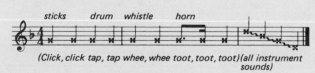

sticks   drum   whistle   horn

(Click, click tap, tap whee, whee toot, toot, toot)(all instrument
sounds)

Lesson Focus

Harmony: A series of simultaneous sounds may alternate between activity and rest. **(P–E)**

Materials

o **Record Information:**
  • John the Rabbit
    Record 7 Side A Band 2
    Voices: children's choir
    Accompaniment: bass harmonica, guitar, electric bass, electric piano, percussion

o **Instruments:** resonator bells D and A or xylophones with D and A bars for several children; two xylophone or bell mallets for each player; autoharp

o **Extends Lesson 56,** page 122

The Lesson

1. Play the recording of "John the Rabbit" and help the children learn to sing the song. Discuss the words of the song; replay the recording and ask the children to join in on the repeated words, "oh yes."

2. When the children know the song, ask them to show the form of the song by raising their hands to the sky as they sing the first part of each phrase and by patting both knees in the rhythm of the words as they sing "oh yes."

3. Choose a child to play D and A on the xylophone or resonator bells (both pitches simultaneously) on the words "oh yes" while the other children sing the song.

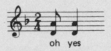

oh yes

John the Rabbit

American Folk Song

4. At another time the children may play an accompaniment on the autoharp. Two children may work together. One child presses the D minor button down firmly; the other child strums the strings from low to high on the accented first beat of each measure.

5. Add new verses to the song. Ask the children to suggest other things rabbits might eat, such as other vegetables and fruits and silly things such as socks or tin cans.

6. Continue to explore "times to play, times not to play" by having the class add instrumental parts to the following chant.

OPTIONAL

Start by having the children rhythmically chant the rhyme, reaching toward the sky on the words "Pitch, patch, pepper" and patting their knees on all other words. Then choose children to play pitches D and A on the xylophone or resonator bells. Both pitches should be played simultaneously; instrument players hold their mallets in the sky on "Pitch, patch, pepper" and play on all other words while the rest of the class chants and moves.

PITCH, PATCH, PEPPER
by B. A.

Pitch, patch, pepper, one, two, three,
Pitch, patch, pepper, four, five, six,
Pitch, patch, pepper, seven, eight, nine,
Pitch, patch, pepper, pooof!

sweet po-ta-toes oh yes, And my ripe to-ma-toes oh yes. Well if I live__ to see next fall, My gar-den won't have__ an-y vege-ta-bles at all.

Describe Music

Responding to the Musical Sound

Young children grow in their understanding of music as they learn to describe the musical sounds produced by others. They may describe music through movement, visual representations, and words. Their early responses to music will likely be expressed through movement. After many nonverbal experiences, the children will begin to make appropriate connections between musical sounds and visual representations, such as pictures, ikons, and musical notation.

The children will develop verbal skills gradually. Help them acquire a vocabulary to describe their understanding of musical concepts; use relevant terminology regularly to provide them with a model. As the children develop verbal skills and acquire relevant concepts, they will begin to use musical terminology appropriately.

Describe with Movement

Expressive Movement Provide many opportunities for the children to respond to music through expressive movement. Help them to explore how their bodies move in space and in relation to other people and objects. As the children explore they will acquire a repertoire of movements that can be used to express musical ideas.

The children will gradually acquire more precise discriminatory skills and will be able to recognize specific elements of music. For most children the sequence of recognition will be: timbre, then volume, tempo, rhythm, melodic organization, form, harmonic change.

Patterned Movement In addition to expressive movement, young children should be given the opportunity to learn specific patterns of movement, such as finger plays, singing games, and simple dances. Begin by helping the children sense the beat and accent of the music as well as the phrase structure. This is particularly important for patterned dance movements, since most dance figures are based on the rhythm and form of the music.

Structured Movement To help the children grow in their ability to discriminate musical elements, introduce structured movements to show melody, rhythm, and form.
1. Melodic organization
   a. Use hand and arm gestures to show contour.
   b. Introduce the body scale to show tonal relationships. (See bottom of page.)
2. Rhythmic organization
   a. Use a variety of motions to show beat, accent, and shortest sound, such as:
      • tapping one hand on a thigh
      • tapping both hands on thighs or knees, either simultaneously or alternately
      • tapping one finger against a palm
   b. Show the rhythm of the melody by:
      • tapping the shortest sounds on fingertips
      • clapping long sounds
      • sliding palms to represent lo-ong sounds

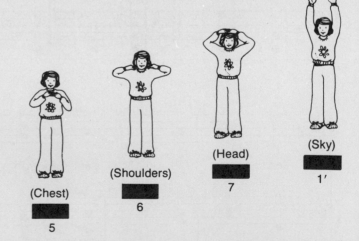

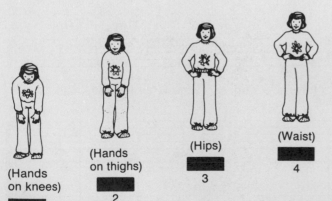

(Hands on knees) 1

(Hands on thighs) 2

(Hips) 3

(Waist) 4

(Chest) 5

(Shoulders) 6

(Head) 7

(Sky) 1′

- stepping the rhythm of the melody, making sure to match the length of the step to the length of the note
3. Formal structure
   a. Show phrases by moving one arm in an arc; start a new arc with each new phrase.
   b. Show sections by walking around the room, turning, and stepping in a new direction as each new section begins.

Describe with Visual and Verbal Representations

When the children can demonstrate their understanding of music through appropriate gestures they are ready to begin to associate what they hear with "pictures of sound," or **ikons**. At this stage, children will also begin to spontaneously use verbal imagery to describe what they hear. Words such as "up," "down," and "high-low," as well as "fast-slow," "same-different," and "short-long" will become part of their vocabulary as the connection is made between musical sound and visual representation.

In the first grade most of the visual experiences provided in *HOLT MUSIC* are at the **ikonic** level. **Rhythmic relationships** are represented by ikons that show relative length of sounds:

- in relation to each other within a rhythm pattern

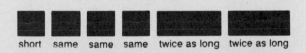

short   same   same   same   twice as long   twice as long

- in relation to the underlying shortest sound, beat, and/or accent

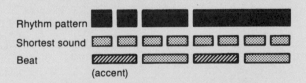

Rhythm pattern
Shortest sound
Beat
(accent)

To introduce the children to notation, ikon and symbol are associated:

Melodic relationships are represented in two ways.

- Overall contour is shown with a continuous line:

- Rhythmic and melodic ikons are combined to show steps and skips:

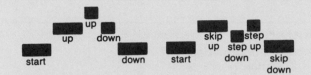

start   up   up   down   down   start   skip up   step up   step down   down   skip down

The ikons are then associated with scale numbers to show the relationship of pitches to a tonal center:

1   3   5   3   1   1   3   2   3   1

Other ikons are used to represent:

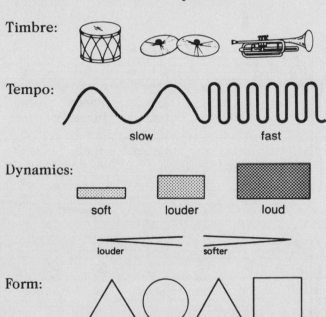

Timbre:

Tempo:

slow   fast

Dynamics:

soft   louder   loud

louder   softer

Form:

The expressive quality of music may be represented abstractly

or by means of representational pictures that suggest the feelings and ideas evoked by the music.

163

Lesson Focus

Form: A musical whole is a combination of smaller segments. *(D–I)*

Materials

o **Record Information:**
  • The Snail
    Record 7 Side A Band 3
    Voices: woman, children's choir
    Accompaniment: four saxophones
o **Other:** paper and pencil for each child
o **Teacher's Resource Binder:**
  • Optional—
    Curriculum Correlation 1, page C1
o **Extends Lesson 41,** page 88

The Lesson

1. Listen to the recording of "The Snail." Suggest to the class that they make a "snail." Begin by forming a circle with everyone but a leader and the child to the leader's left holding hands. Play the recording. As the music begins, the leader walks in a circular direction inside the large circle; everyone follows, gradually creating a spiral.

   As Verse 2 begins the leader reverses direction and leads everyone out of the spiral into one circle, stopping when the music ends.

2. **We've just made a giant snail! This time I'm going to make little snails as we listen to the music! I will make one snail to show each part.** Replay the recording. Draw a snail on the chalkboard to represent each phrase. Try to time your drawing so that you begin and end each snail with the beginning and

The Snail

Traditional

1. Let's join hands and make a shell, A place
   Here's your house; we built it well. Lit- tle
2. Lit- tle snail, now turn a- bout; Find a
   Lit- tle snail, we're out in time; Here we

Fine

for our snail to dwell. Round and round we'll creep and
snail, crawl in your shell. Round and round we'll creep and
hole and lead us out.
are back in our line.

D. C. al Fine

sing, Clos- er, clos- er, wind each ring.
sing, Wind- ing out of ev- ery ring.

end of each phrase. (Each phrase is four measures long.)

3. Ask the children to help you show the parts of the song by "drawing" snails in the air (one snail for each phrase) as they listen to the song again.

4. Hand out a sheet of paper and a pencil to each child. Invite the class to draw snails as you did while listening to the music. **Can you**

OPTIONAL

DESCRIBE 1

start to draw a new snail each time another phrase begins? Play the recording as the children draw their snails. Then invite them to sing the song and draw a new set of snails. (The children should draw six snails—one per phrase.)

Lesson Focus
Rhythm: Music may move in relation to the underlying steady beat. *(D–E)*

Materials
o **Record Information:**
  • This Old Man
    (Record 3 Side A Band 9)
  • *Kid Stuff* (excerpt)
    Record 7 Side A Band 4
    Boston Pops Orchestra
    Arthur Fiedler, conductor
o **Extends Lesson 10,** page 20

The Lesson
1. Review "This Old Man" (Lesson 27, page 56). Lead the children in the following patterned movement while they sing the song.

2. **Listen to this music. Raise your hand when you recognize the melody!** Play the beginning of *Kid Stuff*. When the children recognize "This Old Man," start the recording again and indicate that they are to "do as you do."

   Drum introduction: No movement.
   First statement of melody: Tap beat over heart with fingertips.
   Second statement: Lightly tap beat on chest with fists.
   Third statement: Show beat with elbows.
   Fourth statement: Tap beat on hips with fists.
   Fifth statement: Lightly clap beat.

DESCRIBE 2

When the music changes to "March of the Siamese Children," indicate that the children should do the following motions:

Introduction (8 beats): No movement.
Section A (16 beats): Tap beat on chin with index finger.
Section A' (16 beats): Tap beat on cheekbone with index finger.
Section B (32 beats): Lightly clap beat.
Section A: Gently slide palms on each beat.
Section A': Tap beat on shoulders.

3. Invite the children to take turns being the leader and make up motions for the class to follow while listening to *Kid Stuff*. They must change motions as each new part begins.

Lesson Focus

Rhythm: A series of beats may be organized into regular or irregular groupings by stressing certain beats. *(P–I)*

Materials

o **Record Information:**
   • *Patito*
   ▭ **Record 7 Side A Band 5**
   Voices: children's choir
   Accompaniment: guitar, double bass, harp, accordion, marimba, percussion
o **Instruments:** several C resonator bells; bell mallets
o **Other:** Prepare Spanish-word visuals using construction paper and a marking pen.

o **Extends Lesson 34,** page 70

For Your Information
Pronunciation for the Spanish lyrics:
   pah-**tee**-toh koe-**lohr** day kah-**fay**
   see too noe may **k'air**-race
   may **k'air**-ray hoe-**say**

The Lesson

1. Play the recording of *"Patito."* **Listen to a song about a duck!** (The song is sung in English and in Spanish.) Learn to sing Verse 1.

2. Help the children learn the Spanish verse by first showing visuals for the words *"patito," "color de café," "quieres,"* and "José." (See **Materials.**) Then learn to sing the whole of Verse 2 by displaying the visual reminders of the words at the appropriate times.

3. When the children are familiar with the lyrics, listen to the recording again. Have them decide which pattern of heavy-light beats can be clapped as they sing. (three's)

   two's ▨▭ or three's ▨▭▭

4. Invite the children to clap only on the heavy beat in each measure (first beat) as they sing the song. Distribute the C resonator bells and bell mallets and ask the children to play this sound only on the heavy beat. Use the bell sounds as an accompaniment while all sing the song.

Patito

Words adapted

Mexican Folk Song

1. Lit-tle duck-ie, lit-tle duck-ie, the col-or of ca-fé, If you do not love me, my Jo-sé just may!
2. Pa-ti-to, pa-ti-to co-lor de ca-fé, Si tu no me quier-es me quier-e Jo-sé!

Lesson Focus

Rhythm: Individual sounds and silences within a rhythmic line may be longer than, shorter than, or the same as other sounds within the line. *(D–I)*

Materials

o **Record Information:**
- Bright Stars, Light Stars
  Record 7 Side A Band 6
  Voices: children's choir
  Accompaniment: cello, oboe, French horn, tuba, harp, celesta

o **Instruments:** triangles and strikers, or finger cymbals

o **Teacher's Resource Binder:**
- Optional—
  Curriculum Correlation 11, page C19

o **Extends Lesson 38,** page 82

The Lesson

1. Draw the following pattern of stars on the chalkboard:

Ask the children to describe the stars as short or long. Hand out triangles or finger cymbals to several children. Invite them to play the star pattern while they softly whisper "twin-kly win-kly stars."

twin-kly win-kly stars

2. While the instrument players continue to play the pattern, the other children can move to the pattern. Ask these children to stand in pairs facing one another, with the palms of their hands together. **Tap each other's hands when you hear short sounds. When you hear long sounds, touch palms and move your hands in a circle.**

3. Play the recording of "Bright Stars, Light Stars." Ask the children to listen for all the kinds of stars that are described ("Bright," "Light," "Shining-in-the-night," "Little twinkly winkly," and so on). Play the recording as often as needed until the children are sure of the words; then challenge them to sing the song without the recording.

4. When the class can sing the song correctly, ask them to perform the motions learned in Step 2, while singing the song.

Bright Stars, Light Stars

Words by Rhoda W. Bacmeister

Music by Irving Lowens

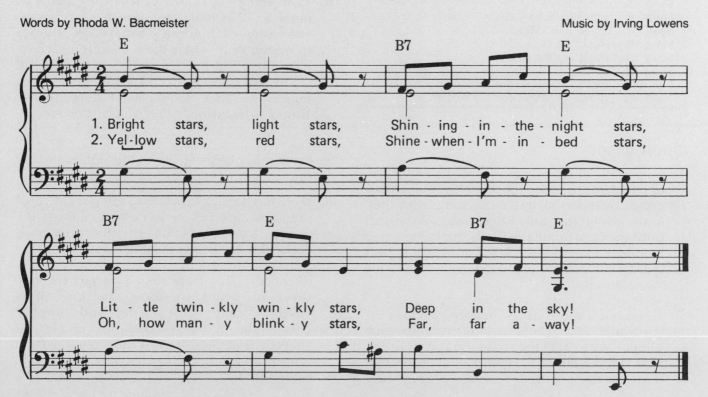

1. Bright stars, light stars, Shin-ing-in-the-night stars,
2. Yel-low stars, red stars, Shine-when-I'm-in-bed stars,

Lit-tle twin-kly win-kly stars, Deep in the sky!
Oh, how man-y blink-y stars, Far, far a-way!

DESCRIBE 5

Lesson Focus

Rhythm: Individual sounds and silences within a rhythmic line may be longer than, shorter than, or the same as other sounds within the line.
Form: A musical whole may be made up of same, varied, or contrasting segments. *(D–I)*

Materials

o **Record Information:**
  • *Children's March*
  by Edwin Franko Goldman, 1878–1956
  Record 7 Side A Band 7
  Northeast Louisiana State College Concert Band
  Joe Barry Mullins, conductor
o **Teacher's Resource Binder:**

  [Activity Sheets] • **Activity Sheets 29a–b**, pages A47–A48
  (Prepare one copy of each activity sheet for each child and cut pictures apart.)
o **Extends Lesson 20**, page 42; **Lesson 59**, page 128

For Your Information

Structure of *Children's March:*
  Introduction
  Song 1: "Mary Had a Little Lamb"
  Song 2: "Jingle Bells"
  Song 3: "Sing a Song of Sixpence"
  Song 4: "The Farmer in the Dell"
  Trumpet and drum interlude
  Song 5: "Lazy Mary"
  Song 6: "Hickory, Dickory, Dock"
  Song 7: "Three Blind Mice"
  Song 8: "Rockabye Baby"
  Song 9: "Pop Goes the Weasel"
  Song 10: "London Bridge Is Falling Down" (first heard at same time as "Pop Goes the Weasel," then alternating with phrases of "Pop Goes the Weasel")

The Lesson

1. Sing each of the songs included in the *Children's March.* Invite the children to sing (as a group or individually) those songs that they know. Sing the unfamiliar songs for them until they are familiar with the melodies. (See Lesson 1, page 1, for "London Bridge Is Falling Down"; see Lesson 54, page 114, for "Jingle Bells.")

2. Hand out a set of cards prepared from Activity Sheet 29a (*Children's March*) to each child. Play or sing the songs in random order; ask the children to find the picture that matches each song.

3. Now I'm going to try to fool you! This time I'm going to sing the melodies without the words. Do you think you can still find the picture that matches each tune?

4. When the children have demonstrated that they can recognize the melodies, tell them that they are going to hear the melodies performed in a very special way. Play the recording of *Children's March* through "Jingle Bells"; ask the children to comment on the different things they noticed. (The tunes are played on instruments and are not sung; there are no words; there are lots of extra sounds, and so on.)

5. Can you put your pictures in a row to show the order of the songs? With what picture should we begin? Start the recording and help the children realize that the music begins with sounds that are not from one of the melodies. **This is called the introduction. It tells us to "Get ready; you're going to hear some music!"** After the children have put the "Get ready" card at the beginning of the row, play the recording through the trumpet and drum interlude. Stop and discuss the order of the melodies; decide that the picture of the trumpet and drum should be the last picture in the row. Suggest that they begin a second row and continue to put pictures in order as they listen to the rest of the music.

6. How many parts are in this long piece of music? (12) Divide the class into ten groups and assign each group a song; each group is to march only when their melody is heard. Help the children realize that at the end of the march, Groups 9 and 10 will march at the same time. (See sequence of songs in **For Your Information**.) Play the entire recording.

7. On another hearing, invite the children to tap the rhythm of each melody as it is heard.

8. Here is a harder task! Hand out a set of cards prepared from Activity Sheet 29b (*Children's March–Rhythm Pictures*) to each child, along with a copy of the pictures for the introduction and the interlude from Activity Sheet 29. **This time, can you put the pictures in order to show the long-short rhythms that you've sung and tapped?** (Note—the rhythm pictures on the activity sheets are in the correct order, reading from left to right; mix the cards up before distributing them.)

169

Lesson Focus

Melody: A series of pitches may move up or down by steps or skips. *(D–I)*

Materials

○ **Record Information:**
  • Had a Little Rooster
  Record 7 Side A Band 8
  Voice: child
  Accompaniment: woodwind quartet, percussion
○ **Instruments:** resonator bells E, F, G, A, B, and C'; bell mallet
○ **Other:** a pencil for each child
○ **Teacher's Resource Binder:**
  |Activity Sheets| • **Activity Sheet 30,** page A49 (Prepare one copy for each child.)
○ **Extends Lesson 33,** page 68

The Lesson

1. Play the recording of "Had a Little Rooster." Ask the children to name the animals. Play the recording again and invite the children to sing each animal's song ("cockadoodle doo," "chick, chick, chick," and so on) while showing the shape of each song with hand movements.

2. Give a copy of Activity Sheet 30 (*Had a Little Rooster*) to each child. Play the recording a third time. **Follow each animal's melody picture with your fingertip while you listen!**

3. Draw attention to the boxes in the lower half of the activity sheet. Give each child a pencil and read the instructions to the class. As the children listen to the recording again, invite them to draw the up-down shape of each animal's song. **How many times will you draw each song?** (rooster—four times; hen—three times; duck—two times; pig—once)

Had a Little Rooster

American Folk Song

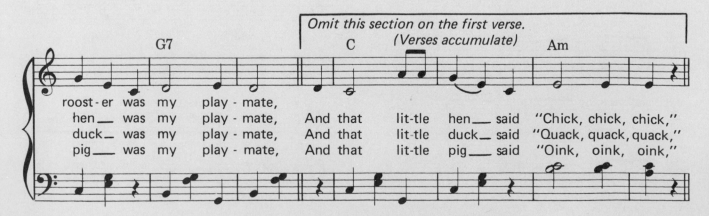

1. Had a lit-tle roost-er by the barn - yard gate, And that lit-tle
2. Had a lit-tle hen___ by the barn - yard gate, And that lit-tle
3. Had a lit-tle duck___ by the barn - yard gate, And that lit-tle
4. Had a lit-tle pig___ by the barn - yard gate, And that lit-tle

Omit this section on the first verse.
(Verses accumulate)

roost-er was my play-mate,
hen___ was my play-mate, And that lit-tle hen___ said "Chick, chick, chick,"
duck___ was my play-mate, And that lit-tle duck___ said "Quack, quack, quack,"
pig___ was my play-mate, And that lit-tle pig___ said "Oink, oink, oink,"

4. When the children know the song well, choose two children to perform the animal songs on resonator bells. One child may play the first part of the rooster's song on bells, F, G, A, B, and C'. The other child can play the other animal sounds on the E bell.

And that lit - tle roost - er said "Cock - a - doo - dle doo, Doo doo doo doo doo doo doo doo, doo doo."

Lesson Focus
Expression: Musical elements are combined into a whole to express a musical or extramusical idea. **(D–E)**

Materials
o **Record Information:**
  • *Green Skirt*
    Record 7 Side A Band 9
    Sung Tso-Liang Orchestra
o **Instruments:** hand drum; two sizes of triangles (or cymbals) with strikers
o **Extends Lesson 47,** page 100

The Lesson

1. Play a hand drum as you invite the children to explore movement ideas.

   • **Crawl into a dark place. Feel the sides of your dark place. If they're smooth, show me!** (Rub drum head.) **If they are rough, show me!** (Strike drum sharply.)
   • **Will you walk, crawl, or slither out of your dark place? Show me!**

2. Use triangles (or cymbals) and invite the children to move to the following ideas.

   • **Go into a bright place. Feel the sides of your bright place. Are they smooth?**

(Make long sustained sounds.) **Or are they lumpy?** (Make short sounds.)
   • **Are you in a high place?** (Use a small triangle.) **or a low place?** (Use a large triangle.)
   • **Step out of your bright place! Do you see the sun?** (Make a long sound.) **Or do you feel three little raindrops?** (Make three short sounds.)

3. Play the recording of *Green Skirt*. Help the children hear the different instruments. (A deep drum begins the music and is joined by a gong. A flute then plays a melody. A bowed stringed instrument plays another melody, accompanied by a plucked stringed instrument. Other instruments finally join in this order: woodblock and deep drum, high plucked stringed instrument, and small bells.)

Ask each child to choose a "special sound." **Listen again. Move only when you hear your sound. Make your movements "look like" your sound.** Play the recording several times until the children can anticipate their sounds and be ready to move.

Lesson Focus

Form: A musical whole may be made up of same, varied, or contrasting segments.
Rhythm: Individual sounds and silences within a rhythmic line may be longer than, shorter than, or the same as other sounds within the line. *(D–I)*

Materials

o **Record Information:**
  • Animal Crackers in My Soup
  Record 7 Side B Band 1
  Voices: children's choir
  Accompaniment: flute, French horn, trumpet, trombone, guitar, double bass, piano, percussion

o **Other:** colored construction paper; four 8" x 10" sheets of oaktag; paste or glue; four Soup Bowls (See instructions on Activity Sheet 31.)
o **Teacher's Resource Binder:**
  Activity Sheets • **Activity Sheet 31,** page A50 (Make copies and cut the pictures apart; prepare enough copies to provide one picture for each child.)
o **Extends Lesson 53,** page 112

The Lesson

1. Play the recording of "Animal Crackers in My Soup." Ask the children to listen carefully and identify all the different animals they might find in their "animal-cracker soup."

2. **Let's make our own animal-cracker soup!** Display the Soup Bowls in the order shown on Activity Sheet 31. (See **Materials.**) Guide the

Animal Crackers in My Soup

Lyrics by Ted Kochler and Irving Caesar

Music by Ray Henderson

children to describe the pattern on each bowl, using "short," "long," and "lo-ong."

3. Give an animal picture from Activity Sheet 31 (*Animal Crackers*) to each child. Help each child chant his or her animal's name, clap the rhythm pattern that emerges, and place the picture in the correct Soup Bowl.

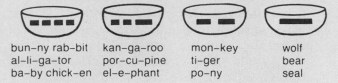

bun–ny rab–bit   kan–ga–roo   mon–key   wolf
al–li–ga–tor   por–cu–pine   ti–ger   bear
ba–by chick–en   el–e–phant   po–ny   seal

4. When all the animal pictures have been placed in a Soup Bowl, ask one child to select four animals and display their pictures in any order he or she wishes. The class then chants the four animal names in order while clapping OPTIONAL

the rhythm pattern that results. Repeat the pattern several times without interrupting the pulse.

5. Play the recording of "Animal Crackers" again. Invite the children to softly chant and tap the animal-cracker pattern from Step 4 as an accompaniment. Then ask another child to prepare a new accompaniment by arranging four different animals in a new order.

6. End the class with an animal-cracker parade. The children should march with the underlying beat, moving as they imagine their favorite animal might move.

push him un-der to drown. Then I bite him in a mil-lion bits, and I gob-ble him right down. When they're in-side me where it's dark, I walk a-roun' like "No-ah's ark." I stuff my tum-my like a "Goop," with an-i-mal crack-ers in my soup.

DESCRIBE 9

Lesson Focus

Melody: A series of pitches may move up, down, or remain the same. *(D–I)*

Materials

o **Record Information:**
- St. Paul's Steeple
  Record 7 Side B Band 2
  Voices: boys' choir
  Accompaniment: handbell choir

o **Instruments:** resonator bells C, D, E, F, G, A, B, and C'; bell mallet

o **Other:** overhead projector; pencil for each child; bell stairsteps for major scale (See Lesson 51, page 108, regarding placement of C major bells on stairsteps.)

o **Teacher's Resource Binder:**

[Activity Sheets] • **Activity Sheet 32**, page A51 (Prepare one copy for each child. Then draw in the melody contours shown below, one on each tree, and prepare a transparency.)

o **Extends Lesson 5**, page 10; **Lesson 25**, page 52

The Lesson

1. Play the recording of "St. Paul's Steeple." Ask the children to "mirror" the up-down contour of the melody with their hands as they listen. (Phrases 1, 2, and 4—down; Phrase 3—up)

2. Display the transparency prepared from Activity Sheet 32 *(St. Paul's Steeple)*. As you play the recording again, trace the contour of the melody on the transparency (each tree equals one phrase) while the children continue to mirror the contour with hand movements. Then challenge the children to sing the melody while you trace the contour on the transparency once more.

3. Distribute a pencil and a copy of the activity sheet to each child. Ask the children to draw their own contours while they sing the song.

4. Place resonator bells on the stairsteps. (See **Materials.**) Choose one child to play the melody of "St. Paul's Steeple." Ask the class to guide the bell player by telling when to move up or down, or by steps or skips.

5. Give several children the opportunity to play the bells while others sing the melody. *OPTIONAL*

St. Paul's Steeple

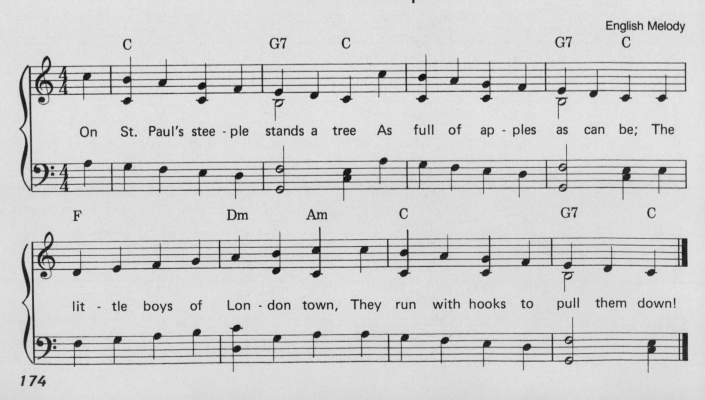

English Melody

On St. Paul's stee-ple stands a tree As full of ap-ples as can be; The lit-tle boys of Lon-don town, They run with hooks to pull them down!

174

Lesson Focus

Rhythm: Individual sounds and silences within a rhythmic line may be longer than, shorter than, or the same as the underlying steady beat. *(D–I)*

Materials

o **Record Information:**
 • Old John Braddleum
 ☐ **Record 7 Side B Band 3**
   Voices: children's choir
   Accompaniment: trumpet, French horn, trombone, tuba
o **Instruments:** resonator bells D, F#, G, and A; bell mallet
o **Other:** rhythm bars (as prepared for Lesson 27, page 56)—melodic rhythm: 4 short bars, 26 long bars; rests: 4 long bars; pulses: 32 long bars
o **Teacher's Resource Binder:**
 • Optional—
   Curriculum Correlation 13, page C21
   Kodaly Activities 6, 7, pages K8, K11
o **Extends Lesson 57,** page 124

The Lesson

1. Display two rows of rhythm bars, using eight pulse bars in each row to show the beat. (See **Materials.**) Establish the beat and sing the first four measures of "Old John Braddleum" while lightly tapping each bar. Ask the children to identify the places where they hear a tap but your voice is silent (Beats 4, 8, and 16).

2. Show the melodic rhythm above the bars that

represent the beat. Sing the first four measures of the song again, this time touching the melodic rhythm bars.

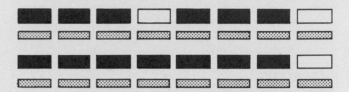

3. Add two more rows of bars to represent the beat (eight in each row) and sing the complete song. **Were there beats where something happened that you hadn't heard before?** Sing the song again if necessary. Help the children recognize that in Row 3 some beats had two sounds ("taddle" and "braddle"). Then show the melodic rhythm of the last four measures of the song with rhythm bars.

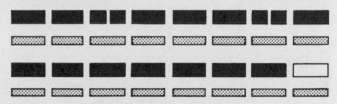

4. **Can you sing the song while I tap the beat?** Establish the tonality by playing D–F#–G–A–D on the resonator bells and encourage the children to sing without your assistance.

Old John Braddleum

Traditional

Num-ber one, num-ber one, This old song has now be-gun.

Rum-tum-tad-dle-um, old John Brad-dle-um, Sail-ing o'er the deep blue sea.

175

DESCRIBE 11

Lesson Focus

Rhythm: Individual sounds and silences within a rhythmic line may be longer than, shorter than, or the same as the underlying shortest pulse. *(D–S)*

Materials

o **Record Information:**
  • Piep, Piep, Mäuschen
  Record 7 Side B Band 4
  Voices: boys' choir
  Accompaniment: string quartet

o **Other:** overhead projector
o **Teacher's Resource Binder:**
  • **Activity Sheets 33a–b**, pages A52–A53 (Prepare a transparency from each activity sheet.)
  • Optional—
  Kodaly Activity 4, page K5
o **Extends Lesson 39**, page 84

For Your Information

Pronunciation for the German lyrics:
  Phrases 1, 3: peep peep **moy**-shen
      blahyb in **dahy**-nem **hoy**-shen
  Phrase 2: **ah**-le **klahy**-nen **moy**-seh-lahyn
      zint in **eeh**-rem **hoy**-seh-lahyn

Piep, Piep, Mäuschen (Peep, Peep, Little Mouse)

Words Adapted

German Folk Song

The Lesson

1. Display the transparency prepared from Activity Sheet 33a (*Piep, Piep, Mäuschen*). Challenge the children to learn a new song by reading the rhythm shown with "rhythm bars." Establish the underlying short sound; then ask the children to chant the rhythm of the melody, using the words "short" and "long."

2. Play the recording of "Piep, Piep, Mäuschen." **Does the rhythm you chanted sound like the rhythm of this melody?** (yes) Place the transparency prepared from Activity Sheet 33b (*Stems*) over the other transparency. **What has happened to our picture?** (Lines or "stems" have been added.) **If I took**

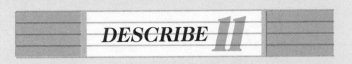

away the rhythm bars, could you still tell when the sounds should be short and when they should be long? (Yes, because when there are two short sounds, the stems are connected across the top with a bar.) Chant the rhythm again with the class, using "short" and "long." Then help them learn the song words.

3. Play the recording again while the children follow the transparency prepared from Activity Sheet 33b. Then challenge them to sing the song. Replay the recording as needed.

Lesson Focus

Expression: The expressiveness of music is affected by the way timbre contributes to the musical whole. *(D–E)*

Materials

o **Record Information:**
- *Sword Dance*
  by Herbert Donaldson, 1918-
  Record 7 Side B Band 5
o **Instruments:** claves; triangle and striker
o **Extends Lesson 1,** page 1

The Lesson

1. Encourage the children to explore movement ideas by responding to your verbal and sound imagery. Play short, sharp clicking sounds on the claves and suggest that the children:

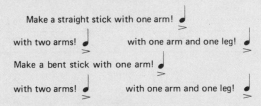

2. Contrast the short clicking sounds with long, ringing sustained sounds played on the triangle:

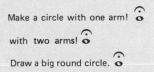

3. Play the recording of *Sword Dance*. Draw attention to the gong that begins the piece, to the heavy accented chords and rapid short sounds, and to the return of the gong at the end of the piece.

4. Play the recording again and invite the children to move to the music. They should begin in a closed position and slowly open up as they hear the sound of the gong. They may move with jabbing, thrusting gestures to represent the heavy accented chords and rapid short sounds. The children should return to a closed position at the end of the music.

Lesson Focus

Rhythm: Individual sounds and silences within a rhythmic line may be longer than, shorter than, or the same as the underlying shortest pulse.
Melody: A series of pitches may move up or down by steps or skips. *(D–I)*

Materials

o **Record Information:**
  • Bow-wow-wow
  Record 7 Side B Band 6
  Voices: solo children's voices, children's choir
  Accompaniment: oboe, trombone, string ensemble, harpsichord, percussion

o **Instrument:** hand drum

o **Teacher's Resource Binder:**

Activity Sheets
  • **Activity Sheets 34a–b**, pages A54–A55 (Prepare one copy of each activity sheet for each child and cut into strips.)
  • Optional—
  Enrichment Activity 12, page E20
  Kodaly Activity 9, page K14
  Orff Activity 11, page O14

o **Extends Lesson 36**, page 78

The Lesson

1. **We are going to play a rhythm game!** Hand each child a copy of Activity Sheet 34a *(Bow-wow-wow—Rhythm)* cut into strips. **Listen to this song. Can you put your pictures in order to show the rhythm of the song?** (correct order, using illustration shown at beginning of each strip—dog, question mark, face, dog) Sing the melody several times while tapping the shortest sound on a hand drum.

2. Discuss each rhythm picture. **What happens at the end of the first picture?** (must be silent for two short sounds) **How is the second picture different from the first?** (includes two short sounds in place of one long sound) **What happens in the third picture?** (short sounds until the last sound, which is long) **in the fourth picture?** (same as first picture)

3. Give each child a copy of Activity Sheet 34b *(Bow-wow-wow—Melody)* cut into strips. Follow the same procedure as in Steps 1 and 2. Discuss the way each melody picture moves, using the words up, down, same, step, or skip.

4. Ask the class to sing the song while following the melody pictures from Step 3.

Bow-wow-wow

Mother Goose Rhyme
Additional Verse by B. A.

Traditional

2. Meow, meow, meow, Whose cat art thou? Little Arabella's cat, Meow, meow, meow.

3. What's this now? Is there a row? Cats and dogs don't mix, I know, Meow, bow-wow!

Lesson Focus

Expression: The expressiveness of music is affected by the way timbre, melody, and harmony contribute to the musical whole. *(D–I)*

Materials

o Record Information:
   • *Peter and the Wolf*
     by Sergei Prokofiev (pruh-**kaw**-fee-yef),
     1891–1953
     Record 8 Side B
     Cyril Ritchard, narrator
     Philadelphia Orchestra
     Eugene Ormandy, conductor
o Teacher's Resource Binder:
   • Optional—
     Biography 8, pages B15–B16
     Enrichment Activity 14, page E21
o **Extends Lesson 17,** page 34

The Lesson

1. **Do you remember a musical story we heard earlier this year?** (*The Three Little Pigs,* Lesson 17, page 34) **Today we're going to hear a new musical story about a boy and a wolf. In this story each person and animal has its own melody played by a special instrument or instruments. I'd like you to meet the people and animals in our story and hear the instruments that play their special melodies.**

2. Play the opening section of *Peter and the Wolf.* Pause after each character has been introduced and name that character's instrument or instrument group for the children. Then help them tell why they think the instrument(s) and melody are good choices for that character. Some possible reasons for choices of instrument and musical sounds are:

   Bird/Flute Light quality of the instrument sound suggests a bird song, as does the quick, high movement of the melody.
   Duck/Oboe Nasal quality of the instrument sound resembles a duck's quacking; the tune seems to "waddle" as it moves up–down–back–forth.
   Cat/Clarinet The clarinet sound suggests a "meow"; the tune seems to "sneak" along softly and more slowly than the other melodies.
   Grandfather/Bassoon Deep, low quality of the instrument sound suggests a grumpy grandfather who may not be too pleased with his grandson's actions.

   Wolf/French horns Dark quality of the instrument sounds suggests a scary wolf.
   Peter/Strings Lilting, "happy-go-lucky" melody bounces around, moving quickly from high to low; suggests someone skipping about, perhaps whistling a happy tune.
   Hunters (rifle shots)/Timpani The roaring sound of the timpani reminds us that the hunters are shooting their guns.

3. When the children are familiar with the characters and the sound of each special instrument and melody, play the remainder of the piece.

4. Ask the children to identify their favorite instrument/character and encourage them to verbalize why they liked that instrument/character the best. **How was your favorite instrument used to make the story more exciting?**

5. On subsequent hearings, emphasize other aspects of the music that help tell the story:
   • the "conversation" between the strings and flute after Peter and the bird have been introduced
   • the argument between the bird and the duck as played by the flute and oboe
   • the sound of the bird flying up into the tree
   • the duck angrily quacking at the cat from the middle of the pond
   • the bird sitting in the tree while the cat circles below
   • the cat scampering up the tree when the wolf appears
   • the sad music when the duck is swallowed
   • the fast music as the bird flies down and circles round the wolf's head
   • the sound of the wolf snapping at the circling bird
   • the sound of the rope being slowly lowered by Peter (played by the strings) and the sound of the brasses as the wolf tries to get free of the rope
   • the marching tune of the hunters as they come out of the woods
   • the sounds of the triumphant procession—Peter's melody played by brasses, the hunters' marching tune played by trumpet
   • the fragment of the oboe melody at the end when the duck is discovered alive inside the wolf

Create Music

Organizing Musical Ideas and Musical Sounds

In *HOLT MUSIC* the term "creative" is used to describe activities that focus on organizing musical ideas and musical sounds in new ways. Children may engage in musical creativity by improvising or by composing. Improvisation occurs when the child simultaneously organizes musical ideas and produces musical sounds. He or she is composer and performer at the same time. Composition can be defined as the act of organizing musical sounds and recording them in some way so that they can be reproduced in exactly the same form at a later time.

Young children should be encouraged to improvise and eventually compose in a variety of ways, using their voices or instruments. As they learn to represent sounds ikonically, they may use this new-found ability to record their musical ideas.

Improvising Music Vocally

Very young children frequently improvise by singing their own "made-up" songs; such songs are often rambling pitched lines. Children improvise vocally as a way of exploring their own abilities; they will experiment with the production of varied sound qualities and will often combine words in ways they might not when speaking. Encourage this experimentation by using any of the following strategies.

- Provide the children with a variety of models for vocal improvisation. For example, announce that everyone has entered Music Land (see Perform 1, page 134) and all conversations must be sung. Sing classroom instructions; make up your own tunes:

- Introduce a chant or easily memorized poem; after the children can easily recite the chant or poem, improvise a melody together. You begin by improvising a melody for the first line; invite the children to respond with their own melodic improvisation for each subsequent line.

DOWN! DOWN!
by Eleanor Farjeon

Down, down!
Yellow and brown
The leaves are falling over the town.

NEW SHOES
by Alice Wilkins

I have new shoes in the fall-time
And new ones in the spring.
Whenever I wear my new shoes,
I always have to sing!

- Provide "silly" ideas for vocal improvisation. **What if all the objects in our room started singing? Let's pretend our pets can sing! What would they say?**
- Use pictures or comic strips as stimulus for vocal improvisation. The children can sing their descriptions of the suggested story or sing the words shown in the comic strip.

Improvising Music Instrumentally

Early instrumental improvisations should be truly exploratory. Create a "Composer's Corner" in the classroom. Each week put a different instrument in the corner; choose instruments that can produce a variety of sound qualities and/or pitches. Give each child time to go to the corner to explore freely. Later leave two instruments in the corner; the children may go there alone or in pairs to engage in "conversations."

Gradually add structure to the explorations.
- Encourage the children to express specific kinds of ideas—sleepy sounds, funny sounds, or scary sounds, the sounds of swinging on the playground swing, sliding down the slippery slide, or riding on the merry-go-round, rainy sounds, sunny sounds, or cloudy sounds.
- Invite the children to improvise introductions, interludes, or codas for familiar songs on pitched or nonpitched instruments.
- Set up resonator bells or xylophone bars for a pentatonic or a whole tone scale; invite the children to create their own melodies.

Pentatonic scales:	C–D–E–G–A
	D–E–F#–A–B
Whole tone scale:	Bb–C–D–E–F#–G#

Later invite two children to work together. One child could play an accompaniment using two pitches from the scale; the other child plays a melody that moves freely over the designated pitches.

Accompanist pitches	Soloist pitches
C, D	C–D–E–G–A
E, F#	Bb–C–D–E–F#–G#

Lesson Focus

Rhythm: Individual sounds and silences within a rhythmic line may be longer than, shorter than, or the same as the underlying shortest pulse. *(C–E)*

Materials

o **Record Information:**
  - Amasee
    Record 7 Side B Band 7
    Voices: man, children's choir
    Accompaniment: synthesizer, electronic drums
o **Instruments:** rhythm sticks; miscellaneous percussion instruments and beaters
o **Extends Lesson 11,** page 22

The Lesson

1. Begin by tapping the shortest sound on your thigh while you chant.

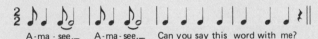

A-ma-see,— A-ma-see,— Can you say this word with me?

Invite the children to join you in tapping and chanting. Repeat the chant several times.

2. Change the words of the chant to "Amasee, Amasee, can you sing this song for me?" Then sing the song "Amasee" while the children continue to tap the shortest sound. Repeat the song several times, each time followed by the chant. Invite the children to sing the melody with you.

3. Help the children learn the actions suggested by the song. Arrange the class in two lines so that each child faces a partner. **Before we begin we must have a player to show us how to go "down the line."** Give one child a set of rhythm sticks. Encourage the child to make up his or her own rhythm pattern; the pattern should last as long as it takes the first set of partners to reach the foot of the line.

4. Perform a complete event. Choose three children to be instrument players. Each child may choose an instrument. (See **Materials.**) Combine chant, instrumental improvisation, and the line dance as follows:

   Introduction: Teacher chants—"Amasee, Amasee, can you play just for me?"
   Player 1 improvises a pattern.
   Song: Class sings Verse 1 of the song while standing in place.
   Interlude: Player 2 improvises a pattern while the head couple moves to the end of the line.
   Song: Class sings Verse 2 of the song.
   Interlude: Player 3 improvises a pattern while all couples go to the center and swing their partners once around.

Amasee

Traditional Black American Song

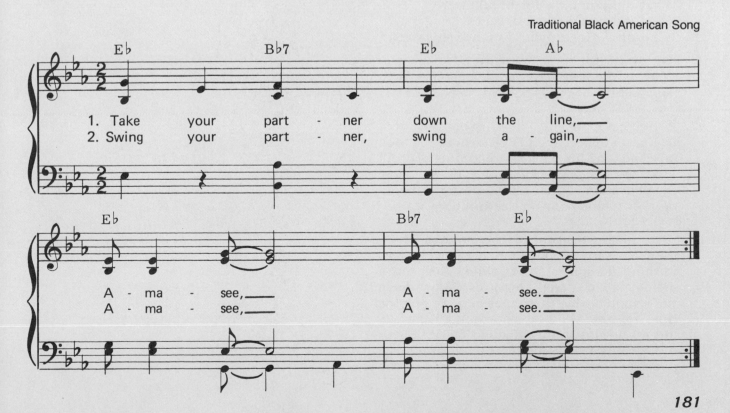

Lesson Focus

Melody: Each pitch within a melody moves in relation to a home tone. *(C–E)*

Materials

o **Record Information:**
  • All That Was Left
    Record 7 Side B Band 8
    Voices: children's choir
    Accompaniment: harmonica, electric guitar, double bass, piano, percussion
o **Instrument:** autoharp
o **Extends Lesson 52,** page 110

The Lesson

1. Begin class with a singing conversation; improvise a melody while giving the following instructions. **We're on our way to Music Land. Here's my magic wand.** (Pretend to wave a wand.) **No one can be heard unless they're using their singing voice.** For the remainder of the class, sing all instructions, questions, and answers.

   Begin by carrying on a conversation with individual children.

   Good morning; how are you feeling today?
   I like that red dress; is it new?
   What did you have for breakfast?
   What did you do during recess?
   What are you studying in math this week?

   You may wish to accompany the conversations on the autoharp; move back and forth between the C and G7 chords.

2. Without stopping the "flow" of conversation, begin to walk around the classroom and then talk and sing (or play the recording of) "All That Was Left." (As the song evolves, follow the chord indications on the music and continue to accompany on the autoharp.)

3. After singing the song for the children, invite them to "turn speaking into singing" by performing this song. Ask one child to make up a melody for the final measures. (Slow down the tempo during these measures to provide time for the child's response.) Encourage, but do not insist, on the child ending his or her melody with a feeling of "closure." Explain that one way to do this is to end on the sound of a home tone. Pluck the C string on the autoharp so the children can hear the home tone for this song.

4. After many children have improvised the final two measures of "All That Was Left," provide an opportunity for them to create another, longer song. Play a different, alternating chordal accompaniment on the autoharp, this time moving between the C and A minor chords. Have the children take turns making up a melody on a neutral syllable. Encourage them to develop longer ideas so that their melodies become more like songs than just short musical patterns. The children may make up words for their melodies if they wish.

All That Was Left

Words and Music by B.A.

I start-ed out talk-in' one warm sum-mer day. Be-

fore I knew what hap-pened, My talk-in' went a-way.

Refrain

All that was left was a song to sing, song to sing, song to sing.

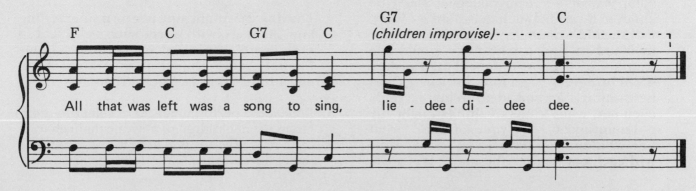

All that was left was a song to sing, lie-dee-di-dee dee.

(children improvise)

183

Lesson Focus

Expression: The expressiveness of music is affected by the way melody contributes to the musical whole. *(C–E)*

Materials

o **Instruments:** drum and mallet
o **Extends Lesson 28,** page 58

The Lesson

1. Tell the children a story about a million cats.

   Once upon a time an old woman decided that she would like a cat. Her husband set out to find her a beautiful cat. As he traveled he not only found one cat, he gathered millions of cats! When he returned home with the cats, the old woman knew that they could not keep them all; so they decided to keep just one, the prettiest one. The cats began to fuss over who was the prettiest, and a great fight ensued. During the fight, the old woman and man noticed one little tiny cat sitting under a tree; she didn't think she was at all pretty and thought that she would never be chosen. The old woman and old man decided that this cat was the prettiest and chose her to live with them.

2. Ask the children to turn the story into a play. Help them follow these steps:
   - Assign roles: Choose children to play the old man, the old woman, and the special cat; everyone else may be the many other cats.
   - Set the stage: Decide where the couple's house should be and where the husband will go on his travels; identify the place for the tree under which the special cat will sit.
   - Develop dialogue: Each character can develop his or her own dialogue. Help the children by asking such questions as: **What will the old woman say when she asks her husband to find a cat? Why would she want a cat? What will the old man answer when he agrees to go look for a cat? Does he think it's a good idea? When he finds each cat, what kinds of things might the old man say?** ("I like your soft fur," "what fine whiskers you have," and so on.) **How will each cat answer the man? When the** **fight begins, will the cats take turns talking or will they all talk at the same time?**
   - Plan movement: Discuss where the old man and woman will be as the play begins—will they be seated? standing? How will the old man move as he walks around the room? What are some ways each cat might move? How will the cats show with movements that each thinks he or she is the most beautiful? Will the cats move the same way when they are fighting? What will happen when the old man and woman choose the special cat? What will that cat do? What will the other cats do?

3. After planning the dialogue and movement, tell the children that they may sing their dialogue as they act out the story. **All the people and cats get to sing their words rather than just speak them.**

4. After performing the play once, discuss ways the dialogue, movement, and improvised songs might be improved. To help the children refine their parts, ask such questions as: **Will the old man sing his words very high or very low? what about the old woman? Could we add some sounds as the old man is walking around the room?** (a drum beat —going faster, slower; stopping and starting) **Would you use the same sound to accompany the cats as they walk?**

   Experiment to help the children develop a "Cat-Singing Vocabulary." Explore patterns such as the following:

   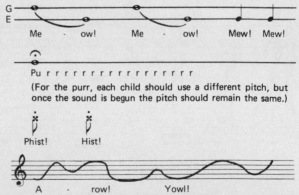

   The tiny cat might sing her own song telling how she feels, with words such as: "I feel so sad. There's no point in fighting; I know I'm not pretty. I'll just sit and watch; if you don't mind, that is. Then I'll go away . . ."

5. Repeat the performance, after selecting a different set of children to play the main characters. After the second rendition, encourage the children to evaluate their performance.

Lesson Focus

Harmony: Two or more musical lines may occur simultaneously.
Expression: The expressiveness of music is affected by the way melody and rhythm contribute to the musical whole. *(C–I)*

Materials

o **Instruments:** resonator bells, glockenspiels, or xylophones—use pitch combinations C, D, E, G, and A or D, F, G, A, and B or E♭, F, G, A, B, and D♭ in as many octaves as available, or piano, using only black keys; mallets
o **Other:** paper and pencil for each child
o **Extends Lesson 49,** page 104

The Lesson

1. Teach the children the rhyme, "Tillie Tassle."

> Tillie Tassle went on a trip,
> Up the hills, down the dips.
> She twisted and turned,
> Bounced up and down,
> Hit the ceiling,
> Then fell on the ground!

2. When the children can chant the rhyme easily, put out a pitched instrument. (See **Materials.**) Invite one child to improvise a melody while the other children continue to chant. **Which way should the melody go at first? Then what should happen? Will the melody move up for a long time before changing direction?**

3. Choose another child to improvise a melody; perform the rhyme again. This time, draw a picture of the contour on the chalkboard as the child improvises. Your contour might look like this:

Look, I've made a picture of your music! I wonder if someone else could play this same picture! Choose another child to perform while the class listens. Discuss the pattern just played; all may agree that it was similar to the previous pattern but probably not exactly the same.

4. Hand out a sheet of paper and a pencil to each child. Invite the children to "compose" another melody for the rhyme by drawing the ups and downs. Give several children the opportunity to play their melodies for the class.

5. Invite the children to prepare a second melody to play with the rhyme. This accompanying melody might move in a different way, with only a little movement up and down.

While one child plays a melody based more closely on the up-down ideas in the rhyme, a second child can play the other "strand of sound" on a different quality instrument; both children should use pitches from the same group. For example, Child 1 might play on a glockenspiel while Child 2 plays on a bass xylophone. Or Child 1 might play on the upper pitches of the piano while Child 2 plays on the lower pitches. **Can you make your melodies move with different rhythms?** Suggest that Child 1 use mostly short sounds while Child 2 uses mostly long or lo-ong sounds. Have each pair of children perform their melodies while the class chants the rhyme.

6. *OPTIONAL* The following are some other poems that suggest melodic directions. Use these poems for additional improvisational activities; follow a similar sequence as in Steps 1 through 5.

THE WIND

> The Wind blew low;
> The Wind blew high;
> It touched everything
> As it went by.

LIKE A LEAF
by Emilie Poulsson

> Like a leaf or a feather
> In the windy, windy weather,
> We'll whirl about and twirl about
> And all sink down together.

TOMMY TAMBER
by E. B.

> Tommy Tamber went to town,
> Sometimes up and sometimes down;
> All along the street he wound,
> Twisting, turning,
> Up and down.

Lesson Focus

Expression: Musical elements are combined into a whole to express a musical or extramusical idea. *(C–I)*

Materials

o **Instruments:** assorted classroom instruments such as the following—glockenspiels; xylophones (any size); sand blocks; woodblock; guiro and scratcher; finger cymbals; large cymbals; large and small drums and beaters; temple blocks; cowbell; maracas; ratchet (optional); autoharp; piano; mallets

o **Other:** overhead projector; tape recorder and recording tape

o **Teacher's Resource Binder:**

Activity Sheets
 • **Activity Sheet 35,** page A56 (Prepare a transparency from the activity sheet.)
 • Optional—
 Curriculum Correlation 6, page C9

o **Extends Lesson 8,** page 16

The Lesson

1. Read the following story to the children as expressively as possible.

A GHOST STORY
by Bill Martin Jr.

In a dark dark woods there is a dark dark house.

In the dark dark house there is a dark dark stair.

Down the dark dark stair there is a dark dark cellar.

In the dark dark cellar there is a dark dark cupboard.

In the dark dark cupboard there is a dark dark bottle.

In the dark dark bottle there is an evil spirit.

Slowly, slowly the evil spirit pushes out the cork.

Now he floats . . .

. . . out of the dark dark bottle through the dark dark cupboard,

out of the dark dark cupboard through the dark dark cellar,

out of the dark dark cellar up the dark dark stair,

out of the dark dark stair through the dark dark house,

out of the dark dark house through the dark dark woods,

out of the dark dark woods into your dark dark . . . pocket.

He's got you!

2. Discuss the story and the suggested mood. Then display the transparency prepared from Activity Sheet 35 (*A Ghost Story*). Discuss each picture and the kind of sounds that might suggest it. Invite the class to select and experiment with a variety of classroom instruments as well as body sounds. Direct the children's exploration so as to focus on which sounds will be most appropriate and how they should be played to be most effective. Choose the best sound(s) for each box. Some possible ideas follow.

Box 1: large cymbal played softly; big drum touched rapidly to create a "rolling sound"; low keys played on the piano

Box 2: high-pitched drum; woodblock

Box 3: same as for Box 2 but with faster rhythm

Box 4: guiro

Box 5: squeaking or scratchy sound to suggest a door opening, such as scraping a cowbell

Box 6: descending sounds on mallet instrument

Box 7: low-pitched sounds, such as moving downward on bass xylophone or piano

Box 8: temple blocks

Box 9: finger cymbals

Box 10: run fingers over autoharp or shake a maraca

Box 11: single sound on woodblock

Box 12: glissandos on glockenspiel

Box 13: loud clap on cymbals

3. When the class has decided on the sounds and playing techniques for each part of the story, read the story again and have the children add the sounds at the appropriate times. (The children may decide where to perform the sounds for Boxes 1–3.) Suspense may gradually be built up to the point of a surprise ending by getting faster or slower and/or louder or softer, beginning with the words, "Now he floats."

4. After exploring sounds and carefully practicing each part of the story, tape the children's performance. Have them listen to the tape recording and each choose a favorite part. **Why do you like this part best?** Help them realize that it may be because the sounds/patterns are particularly effective during that part of the story. Discuss ways of improving other sections.

Perform the story again and retape. Give the children as many opportunities as they wish to modify the composition until they are pleased with the final musical effect.

Lesson Focus

Form: A musical whole may include an introduction, interludes, and an ending segment. *(P–E)*

Materials

o **Record Information:**
  • An Amer"I"can
    Record 7 Side B Band 9
    Voices: children's choir
    Accompaniment: piccolo, trumpet, French horn, trombone, guitar, double bass, piano, percussion
o **Instruments:** drum
o **Teacher's Resource Binder:**
  • **Activity Sheets 41–42**, pages A62–A63 (Prepare a copy of each sheet for display.)
o **Extends Lesson 43**, page 92

The Lesson

1. Play the recording of "An Amer'I'can." The children may form a line and march around the room while listening. **Can you march proudly and step with the steady beat?**

2. Listen again and discuss the words. Invite the children to join in on the spoken phrase, "Yes, sir" as they listen again. After several hearings, ask them to sing the song.

3. Expand the parade from Step 1 by adding a chant as an introduction, interlude, and coda. Help the children think of Presidents and other people who have helped make our country great. Insert their names in a chant:

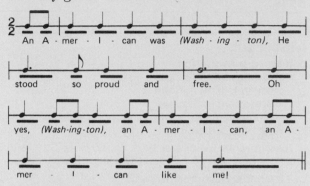

4. Add an accompaniment to the parade.

5. Throughout the year encourage the children to think about each individual's importance to our country by celebrating each child's birthday. Use Activity Sheets 41–42 (*Each Person Is Important* and *Birthday Calendar*) to create a bulletin-board display. The birthday child could be invited to point to the rhythm bars on Activity Sheet 42 while the other children sing "Happy Birthday."

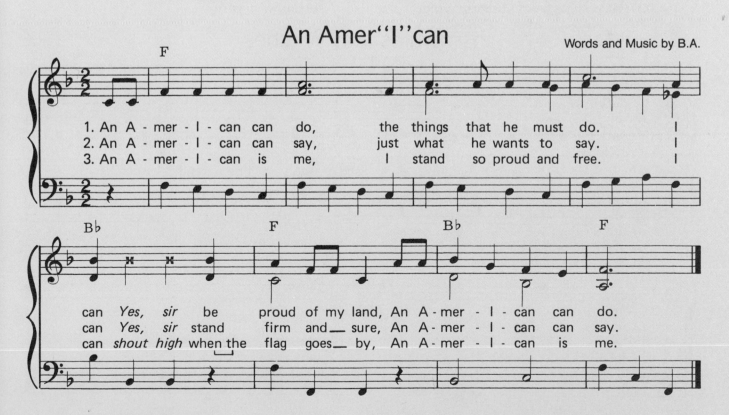

An Amer"I"can

Words and Music by B.A.

1. An A-mer-I-can can do, the things that he must do. I can *Yes, sir* be proud of my land, An A-mer-I-can can do.
2. An A-mer-I-can can say, just what he wants to say. I can *Yes, sir* stand firm and sure, An A-mer-I-can can say.
3. An A-mer-I-can is me, I stand so proud and free. I can *shout high* when the flag goes by, An A-mer-I-can is me.

187

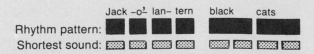

SPECIAL TIMES 2

Lesson Focus

Expression: The expressiveness of music is affected by the way rhythm and melody contribute to the musical whole. *(P–E)*

Materials

o **Record Information:**
  • Brownies and Witches
  Record 8 Side A Band 1
  Voices: children's choir
  Accompaniment: bowed piano, prepared piano, sound effects, percussion

o **Instruments:** resonator bells C#, D, E, F, G, A, and B♭; xylophone with D, E, F, and D' bars in place; mallets

o **Teacher's Resource Binder:**
  Activity Sheets • **Activity Sheets 43–44,** pages A64–A65 (Prepare a copy of each sheet for display.)

o **Extends Lesson 13,** page 26

The Lesson

1. Ask the children to name the things they think of when someone says "Halloween." List the words on the chalkboard. They might include: Jack-o'-lantern, trick or treat, black cats, goblins, witches, scary sounds, ghosts. *OPTIONAL*

2. Chant the words listed on the chalkboard while tapping the shortest sound. Speak expressively, using a scary, breathy voice.

Invite the children to chant with you. Encourage them to change the pitch level of their voices as they chant.

3. Put out resonator bells (see **Materials**) and invite one child to play a scary accompaniment while the other children continue to chant.

   Sing "Brownies and Witches." Add an expressive "Boo!" at the end. Ask the children to show the melodic shape as you sing the song again. They may join in on the "Boo!". Then invite the class to sing the song for you.

4. Perform the song while one child adds the following accompaniment on a xylophone.

   Add the scary chant from Step 2 as an introduction and coda.

5. Use Activity Sheets 43–44 (*Special Times Need Music* and *Special-Times Shapes*) to create a bulletin-board display for use throughout the year. Attach the appropriate shapes from Activity Sheet 44 for each holiday. You might also display holiday-relevant chants with rhythm bars or melodic contours shown with yarn.

Brownies and Witches

Words and Music by Mayme Christenson and J. Wolverton

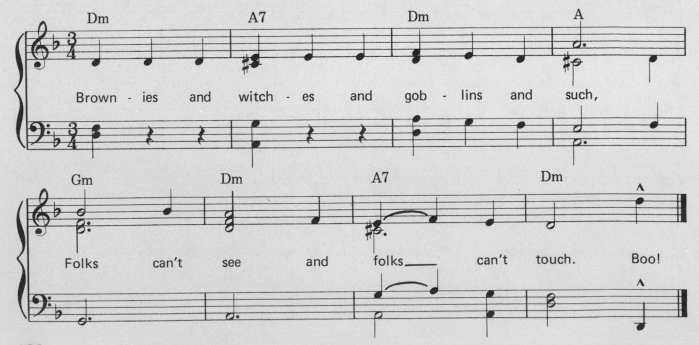

Lesson Focus

Expression: The expressiveness of music is affected by the way melody contributes to the musical whole. *(C–E)*

Materials

o **Extends Lesson 28**, page 58

The Lesson

1. Discuss with the children their plans for Halloween costumes. **Will you be a ghost, a goblin, a space traveler?** After talking about the children's Halloween costumes, begin to sing:

Hey, old ghost, are you com-ing out to-night?

2. Choose one child to be the ghost. The ghost may answer your sung question by singing any words and melodic pattern he or she wishes. The melody may be random with little organization:

Lesson Focus

Expression: Musical elements are combined into a whole to express a musical or extramusical idea. *(D–E)*

Materials

o **Record Information:**
  • Polka from *Age of Gold Ballet Suite* by Dimitri Shostakovich (shawss-tah-**kaw**-vich), 1906–1975
    Record 8 Side A Band 2
    André Kostelanetz and his Orchestra
o **Extends Lesson 2**, page 4

For Your Information

Form of "Polka":
Section 1: Introduction—clarinet, then brass.
Section 2: Xylophone plays main melody.
Section 3: Clarinet plays variation on melody from Section 2.
Section 4: Clarinet plays a new melody; tempo increases; melody is extended by English horn.
Section 5: Trumpet plays a new tune with string and snare drum accompaniment.
Section 6: Clarinet, flute, woodblock, and triangle develop tune from Section 5; section is repeated.
Section 7: Strings play another melody.
Section 8: Flute plays with string accompaniment.
Section 9: Bridgelike section—various instruments "comment," playing short phrases; ends with contrabassoon solo.

SPECIAL TIMES 3

No!
absolutely NOT! of course NOT!
I wouldn't come out if you begged me.
Wild horses couldn't make me come out.

3. Invite the class to respond to the ghost:

Why not, old ghost?

The ghost then improvises another sung answer:

I'm busy haunting a house.
I'm cookin' supper... watching TV
I'm afraid of the dark!

4. Repeat the game with another child, substituting the term that describes the costume that child plans to wear.

SPECIAL TIMES 4

Section 10: Coda—xylophone recalls original melody; tempo increases briefly; brass recalls trumpet melody from Section 5.

The Lesson

1. Play the "Polka" from the *Age of Gold Ballet Suite.* Suggest that the children create a Halloween parade with each child portraying a funny character. Then play the recording once again. **Can you decide when someone new enters the parade?** Guide the class to sense the changes in instrumentation and melody. (See **For Your Information.**)

2. Divide the class into eight groups to represent Sections 2 through 9 of the "Polka." Everyone stands still during the Introduction. Each group then moves only during "their" music. Groups 2 and 5 will move during the Coda because their melodies return. Play the recording again and guide the groups to move appropriately.

SPECIAL TIMES 5

Lesson Focus

Texture: Musical quality is affected by the number of musical lines occurring simultaneously.

Timbre: The total sound is affected by the number and qualities of sounds occurring at the same time. *(D–I)*

Materials

o **Record Information:**
  • Thank You
    Record 8 Side A Band 3
    Voices: children's choir
    Accompaniment: trumpet, French horn, trombone, tuba, harp
o **Other:** a pencil for each child
o **Teacher's Resource Binder:**
  [Activity Sheets] • **Activity Sheet 36,** page A57 (Prepare a copy for each child.)
o **Extends Lesson 14,** page 28

For Your Information

Form of recording of ''Thank You'':
  Section 1: Introduction—brass quartet
  Section 2: Verse—brass and choir
  Section 3: Instrumental Verse—harp
  Section 4: Verse—brass and choir
  Section 5: Verse—choir, brass, and harp
  Section 6: Coda—brass and harp

The Lesson

1. Play the recording of "Thank You." Discuss the different things the children might be thankful for. Play the recording again after asking the children to think about the feelings suggested by the different sounds heard on the recording. **Does the music always sound the same?** (Answers will vary.)

2. Distribute a copy of Activity Sheet 36 (*Thank You*) to each child. Discuss the different pictures; identify the instruments for the children (brass quartet: trumpet, French horn, trombone, tuba; harp). Talk about the differences in sound between the brass and the harp. Invite the children to suggest words that describe the different qualities of sound. (There are no "correct" terms; encourage the children to devise their own.)

3. Give each child a pencil. Play the Introduction and identify the sound as that of the brass quartet. Show the children how to circle the correct picture.

4. Play the recording, pausing after each section to allow the children time to circle a picture. When the activity sheet has been completed, discuss the answers. (See **For Your Information.**)

5. Invite the children to sing the melody during Section 3 (when the choir is not singing).

Thank You

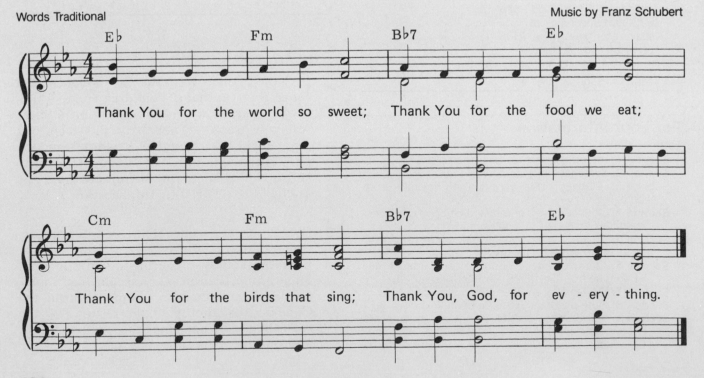

Words Traditional

Music by Franz Schubert

Thank You for the world so sweet; Thank You for the food we eat;

Thank You for the birds that sing; Thank You, God, for ev - ery - thing.

Lesson Focus

Rhythm: Music may move in relation to the underlying shortest pulse. *(D–I)*

Materials

o **Record Information:**
  - Hanukah Hayom
  - **Record 8 Side A Band 4**
    Voices: children's choir
    Accompaniment: clarinet, trumpet, trombone, tuba, violin, double bass, mandolin, cimbalom, accordion, percussion
o **Teacher's Resource Binder:**
  - **Activity Sheet 37**, page A58 (Cut apart the four segments, or copy each pattern onto an 8″ × 11″ sheet.)
o **Other:** rhythm bars (as prepared for Lesson 27, page 56)—melodic rhythm: 4 short bars, 2 long bars
o **Extends Lesson 35**, page 72

For Your Information

Hanukah, the Festival of Lights, is a Jewish holiday that is celebrated in December and lasts eight days. The holiday commemorates a time when the Jews drove their Syrian oppressors from the temple in Judea. An important part of the celebration is the Menorah, a candleholder with eight branches; one additional candle is lit each evening at sunset as part of the celebration. Children celebrate Hanukah by eating special foods, playing games, and giving and receiving gifts.

Pronunciation for the Hebrew lyrics:
  hah-noo-kah hah-yawm.
  yawm-sim-hah, hahg hah hah-noo-kah.
Translation: Today is Hanukah—a happy day.

The Lesson

1. Listen to the recording of "Hanukah Hayom." Discuss the holiday, Hanukah, and translate the song lyrics for the children. (See **For Your Information**.)

2. Listen again and invite the children to lightly tap the underlying short pulse. As they tap and listen, show the rhythm of the first two measures with rhythm bars. (See **Materials**.)

3. Ask the children to listen once again and show the rhythm of the words. They should tap on the short sounds, clap on the long sounds, and slide palms together on the lo-ong sounds.

4. Hand out the four phrases shown on Activity Sheet 37 (*Hanukah Hayom*) to four children, in random order. Ask the class to listen carefully to the music and arrange the phrases in the correct order (A D B C).

5. **Can you sing the song?** Choose one child to be the conductor and to point to the patterns. Listen to the recording again as necessary.

Hanukah Hayom

Words and Music by Judith K. Eisenstein and Frieda Prensky

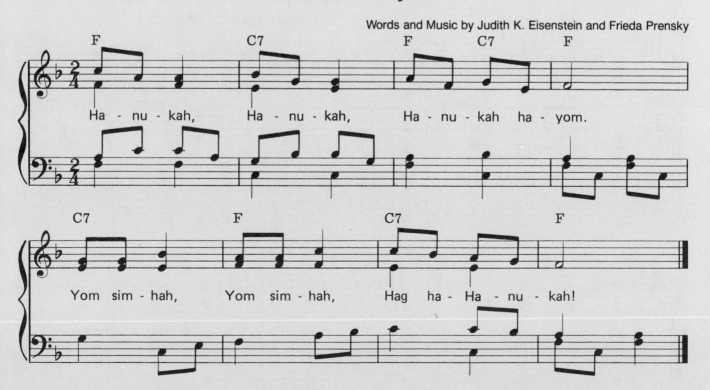

Ha - nu - kah, Ha - nu - kah, Ha - nu - kah ha - yom.

Yom sim - hah, Yom sim - hah, Hag ha - Ha - nu - kah!

o **Teacher's Resource Binder:**

Activity Sheets
- **Activity Sheet 38**, page A59 (Make one copy for each child and cut apart the pictures. Mix up each set of pictures before distributing.)
- Optional—
Mainstreaming Suggestion 20, page M18

o **Extends Lesson 54**, page 114

Lesson Focus

Form: A musical whole is a combination of smaller segments. *(D–I)*

Materials

o **Record Information:**
- Must Be Santa
- **Record 8 Side A Band 5**
  Voices: man, children's choir
  Accompaniment: flute, electric guitar, electric bass, electric piano, percussion

The Lesson

1. Ask the children the questions posed in the song: **Who's got a beard that's long and white? Who comes around on a special night? Who's got boots and a suit of red?** When the children have given the answers, play the recording of "Must Be Santa."

Must Be Santa

Words and Music by Hal Moore and Bill Fredericks

1. Who's got a beard that's long and white? San-ta's got a beard that's long and white. Who comes a-round on a spe-cial night? San-ta comes a-round on a spe-cial night.

*Repeat melody with added text, starting with Verse 2

Spe-cial night, beard that's white,

192

2. **Listen again; something unusual happens in this song. Can you tell me what it is?** Help the children conclude that the unusual "happening" is that each verse is longer than the one before because more words are repeated in the middle section.

3. Hand out a set of pictures from Activity Sheet 38 (*Must Be Santa*) to each child. Play the recording again and ask the children to put the pictures in order. (Replay the recording as necessary.)

4. **If we watch the pictures, it should help us remember the song!** Sing the song as a dialogue (as on the recording): You sing the questions and the children sing the answers. All sing the repeated section and the refrain together.

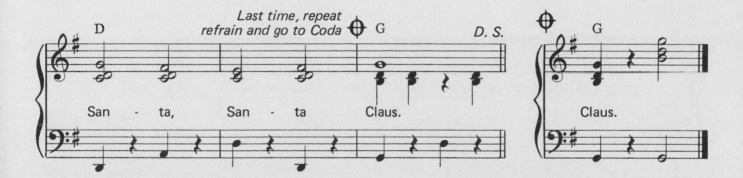

2. Who's got boots and a suit of red?
   Santa's got...
   Who wears a long cap on his head?
   Santa wears...
   * Cap on head, suit that's red,
   Special night, beard that's white,
   Refrain

3. Who's got a great big cherry nose?
   Santa's got...
   Who laughs this way, "Ho, ho, ho?"
   Santa laughs...
   * Ho, ho, ho, cherry nose,
   Cap on head, suit that's red,
   Special night, beard that's white,
   Refrain

4. Who very soon will come our way?
   Santa very...
   Eight little reindeer pull his sleigh,
   Santa's little...
   * Reindeer sleigh, come our way,
   Ho, ho, ho, cherry nose,
   Cap on head, suit that's red,
   Special night, beard that's white,
   Refrain twice

193

SPECIAL TIMES 8

Lesson Focus

Rhythm: Music may move in relation to the underlying steady beat or shortest pulse. *(D–E)*

Materials

o **Record Information:**
  • Jingle Bells
    Record 8 Side A Band 6
    Voices: children's choir
    Accompaniment: electric guitar, electric bass, piano, percussion
o **Instruments:** woodblocks and mallets
o **Teacher's Resource Binder:**
  • Optional—
    Mainstreaming Suggestion 21, page M18
o **Extends Lesson 7,** page 14

The Lesson

1. Play the recording of "Jingle Bells"; invite the class to sit on the floor or at their desks and pretend they are driving a horse and sleigh. They should gently bounce up and down, moving with the short sounds.

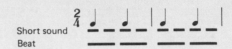

2. Play the recording again; this time, invite some children to move in a slow trot around the room, stepping with the beat.

Jingle Bells

Traditional

Dash - ing through the snow In a one - horse o - pen sleigh,

O'er the fields we go, Laugh - ing all the way;

Bells on bob - tail ring, Mak - ing spir - its bright, What

3. The children may know the refrain; turn the balance on the record player so that they hear only the accompaniment and invite them to sing the refrain. Then turn the balance back to normal and listen to the verse.

4. When the children can sing the refrain easily, add an accompaniment on woodblocks to suggest the sound of horse's hooves and jingling harness bells. The children should experiment to find high and low sounds on the woodblock.

fun it is to ride and sing A sleigh-ing song to-night!

Refrain

Jin-gle bells, jin-gle bells, jin-gle all the

way! Oh, what fun it is to ride in a

1. one-horse o-pen sleigh!____ **2.** one-horse o-pen sleigh!

195

o **Instruments:** two bass (or alto) xylophones with C, D, and G bars in place; glockenspiel with E, F, G, A, and B bars in place; five mallets (two for each xylophone player, one for the glockenspiel player)

o **Extends Lesson 11,** page 22

Lesson Focus

Rhythm: Individual sounds and silences within a rhythmic line may be longer than, shorter than, or the same as the underlying shortest pulse. *(D–E)*

Materials

o **Record Information:**
  • Rudolph the Red-Nosed Reindeer
🔊 **Record 8 Side A Band 7**
  Voices: children's choir
  Accompaniment: synthesizer, piano, electric piano, electric organ, harpsichord, celesta, percussion

The Lesson

1. Play the first statement of "Rudolph the Red-Nosed Reindeer" (recorded with instruments only). Many children may recognize the song and may wish to sing it; involve them in activities that will ensure that they listen carefully to the music before you invite them to sing the song.

Rudolph the Red-Nosed Reindeer

Words and Music by Johnny Marks

1. Ru-dolph, the red - nosed rein - deer had a ver-y shin - y
2. All of the oth - er rein - deer used to laugh and call him
3. Then how the rein - deer loved him as they shout - ed out with

nose, And if you ev - er saw it,
names, They nev - er let poor Ru - dolph
glee: "Ru-dolph, the red - nosed rein - deer,

1. you would e-ven say it glows.
2. join in an-y rein-deer games. *to next section*

Begin by asking the children to lightly tap the rhythm of the reindeer's hooves on their desktops with fingertips. (They could cup their hands to suggest the hooves.) The children should tap to show the underlying short sound (the eighth note).

2. While half of the class continues to tap the short sound, invite others to listen for words that last for eight short sounds. **When you hear such a very long sound, show me by sliding your palms together. Your slide should last for eight short sounds!** After the children have listened, ask them to identify the words that lasted for eight short sounds: nose, glows, names, games, say, and glee.

3. When the children know the song well, they may add the following accompaniment.

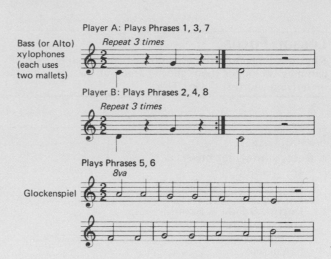

Lesson Focus

Rhythm: Individual sounds and silences within a rhythmic line may be longer than, shorter than, or the same as the underlying shortest pulse. *(D–I)*

Materials

o **Record Information:**
- The Muffin Man
  (Record 6 Side A Band 5)
- I'm Gonna Mail Myself
  Record 8 Side A Band 8
  Voices: children's choir
  Accompaniment: tenor banjo, double bass, tack piano, percussion
o **Instruments:** autoharp; guiro and scraper; finger cymbals; woodblock and mallet; sand blocks
o **Other:** construction-paper hearts or valentines
o **Teacher's Resource Binder:**
  Activity Sheets • **Activity Sheet 39**, page A60 (Make two copies and cut into strips.)
o **Extends Lesson 10, page 20**

The Lesson

1. Ask the class to put their heads down on their desks and close their eyes. Walk around the classroom singing the following words to the tune of "The Muffin Man" (see Perform 4, page 137, for melody):

   Oh, will you be my valentine,
   My valentine, my valentine.
   Oh, will you be my valentine,
   My valentine today.

2. Place a heart (or valentine) beside a chosen child who answers:
   Oh, yes, I'll be your valentine . . .
   Ask the child to walk around the room and sing to a friend ("Oh, will you be my valentine," and so on). The child then places a valentine beside the chosen child and the game continues.

3. **Here's another song for Valentine's Day.** Play the recording of "I'm Gonna Mail Myself." Discuss the words and enjoy the amusing idea of "mailing oneself." Replay the recording as needed until the children can identify the main ideas in each phrase.

4. Give six children the six strips prepared from Activity Sheet 39 (*I'm Gonna Mail Myself*).

Ask the class to listen to the recording again and arrange their classmates in the correct order to show the rhythm of the melody. Play the recording (first verse only) as often as needed until the children have determined the order. Discover that only four of the patterns are needed. The patterns should be arranged as follows: heart, package, cupid, package.

5. Ask the children to chant the rhythm using the words "short," "long," and "lo-ong." (The "heart" pattern should be chanted as follows: long–short–short–long–long–long–long–long–long.) Listen to the recording once more; then challenge the children to sing the song while you accompany on autoharp.

6. When the children can sing the melody easily, they may add an accompaniment to suggest the sounds implied by the words.

   OPTIONAL

   guiro scraping—"wrap myself in paper"
   finger cymbals—"daub myself with glue"
   wood block—"stick some stamps"
   sand blocks—"mail myself" (letter sliding into mailbox)

Each player may devise his or her own rhythm pattern using short or long sounds.

I'm Gonna Mail Myself

Words and Music by Woody Guthrie

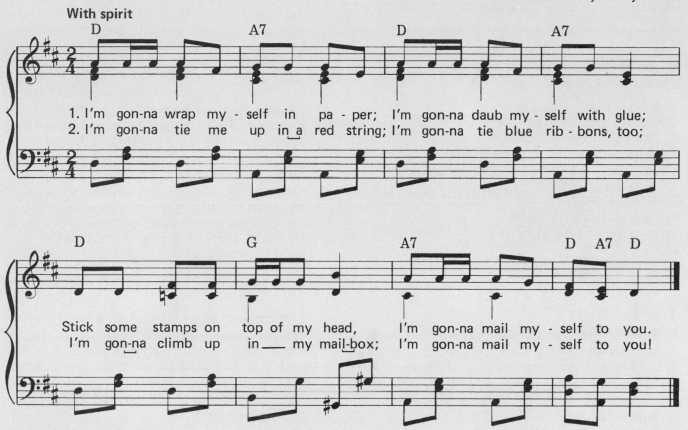

With spirit

1. I'm gon-na wrap my-self in pa-per; I'm gon-na daub my-self with glue;
2. I'm gon-na tie me up in a red string; I'm gon-na tie blue rib-bons, too;

Stick some stamps on top of my head, I'm gon-na mail my-self to you.
I'm gon-na climb up in my mail-box; I'm gon-na mail my-self to you!

Lesson Focus

Melody: A series of pitches may move up or down by steps or skips.
Harmony: Two or more musical lines may occur simultaneously. *(P–I)*

Materials

o **Record Information:**
  • Summer Morning
  Record 8 Side A Band 9
  Voices: children's choir
  Accompaniment: piccolo, string quartet
o **Instruments:** set up each of the following with C, D, F, G, A, C', and D' bars in place—alto xylophone, bass xylophone, glockenspiel; mallets
o **Other:** overhead projector
o **Teacher's Resource Binder:**
  Activity Sheets • **Activity Sheet 40,** page A61 (Prepare a transparency from the activity sheet.)
o **Extends Lesson 35,** page 72

The Lesson

1. Display the transparency prepared from Activity Sheet 40 (*Summer Morning*). **Can you find some patterns in this song that will sound the same?** (first pattern in each row; all patterns in Rows 1 and 3; all patterns in Rows 2 and 4)

2. Ask one child to play the first pattern in Row 1 on the alto xylophone, beginning on F. **Can we sing what (Gerald) just played?** Sing the pattern on "loo"; then sing with the words.

3. **Look at the second pattern in Row 1. Can we play this pattern with the same pitches as the first pattern?** (no, need two higher pitches) Help a performer find this pattern on the alto xylophone, starting on A. Follow a similar procedure until all the patterns have been performed; then challenge the class to sing the complete song.

4. Play the recording and draw attention to the accompaniment. **Sometimes there are high sounds and sometimes there are low sounds accompanying the voices.** Divide the class into three groups. The first group stretches up high when they hear the high sounds of the piccolo; the second group bends over when they hear the low sounds of the strings; the third group stands when voices are heard. Discover that at times there is only one sound; sometimes two sounds are heard, and sometimes three sounds are heard at the same time.

5. Invite two children to improvise an accompaniment for the song. Child 1 should improvise a pattern on the bass xylophone that moves with the beat. Child 2 may improvise a pattern on the glockenspiel that moves with the short sounds. They may play their patterns as the class sings the song.

Summer Morning

Words by Barbara Young

Music by William S. Haynie

Piano Accompaniments

26. That's Nice

Words and Music by B.A.

Did you come to
1. vis - it
2. sing with
3. clap with me? Oh, that's nice! Did you
4. walk with
5. talk with
6. play with

come to
vis - it
sing with
clap with me, sweet as su-gar and spice? Did you come to
walk with
talk with
play with

vis - it
sing with
clap with me, sing - ing
walk with
talk with
play with

Hi - de - lee, Hi - de - lee, Hi - de - lee? That's nice!

28. Knock! Knock! Anybody There?

Words by Clyde Watson

Traditional Melody

Knock! Knock! An-y-bod-y there? I've feath-ers for your caps and rib-bons for your hair. If you can't pay you can sing___ me a song. But if you can't sing I'll just run a-long!

30. Little Sir Echo

Original Version by Laura R. Smith and J.S. Fearis
Verse and Revised Arrangement by Adele Girard and Joe Marsala

hel - lo   hel - lo

lo,_____ hel - lo,_____   Won't you come o - ver and

play?_____   You're a   nice lit - tle fel - low, I know by your

a - way

voice,   But you're al - ways so far a - way._____

38. The Hurry Song

By B.A.

Two, four, six, eight, Man-y legs I see, They real-ly are pe-
cu-liar when they aren't on me! Hur-ry, hur-ry; run-ning fast then
slow-ly 'til we're through, Eight, six, four legs do just like my two!

40. Happy Birthday

Words and Music by Mildred and Patty Hill

Hap - py birth - day to you. Hap - py birth - day to you. Hap - py

birth - day dear *(insert name),* Hap - py birth - day to you.

44. Miss Polly

Old English Nursery Song

1 Miss Pol - ly had a dol - ly who was sick, sick, sick, So she
2. She looked___ at the dol - ly and she shook her head; Then she

phoned for the doc - tor to be quick, quick, quick. The doc - tor came___ with her
said, "Miss___ Pol - ly, put her straight to bed." She wrote on a pa - per for a

bag and her hat, And she rapped at the door___ with a rat - ta - tat.
pill, pill,___ pill. "I'll be back in the morn - ing with my bill, bill, bill."

52. *Hakof* (The Monkey)

Words by Judith Eisenstein

Hebrew Folk Song

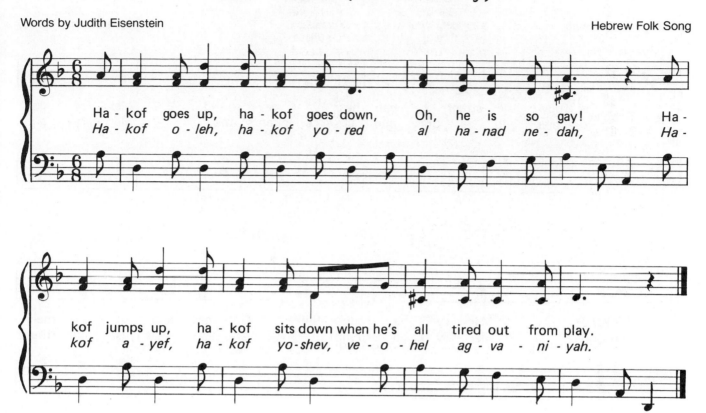

Ha - kof goes up, ha - kof goes down, Oh, he is so gay! Ha -
Ha - kof o - leh, ha - kof yo - red al ha - nad ne - dah, Ha -

kof jumps up, ha - kof sits down when he's all tired out from play.
kof a - yef, ha - kof yo - shev, ve - o - hel ag - va - ni - yah.

58. The Merry-go-round

Words by J. W. Beattie

Traditional Melody

1. Far down the street I can hear a gay sound, Mer-ry-go-round! Mer-ry-go-round! Or-gan and an-i-mals whirl-ing a-round, Rid-ing the mer-ry-go-round._____

2. Po-nies and ze-bras and el-e-phants too, Mer-ry-go-round! Mer-ry-go-round! An-i-mals just like the ones in the zoo, Ride on the mer-ry-go-round._____

68. Loopidee Loo

English Singing Game
Adapted by B.A.

Refrain

Here we go loop-i-dee loo,   Here we go loop-i-dee

lie,   Here we go loop-i-dee loo,

All on a Sat-ur-day night.   1. You night.

Verse (not shown on pupil page)

put your left hand in,   You take your left hand out,   You

give your hand a shake, shake, shake, and turn your-self a-bout.

D. C.

2. right hand   3. left foot   4. right foot   5. whole self

72. Have You Seen My Honey Bears?

Original English Text by Ruth Rubin

Traditional Yiddish Tune

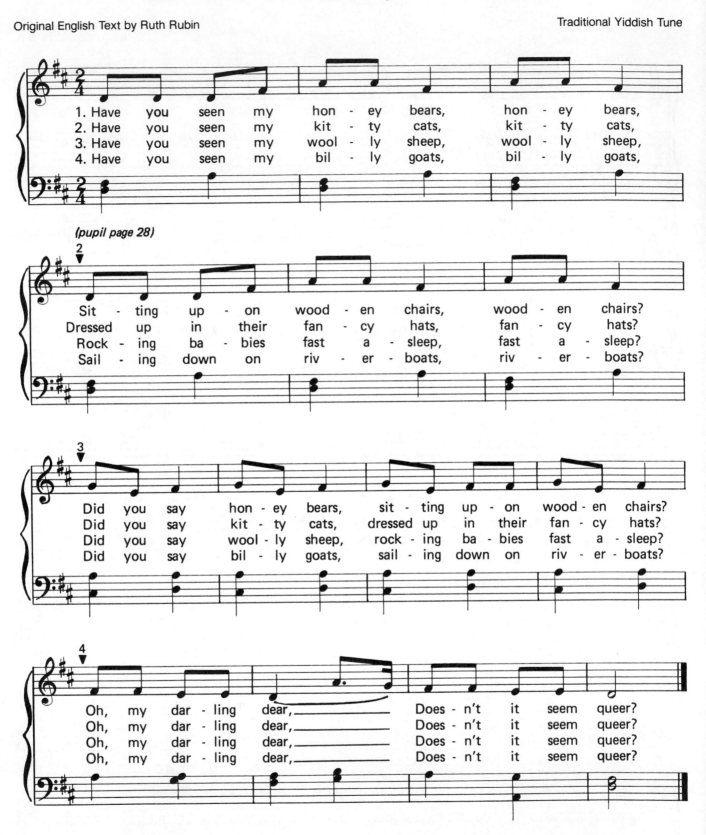

1. Have you seen my hon - ey bears, hon - ey bears,
2. Have you seen my kit - ty cats, kit - ty cats,
3. Have you seen my wool - ly sheep, wool - ly sheep,
4. Have you seen my bil - ly goats, bil - ly goats,

(pupil page 28)

Sit - ting up - on wood - en chairs, wood - en chairs?
Dressed up in their fan - cy hats, fan - cy hats?
Rock - ing ba - bies fast a - sleep, fast a - sleep?
Sail - ing down on riv - er - boats, riv - er - boats?

Did you say hon - ey bears, sit - ting up - on wood - en chairs?
Did you say kit - ty cats, dressed up in their fan - cy hats?
Did you say wool - ly sheep, rock - ing ba - bies fast a - sleep?
Did you say bil - ly goats, sail - ing down on riv - er - boats?

Oh, my dar - ling dear,_____ Does - n't it seem queer?
Oh, my dar - ling dear,_____ Does - n't it seem queer?
Oh, my dar - ling dear,_____ Does - n't it seem queer?
Oh, my dar - ling dear,_____ Does - n't it seem queer?

84. Yankee Doodle

Traditional American Song

Verse

Yan - kee Doo - dle came to town, Rid - ing on a po - ny;

Stuck a feath - er in his cap And called it Mac - a - ro - ni.

Refrain (not shown on pupil page)

Yan - kee Doo - dle, keep it up, Yan - kee Doo - dle dan - dy,

Mind the mu - sic and the step And with the girls be hand - y.

86. Clapping Land

Danish Folk Song

90. Riding in My Car

Words and Music by Woody Guthrie

104. Heigh-Ho

Words and Music by Larry Morey and Frank Churchill

"Heigh - Ho, Heigh - Ho," To make your trou - bles go, Just
Ho, Heigh - Ho," It's home from work we go. (whistle)

keep on sing - ing all day long "Heigh - Ho,

Heigh - Ho, Heigh - Ho, Heigh-
"Heigh - Ho, Heigh - Ho, Heigh-

Ho, Heigh-Ho," For if you're feel - ing low, You pos - i - tive - ly
Ho, Heigh-Ho," All sev - en in a row, (whistle)

can't go wrong with a "Heigh, Heigh - Ho, Heigh - Ho, Heigh-
with a "Heigh, Heigh -

Ho."

106. It Rained a Mist

Virginia Folk Song

Smoothly *(8va throughout)*

(melody)

1. It rained a mist, it rained a mist, It
2. The sun came out, the sun came out, It
3. And then the grass be - gan to grow, It
4. And then the flow - ers be - gan to bloom, They

rained all o - ver the town, town, town, It
shone all o - ver the town, town, town, It
grew all o - ver the town, town, town, It
bloomed all o - ver the town, town, town, They

rained___ all o - ver the town._____
shone___ all o - ver the town._____
grew___ all o - ver the town._____
bloomed___ all o - ver the town._____

108. Taffy

Traditional

Taf - fy was a hound - dog, Taf - fy was a thief,

Taf - fy came to our house and stole a leg of beef. I went to Taf - fy's house,

Taf - fy was in bed; I took a feath - er and tick - led his head!

110. To London Town

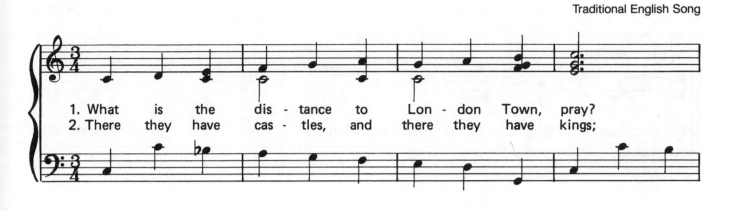

1. What is the dis - tance to Lon - don Town, pray?
2. There they have cas - tles, and there they have kings;

You could not walk there in man - y a day.
There they have thou - sands of won - der - ful things.

110. Rain

Traditional Rhyme

Music by Josephine Wolverton

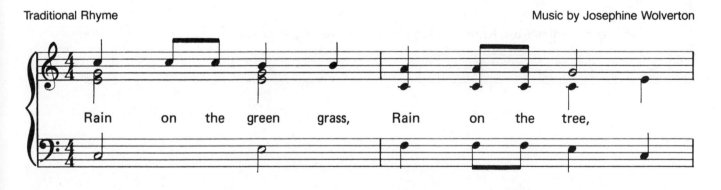

Rain on the green grass, Rain on the tree,

Rain on the house - top, But not on me!

112. Knock Along

American Folk Song

Brightly
Refrain

(pupil page 46) 2

Knock a - long, broth - er rab - bit, knock a - long! Knock a -

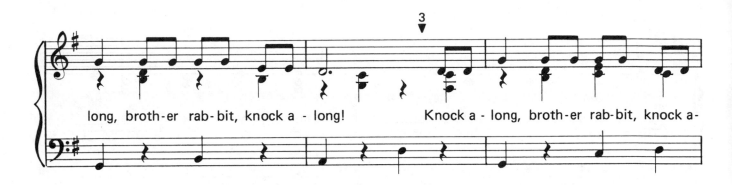

3

long, broth - er rab - bit, knock a - long! Knock a - long, broth - er rab - bit, knock a-

4

1. 2. *Fine*

long, broth - er rab - bit, Knock a - long, broth - er rab - bit, knock a - long.   long.

220

Verse (not notated on pupil page)

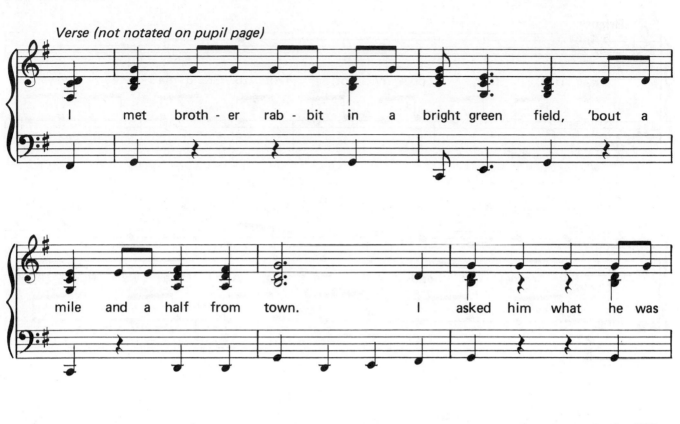

I met broth - er rab - bit in a bright green field, 'bout a

mile and a half from town.   I asked him what he was

D. C. al Fine

do - ing,_____ "I'm eat - ing those car - rots down."

118. Trot, Pony, Trot

Chinese Folk Song

Trot, trot, po - ny trot, Trot to Grand-ma's gate - way.

She comes out and calls the dog, And then we ride on,

jog - a - jog. Trot, trot, trot, trot, trot, trot.

124. Little Tommy Tucker

Traditional

Lit - tle Tom - my Tuck - er, Sing for your sup - per.

"What shall I be ask - ing for?" White bread and but - ter.

126. Redbird

Additional verse by B.A.

New words and new music arrangement by Huddie Ledbetter
Edited with new additional material by Alan Lomax

(pupil page 58)

Refrain

Red - bird, soon in the morn - ing, Red - bird, soon in the morn - ing, Red - bird, soon in the morn - ing, Red - bird,

1. 3. 4. *Fine* 2.

soon in the morn - ing. *[last time only]* soon in the morn - ing.

2. What's the

225

128. Who's That Tapping at the Window?

American Folk Song

Who's that tap - ping at the win - dow?

Who's that knock - ing at the door?

130. One Day My Mother Went to the Market

Words by Leo Israel

Music collected and adapted by Rudolph Goehr

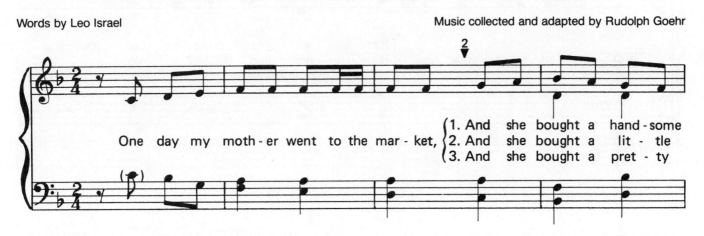

One day my moth-er went to the mar-ket,
1. And she bought a hand-some
2. And she bought a lit-tle
3. And she bought a pret-ty

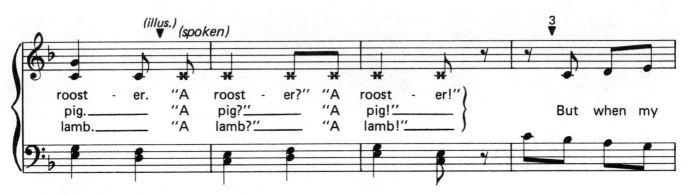

roost - er. "A roost - er?" "A roost - er!" But when my
pig._____ "A pig?"_____ "A pig!"
lamb._____ "A lamb?"_____ "A lamb!"

(illus.) (spoken)

(spoken)

moth-er start-ed to cook him,
{ He did ev-ery-thing he use-ter. "He
{ He got up and danced a jig.____ "A
{ He said,"Do you know who I am?"____ "I

use - ter?" "He use - ter!"   "Oh," he said, "Cock - a - doo - dle -
jig?"____ "A jig!"____   "Oh," he said, "Oink, oink, oink, oink,
am?"____ "I am!"____   "Oh," he said, "Baa, baa, baa, baa,

doo, Tho' I love you true, Tho' I love you true." "Oh," he said,
oink, How I'd like to stay, How I'd like to stay." "Oh," he said,
baa, I'm the queen's es - cort, I'm the queen's es - cort." "Oh," he said,

"Cock - a - doo - dle - doo, I must say a - dieu, I must say a - dieu!"
"Oink, oink, oink, oink, oink, But I must a - way, But I must a - way!"
"Baa, baa, baa, baa, baa, And I'm due at court, And I'm due at court!"

Accidental A notational sign indicating that single tones within a measure should be raised or lowered a half step.

Accompaniment The musical background provided for a principal part.

Aerophone An instrument whose sound is made by blowing into an opening to vibrate a column of air.

Arpeggio The sound produced when the notes of a chord are sounded one after another rather than simultaneously.

Articulation The manner in which a tone is produced, smoothly (*legato*) or detached (*staccato*).

Beat The basic unit of time in music, usually organized within a certain meter into groups of two or three. The underlying pulse of the music.

Brass family Instruments made of brass or other metal on which sound is produced by blowing into a mouthpiece. Pitch changes result from altering the length of tubing through which the air moves. This family includes the trumpet, French horn, and tuba.

Call-response A musical form in which a musical idea is stated (usually by one voice) and echoed (usually by a group).

Canon A composition in whch one line of music is imitated strictly in another line of music at any pitch or time interval.

Chamber music Music for small instrumental ensembles in which one instrument plays each part.

Chord The simultaneous sounding of three or more tones.

Chordophone An instrument whose sound is produced by the vibration of stretched strings.

Chromatic scale In Western music the octave is divided into twelve half steps. When these half steps are played one after the other, they form a chromatic scale.

Coda A section added to the end of a composition as a conclusion.

Concerto A piece of music for one or more soloists and orchestra, usually in symphonic form with three contrasting movements.

Consonance A combination of tones within a given musical system that creates an agreeable effect or a feeling of repose.

Countermelody A melody added to another to provide rhythmic or harmonic contrast, or harmonic tone color.

Crescendo A gradual increase in volume.

Da Capo (D.C.) From the beginning. Indicates that the composition should be repeated from the beginning to the end or until the word *Fine* appears.

Dal Segno (D.S.) From the sign. Indicates that the composition should be repeated from the sign until the word *Fine* appears.

Decrescendo A gradual decrease in volume.

Descant A countermelody usually played or sung above the main melody of a song.

Dissonance A combination of tones within a given musical system that creates a disagreeable effect or a feeling of tension.

Dynamics The expressive markings used to indicate the degree of intensity of sound or volume. The most common are pianissimo (*pp*): very soft; piano (*p*): soft; mezzo piano (*mp*): moderately soft; mezzo forte (*mf*): moderately loud; forte (*f*): loud; fortissimo (*ff*): very loud; crescendo: increase in loudness; decrescendo or diminuendo: decrease in loudness.

Fermata Hold or pause.

Fine End or close.

Fugue A composition in which one or two themes are repeated or imitated by successively entering voices.

Glissando A rapid slide over the scale on a keyboard instrument or harp; also a "smeared" slur of no definite pitch intervals, possible on stringed instruments and the trombone.

Harmony The sound that occurs when two or more tones are produced simultaneously.

Home tone The tonal center, or first tone of a scale.

Idiophone An instrument whose sound is produced by the vibration of a solid material; the sound is initiated by striking, scraping, or rattling.

Imitation The repetition by one voice or instrument of a theme or melody previously sung or played by another voice or instrument, as in a round, canon, or fugue.

Improvisation Performing or creating music spontaneously without the use of printed music, notes, or memory.

Interlude A section of music inserted between the parts of a long composition. In this text, it often refers to brief instrumental sections between verses of songs on the recordings.

Interval The distance in pitch between two tones.

Introduction An opening section of a composition.

Key The key of a composition indicates the scale on which the work is based.

Key signature A number of sharps or flats present on a staff at the beginning of a piece or section that indicates its key or tonality.

Legato An indication that tones should be performed in a smooth, connected manner.

Major scale A scale consisting of seven different pitches and an eighth pitch that is a higher repetition of the first. All of the pitches, except the third and fourth and the seventh and eighth, are separated from each other by one whole step. The remaining pitches are separated from each other by a half step.

Marcato The performance of a tone in a marked or stressed manner.

Measure A group of beats, the first of which is usually accented. The number of beats in the group is determined by the meter signature. Measures are separated from each other by bar lines.

Melodic contour The shape of a succession of musical tones.

Melody A succession of tones having both motion and rhythm.

Membranophone An instrument whose sound is produced by vibrating a stretched skin or membrane.

Meter The organization of a specific number of beats into a group. The groupings are determined by the frequency of the underlying accents.

Meter signature A numerical indication found at the beginning of a piece of music or section that tells the number of beats and type of beat found in each measure.

Minor scale A scale consisting of seven different pitches and an eighth pitch that is a higher repetition of the first. All of the pitches except for the second and third and the fifth and sixth are separated from each other by one whole step. The remaining pitches are separated by a half step.

Mode A scalewise arrangement of tones that may form the basic tonal material of a composition; specifically refers to the medieval church modes.

Modulation The process of changing from one key to another during the course of a composition.

Motive The shortest recognizable unit of notes of a musical theme or subject.

Movement An independent section of a larger instrumental composition such as a symphony or concerto.

Octave The interval between two tones having the same name and located eight notes apart.

Ostinato A short pattern, repeated over and over.

Patschen A physical movement in which one slaps his or her thighs rhythmically.

Pentatonic scale A five-tone scale with no half steps between any two tones. The five tones include one group of two tones and one of three, separated by an interval of one and one-half steps. The scale can be produced on the piano by playing only the black keys.

Percussion family A group of instruments played by shaking or striking. This family includes the celesta, orchestra bells, timpani, maracas, woodblock, castanets, cymbals, drums, xylophone, glockenspiel, tambourine, and claves.

Phrase A natural division of the melodic line, comparable to a sentence in speech.

Pitch The highness or lowness of a musical sound, determined by the frequency of the sound waves producing it.

Pizzicato In string music, the sound produced by plucking the strings rather than bowing them.

Prime mark A marking that indicates the upper octave of notes; e.g. 1′ is higher than 1. Also used to describe sections of music that are similar; e.g. A′ is similar to A.

Pulse See *Beat*.

Rallentando A slowing down of tempo.

Rest A sign indicating silence in music.

Ritard A gradual slowing of tempo.

Rondo A musical form resulting from the alternation of a main theme with contrasting themes (**A B A C A** etc.)

Root The note on which a chord is built. A chord is said to be in root position if the root is the lowest sounding note.

Round A melody sung or played by two or more musicians. Each musician or group starts at a different time and repeats the melody several times.

Scale A series of tones arranged in ascending or descending order according to a plan.

Score Printed music.

Sequence Immediate repetition of a tonal pattern at a higher or lower pitch level.

Slur A curved line placed above or below two or more notes of different pitch to indicate that they are to be sung or played without separation.

Sonata A composition for piano or some other instrument (violin, flute, cello, etc.), usually with piano accompaniment, which consists of three or four separate sections called movements.

Staccato An indication that tones should be performed in a short, detached manner.

Staff A group of five horizontal lines on and around which notes are positioned.

String family A group of instruments on which sound is produced by rubbing a bow against strings. Includes the violin, viola, cello, and double bass (bass viol).

Suite A musical form consisting of a set of pieces or movements.

Symphony A sonata for orchestra.

Syncopation The temporary displacement of a regular rhythmic pulse.

Tempo Rate of speed.

Texture The density of sound in a piece of music. This thickness or thinness of sound is created by the number of instruments or voices heard simultaneously.

Theme A complete musical idea that serves as the focus or subject of a musical composition.

Tie A curved line between two or more successive tones of the same pitch. The tones so connected are sounded as one tone that is equal in length to the combined duration of the individual tones.

Timbre The quality or "color" of a tone unique to the instrument or voice that produces it.

Tonal center The first degree of the scale on which a melody is constructed. Also called the *tonic*.

Tonality Feeling for a key or tonal center.

Unison All voices or instruments singing or playing the same pitch. The playing of the same notes by various instruments, voices, or a whole orchestra, either at the same pitch or in different octaves.

Variation The modification of a musical theme ate a new musical idea. This modification result of melodic, rhythmic, or

Whole-tone scale between

Woo

Acknowledgments and Credits

ACKNOWLEDGMENTS

Grateful acknowledgment is made to the following copyright owners and agents for their permission to reprint the following copyrighted material. Every effort has been made to locate all copyright owners; any errors or omissions in copyright notice are inadvertent and will be corrected as they are discovered.

"Animal Crackers in My Soup," words by Ted Kochler and Irving Caesar, music by Ray Henderson. Copyright © 1935 and 1963 by Movietone Music Corporation, New York, N.Y. This arrangement Copyright 1987 Movietone Music Corporation, New York, N.Y. Sam Fox Publishing Company, Inc., Santa Maria, CA, Sole Agent. Made in U.S.A. International Copyright Secured. All Rights Reserved. Reprinted and recorded by permission of the Sam Fox Publishing Company, Inc., Music Publishers.

"Bright Stars, Light Stars," from the poem "Stars," from STORIES TO BEGIN ON by Rhoda W. Bacmeister. Copyright 1940 by E. P. Dutton, renewed 1968 by Rhoda W. Bacmeister. Words reprinted and recorded by permission of the publisher, E. P. Dutton, a division of New American Library. Set to music by Irving Lowens, from *We Sing Of Life,* copyright 1955 by Irving Lowens. Music reprinted and recorded by permission of Margery Morgan Lowens, personal representative of the Estate of Irving Lowens.

"Brownies and Witches," by Mayme Christenson and Josephine Wolverton, from *The American Singer,* Second Edition, Book 1, by John W. Beattie, Josephine Wolverton, Grace V. Wilson and Howard Hinga. Copyright 1954 by American Book Company. Reprinted and recorded by permission of D.C. Heath & Co.

"Caterpillar, Butterfly," by Sharon Beth Falk, copyright by Sharon Beth Falk. Reprinted by permission of the author.

"Clues," rhyme by Nancy Kilpin. Copyright © 1978 by Nancy Kilpin. Reprinted by permission of the author.

"Come, All You Playmates," from *Sally Go Round the Sun* by Edith Fowke. Used by permission of The Canadian Publishers, McClelland and Stewart Limited, Toronto. Recorded by permission of Edith Fowke.

"Dog and Cat," from *American Folk Songs For Young Singers* by Maurice Matteson, copyright © 1947 by G. Schirmer, Inc. Reprinted and recorded by permission of Hal Leonard Publishing Corp. for G. Schirmer, Inc.

"Down, Down!," a poem by Eleanor Farjeon, from ELEANOR FARJEON'S POEMS FOR CHILDREN (J.B. Lippincott Company) Copyright 1926, renewed 1954 by Eleanor Farjeon Reprinted by permission of Harper & Row, Publishers, Inc. Reprinted outside the United States by permission of Harold Ober Associates, Inc.

"Five Angels," a German folk song, English words by Adina Williamson, arranged by Georgette LeNorth, from *Making Music Your Own,* Book 1, by Beatrice Landek *et al.,* copyright © 1964, 1971 Silver Burdett Company. Reprinted and recorded by permission of the publisher.

"Goin' to the Zoo," words and music by Tom Paxton, © Copyright 1961 Cherry Lane Music Publishing Co., Inc. This arrangement © Copyright 1980 Cherry Lane Music Publishing ... ght Secured. All Rights Re- ...

"Goodnight, fr... G. Buttolph, ... printed by perm... Jobbers. Recor... licensed ...the publisher. Recording

... Walk with a ... © 1959 by ...sion of

Line... Dough... Doubled...

"Grandma Moses," from *Circle Round the Zero* by Maureen Kenney, copyright © 1975 by MMB Music, Inc. and Maureen Kenney. Reprinted and recorded by permission of the publisher.

"Hakof," words by Judith K. Eisenstein, from *Songs of Childhood* by Judith K. Eisenstein and Frieda Prensky. Copyright © 1949 by the United Synagogue Commission on Jewish Education. Reprinted and recorded by permission of the United Synagogue Commission on Jewish Education.

"Hanukah Hayom," words and music by Judith K. Eisenstein and Frieda Prensky, from *Songs of Childhood* by Judith K. Eisenstein and Frieda Prensky. Copyright © 1949 by the United Synagogue Commission on Jewish Education. Reprinted and recorded by permission of the United Synagogue Commission on Jewish Education.

"Happy Birthday to You," by Mildred J. and Patty S. Hill. © Copyright 1935 by Birch Tree Group Ltd. All rights reserved. Used by permission of Birch Tree Group, Ltd. All rights reserved. Used by permission. Recording licensed through the Harry Fox Agency.

"Happy Train," words and music by Ruth Roberts and Ralph Stein, copyright © 1968 by Michael Brent Publications, Inc. Reprinted and recorded by permission of the publishers.

"Have You Seen My Honey Bears?," a traditional Yiddish tune, English lyrics by Ruth Rubin. Copyright © 1964 by Ruth Rubin. Reprinted and recorded by permission of the author.

"Heigh-Ho," by Larry Morey and Frank Churchill, copyright 1936 by Bourne Co., Music Publishers. Reprinted by permission of the publisher. Recording licensed through the Harry Fox Agency.

"Hello," words and music by Ella Jenkins, copyright © 1966 by Ella Jenkins. Reprinted and recorded by permission of Ellbern Publishing Company.

"Hello Ev'rybody," words by Eunice Holsaert, music by Charity Bailey, from *Sing A Song With Charity Bailey,* copyright © 1955 by Plymouth Music Co., Inc. Reprinted and recorded by permission of the publisher.

"How D'Ye Do and Shake Hands," words by Cy Coben and music by Oliver Wallace (adapted from a book by L. Carroll). © 1951 Walt Disney Music Company. Used by Permission. Recording licensed through the Harry Fox Agency.

"I'm Gonna Mail Myself," originally titled "Mail Myself to You," words and music by Woody Guthrie. TRO— © Copyright 1962 and 1963 Ludlow Music, Inc., New York, NY. Used by Permission of The Richmond Organization. Recording licensed through the Harry Fox Agency.

"It Rained a Mist," a Virginian folk song adapted by Arthur Kyle Davis, Jr. Copyright 1929 and renewed copyright © 1957 by Arthur Kyle Davis, Jr. Reprinted and recorded by permission of the University Press of Virginia.

"Jack in the Box," from *Singing Fun* by Lucille Wood and Louise B. Scott. Copyright © 1954 by Bowmar Noble. Copyright renewed. Reprinted by permission of Belwin-Mills Publishing Corp. All Rights Reserved. Recording licensed through the Harry Fox Agency.

"Japanese Rain Song," English lyrics by Roberta McLaughlin, from *Sing a Song of Holidays and Seasons* by Roberta McLaughlin and Lucille Wood. Copyright © 1969 by Bowmar Noble. Reprinted by permission of Belwin-Mills Publishing Corp. All Rights Reserved. Recording licensed through the Harry Fox Agency.

"Knock! Knock! Anybody There?," words by Clyde Watson, from *Father Fox's Pennyrhymes* by Clyde Watson. Copyright 1971 by Clyde Watson. Reprinted, set to music and re... by permission of Curtis Brown, Ltd.

Teacher's Edition:

HRW Photos by Elizabeth Hathon appear on pp. ii–iii (top), xvi–xxi.

HRW Photos by Richard Haynes appear on pp. ii–iii (bottom).

ART CREDITS

Pupil Book (page numbers refer to pupil pages):

pp. 6, 7, 44, 45, 57, Marilyn Janovitz; pp. 8, 9, 10, 11, 38, 44, 62, 63, Debbie Dieneman; p. 22, Sally Springer; pp. 24, 25,

Tom Thorspecken; p. 30, Maria Pia Marella; p. 32, Phil Scheuer; pp. 4, 5, 46, 47, Represented by Publishers' Graphics Inc./Julie Durrell; pp. 14, 15, Ethel Gold; pp. 18, 19, Paul Harvey; pp. 12, 13, 39, 58, 59, Repesented by Asciutto Art Representatives/Sal Murdocca; pp. 34, 35, Meryl Henderson; pp. 41, 48, 49, 50, 51, Jan Pyk.

All technical art prepared by Bud Musso.

Teacher's Edition:

All technical art prepared by Vantage Art.

All illustrative art prepared by Jody Wheeler/Represented by Publisher's Graphics, Inc.

Classified Index of Music, Art, and Poetry

*Topics of special interest to teachers who use the Kodaly and Orff methods are indicated with a **K** and an **O**.*

Classified Index of Activities and Skills

*Topics of special interest to teachers who use the Kodaly and Orff methods are indicated with a **K** and an **O**.*

156, 160–61, 180, 185, 186, 187, 196–97, 200

INSTRUMENTAL SKILLS
alternating playing and resting, 6, 16, 123, 155, 159, 161
echoing, 26, 56, 82, 85, 108, 147
playing a steady rhythm or beat, 6, 17, 64, 122, 195
playing two or more pitches simultaneously, 151, 153, 155, 156, 160–61

INSTRUMENTS FEATURED IN LISTENING LESSONS

Band
Children's March (*E.F. Goldman*), 168
Semper Fidelis (*J.P. Sousa*), 84–85

Bassett Horn
Menuetto from Five Divertimenti in B-Flat Major (*W.A. Mozart*), 50–51

Bassoon
Peter and the Wolf (*S. Prokofiev*), 179

Chamber Ensemble
Ghost Dance from Ancient Voices of Children (*G. Crumb*), 18
Staines Morris Dance (*Anonymous*), 82–83

Chinese Orchestra
Green Skirt (*Chinese Folk Tune*), 171

Clarinet
Cuckoo in the Woods, The, from The Carnival of the Animals (*C. Saint-Saëns*), 104
Peter and the Wolf (*S. Prokofiev*), 179

Coconut Grater
Mango Time (*Trinidad Folk Tune*), 14, 20

Finger Cymbals
Song of the Narobi Trio, (*R. Maxwell*), 87, 91

Flute
Peter and the Wolf (*S. Prokofiev*), 179

French Horn
Peter and the Wolf (*S. Prokofiev*), 179

Gong
Sword Dance (*H. Donaldson*), 177

Jazz Trio
Happy Birthday, 40

Mandolin
Ghost Dance from Ancient Voices of Children (*G. Crumb*), 18

Maracas
Ghost Dance from Ancient Voices of Children (*G. Crumb*), 18

Music Box
Happy Birthday, 40

Oboe
Peter and the Wolf (*S. Prokofiev*), 179

Orchestra
Children's Symphony (*H. McDonald*), 2–3, 4–5, 22–23, 114–15
Circus Music from The Red Pony (*A. Copland*), 6–7, 58–59
Cuckoo in the Woods, The, from The Carnival of the Animals (*C. Saint-Saëns*), 104
Kid Stuff, 165
Peter and the Wolf (*S. Prokofiev*), 179
Polka from Age of Gold Ballet Suite (*D. Shostakovich*), 189
Sword Dance (*H. Donaldson*), 177
Walking Song from Acadian Songs and Dances (*V. Thomson*), 68

Piano
Cuckoo in the Woods, The, from The Carnival of the Animals (*C. Saint-Saëns*), 104
Prelude in A Major (*F. Chopin*), 88
Run, Run! from Scenas Infantis (*O. Pinto*), 38–39

Strings
Peter and the Wolf (*S. Prokofiev*), 179

Timpani
Fanfare for Three Trumpets, Three Trombones, and Timpani (*D. Speer*), 30
Peter and the Wolf (*S. Prokofiev*), 179

Trumpet
Fanfare for Three Trumpets, Three Trombones, and Timpani (*D. Speer*), 30

Trombone
Fanfare for Three Trumpets, Three Trombones, and Timpani (*D. Speer*), 30

Violin
Happy Birthday, 40

Woodblock
Song of the Narobi Trio, (*R. Maxwell*), 87, 91

Wooden Trumpet
Mango Time (*Trinidad Folk Tune*), 20

LISTENING SKILLS
expressive elements, 4–5, 34, 39, 55, 100–01, 104
following instructions in song, 12, 14, 106
recognizing a melody, 3, 42, 64, 114, 165, 168
recognizing form, 16, 42, 160
recognizing instruments, 18, 40, 91, 104–15, 137, 171, 179, 189, 190
vocal types, 137

MELODY —K
high-low, 21, 64–65, 138, 200
major scale, 110, 122
melodic contour, 10–11, 12, 14, 16, 21, 22, 24–25, 52–53, 54–55, 56, 58–59, 61, 62, 66, 95,143, 185
melodic direction (up-down-same), 18, 24–25, 46, 58–59, 78–79, 81, 106–07, 126–27, 130, 138–39, 140–41, 174, 178, 185
melodic patterns, 94–95
pentatonic scale, 180
step-skip-same, 72, 74, 78–79, 80–81, 106–07, 108–09, 128, 130, 170, 178, 200
tonal center, 182
tonal set, 78–79, 80–81, 108–09, 110
whole-tone scale, 180

MOVEMENT (SEE ALSO CREATIVE ACTIVITIES)— O
action songs, 4–5, 6, 12–13, 14–15, 18, 20, 22–23, 26–27, 32, 39, 44, 46, 48, 57, 64, 69 84–85, 135, 142, 152, 153, 155, 158, 161, 165, 181
body as percussion instrument, 12–13, 22, 26–27, 48, 50, 56–57, 60–61, 64, 96, 122, 123, 147, 150–51, 152, 165
patterned dancing, 96, 157

MUSIC DRAMA, SEE CURRICULUM CORRELATION— LANGUAGE ARTS; CREATIVE ACTIVITIES— CREATIVE DRAMATICS

NOTATING MUSIC
with ikons, 69, 70, 82, 86, 120, 122, 141, 170, 174, 185, 187
with pictures, 88–89, 164–65

READING MUSIC
melodic ikons, 41, 47, 54, 58–59, 61, 62, 66, 74, 75, 78–79, 95, 102, 106–07, 141, 142, 163, 170, 174, 185
musical pictures, 32, 34–35, 38, 44, 52–53, 71, 73, 84, 88, 100–01, 104–05, 106–07, 114–15, 119, 126–27, 143, 163, 164–65

Alphabetical Index of Music

Melodic contour The shape of a succession of musical tones.

Melody A succession of tones having both motion and rhythm.

Membranophone An instrument whose sound is produced by vibrating a stretched skin or membrane.

Meter The organization of a specific number of beats into a group. The groupings are determined by the frequency of the underlying accents.

Meter signature A numerical indication found at the beginning of a piece of music or section that tells the number of beats and type of beat found in each measure.

Minor scale A scale consisting of seven different pitches and an eighth pitch that is a higher repetition of the first. All of the pitches except for the second and third and the fifth and sixth are separated from each other by one whole step. The remaining pitches are separated by a half step.

Mode A scalewise arrangement of tones that may form the basic tonal material of a composition; specifically refers to the medieval church modes.

Modulation The process of changing from one key to another during the course of a composition.

Motive The shortest recognizable unit of notes of a musical theme or subject.

Movement An independent section of a larger instrumental composition such as a symphony or concerto.

Octave The interval between two tones having the same name and located eight notes apart.

Ostinato A short pattern, repeated over and over.

Patschen A physical movement in which one slaps his or her thighs rhythmically.

Pentatonic scale A five-tone scale with no half steps between any two tones. The five tones include one group of two tones and one of three, separated by an interval of one and one-half steps. The scale can be produced on the piano by playing only the black keys.

Percussion family A group of instruments played by shaking or striking. This family includes the celesta, orchestra bells, timpani, maracas, woodblock, castanets, cymbals, drums, xylophone, glockenspiel, tambourine, and claves.

Phrase A natural division of the melodic line, comparable to a sentence in speech.

Pitch The highness or lowness of a musical sound, determined by the frequency of the sound waves producing it.

Pizzicato In string music, the sound produced by plucking the strings rather than bowing them.

Prime mark A marking that indicates the upper octave of notes; e.g. 1' is higher than 1. Also used to describe sections of music that are similar; e.g. A' is similar to A.

Pulse See *Beat*.

Rallentando A slowing down of tempo.

Rest A sign indicating silence in music.

Ritard A gradual slowing of tempo.

Rondo A musical form resulting from the alternation of a main theme with contrasting themes (**A B A C A** etc.)

Root The note on which a chord is built. A chord is said to be in root position if the root is the lowest sounding note.

Round A melody sung or played by two or more musicians. Each musician or group starts at a different time and repeats the melody several times.

Scale A series of tones arranged in ascending or descending order according to a plan.

Score Printed music.

Sequence Immediate repetition of a tonal pattern at a higher or lower pitch level.

Slur A curved line placed above or below two or more notes of different pitch to indicate that they are to be sung or played without separation.

Sonata A composition for piano or some other instrument (violin, flute, cello, etc.), usually with piano accompaniment, which consists of three or four separate sections called movements.

Staccato An indication that tones should be performed in a short, detached manner.

Staff A group of five horizontal lines on and around which notes are positioned.

String family A group of instruments on which sound is produced by rubbing a bow against strings. Includes the violin, viola, cello, and double bass (bass viol).

Suite A musical form consisting of a set of pieces or movements.

Symphony A sonata for orchestra.

Syncopation The temporary displacement of a regular rhythmic pulse.

Tempo Rate of speed.

Texture The density of sound in a piece of music. This thickness or thinness of sound is created by the number of instruments or voices heard simultaneously.

Theme A complete musical idea that serves as the focus or subject of a musical composition.

Tie A curved line between two or more successive tones of the same pitch. The tones so connected are sounded as one tone that is equal in length to the combined duration of the individual tones.

Timbre The quality or "color" of a tone unique to the instrument or voice that produces it.

Tonal center The first degree of the scale on which a melody is constructed. Also called the *tonic*.

Tonality Feeling for a key or tonal center.

Unison All voices or instruments singing or playing the same pitch. The playing of the same notes by various instruments, voices, or a whole orchestra, either at the same pitch or in different octaves.

Variation The modification of a musical theme to create a new musical idea. This modification may be the result of melodic, rhythmic, or harmonic alteration.

Whole-tone scale A six-tone scale with one whole step between any two tones.

Woodwind family A group of instruments on which sound is produced by vibrating one or two reeds. Includes the clarinet, flute, oboe, and saxophone.

Acknowledgments and Credits

ACKNOWLEDGMENTS

Grateful acknowledgment is made to the following copyright owners and agents for their permission to reprint the following copyrighted material. Every effort has been made to locate all copyright owners; any errors or omissions in copyright notice are inadvertent and will be corrected as they are discovered.

"Animal Crackers in My Soup," words by Ted Kochler and Irving Caesar, music by Ray Henderson. Copyright © 1935 and 1963 by Movietone Music Corporation, New York, N.Y. This arrangement Copyright 1987 Movietone Music Corporation, New York, N.Y. Sam Fox Publishing Company, Inc., Santa Maria, CA, Sole Agent. Made in U.S.A. International Copyright Secured. All Rights Reserved. Reprinted and recorded by permission of the Sam Fox Publishing Company, Inc., Music Publishers.

"Bright Stars, Light Stars," from the poem "Stars," from STORIES TO BEGIN ON by Rhoda W. Bacmeister. Copyright 1940 by E. P. Dutton, renewed 1968 by Rhoda W. Bacmeister. Words reprinted and recorded by permission of the publisher, E. P. Dutton, a division of New American Library. Set to music by Irving Lowens, from *We Sing Of Life,* copyright 1955 by Irving Lowens. Music reprinted and recorded by permission of Margery Morgan Lowens, personal representative of the Estate of Irving Lowens.

"Brownies and Witches," by Mayme Christenson and Josephine Wolverton, from *The American Singer,* Second Edition, Book 1, by John W. Beattie, Josephine Wolverton, Grace V. Wilson and Howard Hinga. Copyright 1954 by American Book Company. Reprinted and recorded by permission of D.C. Heath & Co.

"Caterpillar, Butterfly," by Sharon Beth Falk, copyright by Sharon Beth Falk. Reprinted by permission of the author.

"Clues," rhyme by Nancy Kilpin. Copyright © 1978 by Nancy Kilpin. Reprinted by permission of the author.

"Come, All You Playmates," from *Sally Go Round the Sun* by Edith Fowke. Used by permission of The Canadian Publishers, McClelland and Stewart Limited, Toronto. Recorded by permission of Edith Fowke.

"Dog and Cat," from *American Folk Songs For Young Singers* by Maurice Matteson, copyright © 1947 by G. Schirmer, Inc. Reprinted and recorded by permission of Hal Leonard Publishing Corp. for G. Schirmer, Inc.

"Down, Down!," a poem by Eleanor Farjeon, from ELEANOR FARJEON'S POEMS FOR CHILDREN (J.B. Lippincott Company) Copyright 1926, renewed 1954 by Eleanor Farjeon Reprinted by permission of Harper & Row, Publishers, Inc. Reprinted outside the United States by permission of Harold Ober Associates, Inc.

"Five Angels," a German folk song, English words by Adina Williamson, arranged by Georgette LeNorth, from *Making Music Your Own,* Book 1, by Beatrice Landek et al., copyright © 1964, 1971 Silver Burdett Company. Reprinted and recorded by permission of the publisher.

"Goin' to the Zoo," words and music by Tom Paxton, © Copyright 1961 Cherry Lane Music Publishing Co., Inc. This arrangement © Copyright 1980 Cherry Lane Music Publishing Co., Inc. International Copyright Secured. All Rights Reserved. Reprinted by permission of the publisher. Recording licensed through the Harry Fox Agency.

"Going for a Walk," excerpts from *Going For a Walk with a Line* By Douglas and Elizabeth MacAgy. Copyright © 1959 by Douglas and Elizabeth MacAgy. Reprinted by permission of Doubleday & Company, Inc.

"Goodnight," words by Lucy Sprague Mitchell, music by Edna G. Buttolph, from *Music Is Motion* by Edna G. Buttolph. Reprinted by permission of The Willis Music Co., Publishers & Jobbers. Recording licensed through SESAC.

"Grandma Moses," from *Circle Round the Zero* by Maureen Kenney, copyright © 1975 by MMB Music, Inc. and Maureen Kenney. Reprinted and recorded by permission of the publisher.

"Hakof," words by Judith K. Eisenstein, from *Songs of Childhood* by Judith K. Eisenstein and Frieda Prensky. Copyright © 1949 by the United Synagogue Commission on Jewish Education. Reprinted and recorded by permission of the United Synagogue Commission on Jewish Education.

"Hanukah Hayom," words and music by Judith K. Eisenstein and Frieda Prensky, from *Songs of Childhood* by Judith K. Eisenstein and Frieda Prensky. Copyright © 1949 by the United Synagogue Commission on Jewish Education. Reprinted and recorded by permission of the United Synagogue Commission on Jewish Education.

"Happy Birthday to You," by Mildred J. and Patty S. Hill. © Copyright 1935 by Birch Tree Group Ltd. All rights reserved. Used by permission of Birch Tree Group, Ltd. All rights reserved. Used by permission. Recording licensed through the Harry Fox Agency.

"Happy Train," words and music by Ruth Roberts and Ralph Stein, copyright © 1968 by Michael Brent Publications, Inc. Reprinted and recorded by permission of the publishers.

"Have You Seen My Honey Bears?," a traditional Yiddish tune, English lyrics by Ruth Rubin. Copyright © 1964 by Ruth Rubin. Reprinted and recorded by permission of the author.

"Heigh-Ho," by Larry Morey and Frank Churchill, copyright 1936 by Bourne Co., Music Publishers. Reprinted by permission of the publisher. Recording licensed through the Harry Fox Agency.

"Hello," words and music by Ella Jenkins, copyright © 1966 by Ella Jenkins. Reprinted and recorded by permission of Ellbern Publishing Company.

"Hello Ev'rybody," words by Eunice Holsaert, music by Charity Bailey, from *Sing A Song With Charity Bailey,* copyright © 1955 by Plymouth Music Co., Inc. Reprinted and recorded by permission of the publisher.

"How D'Ye Do and Shake Hands," words by Cy Coben and music by Oliver Wallace (adapted from a book by L. Carroll). © 1951 Walt Disney Music Company. Used by Permission. Recording licensed through the Harry Fox Agency.

"I'm Gonna Mail Myself," originally titled "Mail Myself to You," words and music by Woody Guthrie. TRO— © Copyright 1962 and 1963 Ludlow Music, Inc., New York, NY. Used by Permission of The Richmond Organization. Recording licensed through the Harry Fox Agency.

"It Rained a Mist," a Virginian folk song adapted by Arthur Kyle Davis, Jr. Copyright 1929 and renewed copyright © 1957 by Arthur Kyle Davis, Jr. Reprinted and recorded by permission of the University Press of Virginia.

"Jack in the Box," from *Singing Fun* by Lucille Wood and Louise B. Scott. Copyright © 1954 by Bowmar Noble. Copyright renewed. Reprinted by permission of Belwin-Mills Publishing Corp. All Rights Reserved. Recording licensed through the Harry Fox Agency.

"Japanese Rain Song," English lyrics by Roberta McLaughlin, from *Sing a Song of Holidays and Seasons* by Roberta McLaughlin and Lucille Wood. Copyright © 1969 by Bowmar Noble. Reprinted by permission of Belwin-Mills Publishing Corp. All Rights Reserved. Recording licensed through the Harry Fox Agency.

"Knock! Knock! Anybody There?," words by Clyde Watson, from *Father Fox's Pennyrhymes* by Clyde Watson. Copyright © 1971 by Clyde Watson. Reprinted, set to music and recorded by permission of Curtis Brown, Ltd.